The Professional Counselor

The Professional Counselor: Challenges and Opportunities weaves a rich narrative for the inner counselor of self-discovery, mindfulness and self-care, emotional intelligence, counselor identity, ethical issues, career maturation, and future trends in counseling.

Readers will be confronted with professional decision points regarding enrollment in the counselor profession, ethical issues, client treatment, accreditation, and occupational outlook. The text also posits counseling as an emerging global profession and addresses the ways technology will transform professional practice. Each chapter concludes with a Lessons Learned section in which the author uses his personal and professional experiences to address relevant professional issues in mindfulness-based treatment.

The Professional Counselor is an excellent resource and guide for students in graduate counseling programs, those considering the field, and counselors new to the profession.

Shannon Hodges, PhD, is professor of clinical mental health counseling at Niagara University, USA

The Professional Counselor
Challenges and Opportunities

Shannon Hodges

NEW YORK AND LONDON

First published 2021
by Routledge
52 Vanderbilt Avenue, New York, NY 10017

and by Routledge
2 Park Square, Milton Park, Abingdon, Oxon, OX14 4RN

Routledge is an imprint of the Taylor & Francis Group, an informa business

© 2021 Shannon Hodges

The right of Shannon Hodges to be identified as author of this work has been asserted by him in accordance with sections 77 and 78 of the Copyright, Designs and Patents Act 1988.

All rights reserved. No part of this book may be reprinted or reproduced or utilised in any form or by any electronic, mechanical, or other means, now known or hereafter invented, including photocopying and recording, or in any information storage or retrieval system, without permission in writing from the publishers.

Trademark notice: Product or corporate names may be trademarks or registered trademarks, and are used only for identification and explanation without intent to infringe.

Library of Congress Cataloging-in-Publication Data
A catalog record for this title has been requested

ISBN: 978-0-367-00220-6 (hbk)
ISBN: 978-0-367-00221-3 (pbk)
ISBN: 978-0-429-02055-1 (ebk)

Typeset in Goudy
by Newgen Publishing UK

This book is dedicated to Clarence Calvin Bowling. He was my uncle by marriage, but closer than any blood relative could become. An entomologist by training, though as patient a listener as any counselor and was mindfulness embodied before I had ever heard of the term. No matter what endeavor I tried, he was always there for support.

In memory of Clarence C. Bowling (1926–2018)

Contents

	Introduction	1
1	Who Am I? The Power of Self-Discovery	3
2	The Counseling Profession: Critical Information for Consideration	11
3	Should I Become a Counselor?	22
4	Becoming a Counselor: What's Involved?	30
5	Counseling: A Broad Profession in the Twenty-First Century	43
6	Mindfulness and Wellbeing	58
7	Groups, Couples, and Family Counseling	69
8	Emotional Intelligence: The Most Critical Component for Counselors	84
9	Technology and Distance Delivery: Twenty-First Century Realities for Counselors	105
10	Nurturing and Managing Your Career	117
11	The Counselor as Leader and Activist	150
12	Healing the Divided Self	173
13	Gazing into the Future	186
	References	203
	Index	209

Introduction

This text, *The Professional Counselor: Challenges and Opportunities*, represents my effort at introducing the counseling profession to graduate counseling students and those considering the profession. Throughout the pages of this text I have attempted to portray the counseling profession through the windows of my eyes. As I have over two decades of professional counseling experience, including serving as director of a community clinic in the rural Mountain West and director of a university counseling center in the rural upper Midwest, as well as 30 years of teaching experience, I have a particular perspective. I have counseled individuals, couples, families, and groups, at an in-patient psychiatric center, in the remote Outback of Australia, in South African orphanages, and numerous other locations. While I am trying to pass on what I consider the most pertinent information regarding the counseling field, the more important aspects of the chapters are the self-reflective questions and the lessons learned section. The former provides readers the opportunity for intense self-reflection while the latter illustrated some of my challenges, struggles, and successes in the profession and in my life.

It is my sincere hope that this text will be more than a simple course requirement or an assigned text for a book report, but rather a catalyst for a "deeper dive" into the self and the profession by graduate counseling students and readers considering the profession for a career. While I obviously cannot answer all important questions regarding the profession of counseling, I do believe I have addressed some of the challenges, complexities, and rewards the profession offers. As a counseling professional who stumbled into the profession by accident when taking a counseling course when running a university living group, my initial foray was transformed into a life-altering pathway. It is no exaggeration to say the counseling profession has changed my life for the better. That I have had professional and personal success, perhaps more than envisioned, is to a good deal the result of landing in a profession for which I was well suited. In fact, other than teaching, counseling is the only other professional endeavor I have enjoyed. Thankfully, I found my passion and have been able to maintain it 35 years later.

Finally, you just never know where your life's journey will take you. The Quakers have a say that goes, "Way will open." I have found this to be particularly true in my personal and professional life. Truthfully, I have further discovered that sometimes *way will close*, but this has had the same guiding principle in my experience.

2   Introduction

The openings and closings of my life have helped to make me the person, counselor, and counselor educator I have become. I hope my book will serve as a useful guide for readers in counseling programs, those interested in the profession, or simple the curious reader who like me, may have stumbled accidentally into their life profession.

Finally, I would hope that all readers, regardless of whether they become counselors or another profession, will find the meaning and fulfillment I have discovered. Professional life has occasionally been very hard on me but the challenging times only make the smooth one more rewarding. The profession has transported me far from my rural Ozark upbringing and sent me all over the world to teach, counsel, and conduct trainings and seminars. I have had the privilege of meeting amazing people from many cultures and have learned so much from them. Wherever your life journey takes you, I wish for you the same type of meaning and fulfillment as I have found.

1 Who Am I? The Power of Self-Discovery

The year is 1985 in late August and I am sitting in a stuffy classroom in the College of Education building at Oregon State University. Fall term classes had just commenced. With few options, I had enrolled in OSU's graduate Community Counseling program. I cannot recall *which* particular class it was. More embarrassingly, I do not recall which of my professors was teaching the class. What I do remember is the question we were to ponder and then discuss in a small group. The question was "Who am I?"

I was initially puzzled at the assignment. As a young twenty-something person, I had given only vague consideration to my self-identity, often in relation to another person and never had I thought to any great depth on the matter. I do not recall the ensuing discussion though the question lingered with me for some time until the matter faded from conscious thought. Some 15 years later, however, while participating in a workshop at a small college where I served as director of Counseling Services, the question returned. The facilitator, a woman from one of the indigenous tribes in Minnesota, gave us the same assignment. "Tell us who you are in any way you define," she suggested. She went on to model that she was a mother, wife, daughter, sister, tribal member, friend, and neighbor, and continued for several more lines. I was impressed. This woman had really given a lot of thought to the matter! Some 60 participants sat in an oval listening. We were an amalgamation of faculty, staff, and students. I had known several of my colleagues for years, but after the exercise realized I really did not *know* them. I knew their peripheral selves, but not so much their hopes, vulnerabilities, and expectations. As one of the last to speak, I cannot recall what I said. I do remember, however, the impact the exercise had on me. Namely, that I, a professional counselor, needed to engage more in a deep, self-reflective manner on who I was beyond my professional title and family. Therefore, as this is a text for counselors in training, or anyone else reading it, here is who I am. I am the following: a spouse, a brother, an uncle, a friend, a counselor, a professor, a liberal, straight, though not narrow Christian, a man of conviction, of real weakness, strong on patience but with real slip-ups, an empathic type who too often misses injustice before him, a person of love but also one who has struggled to show it to those closest, an idealist with few illusions, to cite several layers of self-hood.

4   *Who Am I? The Power of Self-Discovery*

I am all these and much more, and though it pains me to acknowledge it, I am sometimes far less that who I would like to be. Such is the human experience and thus the necessity for us all, counselors particularly, to engage in ongoing self-reflection and self-discovery. Therefore, here is a suggestion: You ask yourself the same "Who am I?" question. Go as far with it as you feel led to do. In fact, write it down on paper or on a smart phone, a laptop—somewhere it is retrievable. Next, share your list with someone you trust and who knows you well. Ask that person how well your self-view coincides with theirs. The reason for sharing with someone close to you is to check if your self-view is closely aligned with his or hers. It is not necessarily a problem if there is difference, depending on the nature of that difference. Soliciting feedback from key people in our lives is a way to check how well we live out our values. This exercise has brought me both real validation and, on occasion, much disappointment. I would admit that it seems the disappointing feeling motivates me to hold myself more accountable.

Peeling Away Our Defenses: Vulnerability Risks and Rewards

Now that you have considered your identity on a more in-depth level, the next step is to examine your relationships and additional reflective questions. Healthy attachments are encoded in our DNA and are good for our wellbeing (Myers & Sweeney, 2005). Here are some reflective questions to consider:

1. How satisfied are you with your friendships and social relationships (including close family relationships)? If not satisfied, what could you do to create a greater sense of fulfillment?
2. Would you want to make friends with someone such as yourself? Why or why not? If "no," what could you change in order to answer "yes"?
3. If you are single and would like to be in a relationship (e.g., marriage or partnership), what qualities would you want in that person? Then, how well do those qualities match up with your values?
4. Recall a difficult transition in your life. How did you navigate your way through that difficult time?
5. How would a best friend describe you? Then, seek that person out and ask to check your perception.
6. What person (or persons) do you most admire? What qualities about this person (or persons) do you find particularly appealing?
7. Complete this sentence: "What matters most to me in life is …"
8. Complete this sentence: "My greatest challenge in life has been …"
9. Complete this sentence: "My greatest fear in life is …"
10. Complete this sentence: "My most significant accomplishment thus far is …"

Naturally, age and experience make a difference when entertaining questions on personal issues such as those above. Nevertheless, anyone in a counseling program, considering becoming a counselor, or who is a counselor, would be wise to consider questions such as the ones above (and questions well beyond, naturally).

Meaning and Purpose in Counseling

Famed psychiatrist, author, and Holocaust survivor Viktor Frankl theorized that the will to meaning and not sex, power, or aggression was the primary motivating force in human existence (Frankl, 1969). Frankl developed a therapeutic approach he termed "Logotherapy" (Frankl, 1965) or, essentially, a therapy of meaning. While numerous arguments persist regarding the construct of meaning, it appears important in many regards. First, one can hypothesize hope as strongly correlated with optimism. Aaron Beck's research on cognitive therapy, depression, and suicide strongly suggests optimism as key to combat depression and suicide (Beck, 1963; 1967). My own anecdotal experience strongly validates both Frankl and Beck. In more than 20 years of providing counseling in university counseling centers, and community mental health clinics, and other human service agencies, seemingly every person presented with the underlying issues of "My life is less meaningful." Now, few were articulating their presenting problem as such, but as the counseling relationship matured, it seemed life meaning was precisely a chief concern. I would also voice that in ten years of supervising a variety of university-living groups, where a good part of my job was advising, most residents seemed to be presenting for advising with issues about life meaning. In some of my own research, a survey of nearly 500 college students, nearly every respondent agreed meaning was important to very important in their life (Hodges, Denig, & Crowe, 2014).

Thus, a central theme of this book is that meaning in life is very important in the counseling encounter. What I have discovered, however, through finding meaning in my own life, teaching it as a counselor education professor, and working as a counselor in practice, is that meaning seems to be a by-product of relationships and doing good works. So then, for readers interested in becoming counselors, those in counselor education graduate programs, and others in the field, here are some reflective questions for consideration:

1. What role does meaning play in your life?
2. What relationship do you see meaning having in your career (or future career) as a counselor?
3. How, or in what way, is meaning manifest in your life (e.g., family, spiritual life, occupation, etc.)?
4. What is the most meaningful experience you have had? What made that experience so meaningful?
5. Think of someone you admire who appears to have lived a meaningful life. It could be a famous person (e.g., Nelson Mandela, the Dalai Lama, Mother Teresa, Viktor Frankl, etc.) or someone you know very well. What role did meaning appear to have played in their life?
6. If you feel you have less meaning in your life than you would like, how could you begin to rediscover a stronger sense of meaning?
7. Make a list of the ten most important "things" you most value in life. What persons and what things are included on that list? What do you learn from your list? What might you change if anything?

6 Who Am I? The Power of Self-Discovery

8. If you could change anything in your life, what would you change? How could you begin to make that change happen?
9. If you were to ask a close friend or family member whether they see you living a meaning-filled life, what might they say? If you feel so inclined, ask this question of someone close to you.
10. True or false: I have a clear vision for how meaning instructs my personal and professional life. If you answered false, how might you begin to develop a clear vision for meaning in your personal and occupational life?

The Importance of Presence in Counseling

The previous exercises are less about specific answers and more to promote the genesis of an in-depth self-reflection. Readers must be aware they have or may enter a profession where presence arguably far more important than technique or theoretical approach. A challenge I have often encountered as a counselor education professor is how precisely to "teach" presence. Miriam Rose-Baumann, an indigenous elder, retired school principal and former teacher in remote Daly River, Australia teaches workshops on "Dadirri" (pronounced "da-da"), which roughly translates as deep listening. She conducts workshops throughout Australia, in remote aboriginal schools and communities as well as professional conferences for counselors, psychologists, teachers, and others. During June 2018, I visited her community and former school. She invited me to her home, and my colleague and I had an informative conversation with her. We spoke of the similarities of her approach and philosophy to that of counseling. She was familiar with Carl Rogers and agreed his view of presence was akin to deep listening. I explained my challenges in trying to teach and model deep listening to my students and those I have supervised in clinical settings. She admitted she had similar difficulties, especially when instructing children and adolescents. "I tell them, you have to find a way to catch it," she opined (pers. comm., 2018). She went on to say that, in her experience, prayer or meditation, and understanding one's culture and oneself, were critical components in developing deep listening. Deep listening is essential in developing as an educator and likely a counselor, as we must attend to voice tone, body language, eye contact, and what the client does not say as much as what is stated. As Miriam Rose suggests, stillness also is a vestige of presence.

In a similar vein, the author, sociologist, and higher education speaker Parker Palmer writes eloquently on presence and vocation. Vocation, counseling, teaching, nursing, and so forth, do not spring from mere interest and hard work, although these are very important components. One's vocation comes from listening and accepting the authentic self (Palmer, 2000). Thus, your vocation as counselor is not a terminal goal in itself, but an ongoing process where the *gift* lies in living authentically as opposed to any particular external award or recognition. This type of language—gift, deep listening, meaning in life and so forth—may not fit so neatly in a twenty-first-century evolving counseling profession where "evidenced-based" seems to be the primary mantra. However, questions surrounding the deeper subjective responses to the human condition do not necessarily lend themselves easily to empirical research study (Yalom, 1998). Furthermore, when I consider how complicated explaining my therapeutic approach has become, I am tempted to say, "existential-oriented, mindfulness-based cognitive therapy," which some suggest is a contradiction in terms. Perhaps, then, learning how to balance and live consciously within contractions is part and parcel of an authentic life.

So then readers, what is an existential approach and how is it important to your development as a counselor? Professors and researchers alike pepper imprecise responses with terms such as "self-actualization," "humanistic," "grounding," "centering," and the current term du jour, "mindfulness." All these terms may be somewhat related to an existential therapeutic approach, although I find none of them satisfying in the general sense. My own orientation on the matter, honed from my study and experiences in the field during the past 30-plus years, is that existential therapy is more a "being" than a "doing." Existential counseling requires a different understanding of what matters in therapy and flies in the face of evidence-based therapeutic approaches that have become the battle cry among a profession concerned about DSM-5 (*Diagnostic and Statistical Manual of Mental Disorders*, fifth ed., 2013) typologies and insurance reimbursement. No doubt, counselors must generate income in order to continue providing valuable services. I would maintain, however, that authenticity, addressing life meaning, exploring one's condition, and helping clients to author healthy changes in life are all higher callings and likely more important than the diagnosis du jour. Now, I am not opposed to diagnosis per se, but rather the indiscriminate manner whereby it may be used against the client and the fact that the shelf life of diagnostic labels may extend far beyond the actual duration. Consider Borderline Personality Disorder, for example, and the stigma for women, most of whom are trauma survivors (Linehan, 1993). To paraphrase Linehan, women with BPD diagnoses are having a normal reaction to an abnormal experience (1993).

During the initial counseling class I took prior to admission to the counseling program, we studied Fritz and Laura Perl's Gestalt Therapy. After an extended discussion on the chapter, someone in the class (someone braver than yours truly) asked, "What does the term gestalt mean?" The professor replied that a gestalt implied a whole that was more than the sum of its parts. We all nodded our heads in agreement and understanding, although from the furrowed brows evidenced, I wonder how many actually understood. Finally, someone else asked for an example of gestalt. The professor pondered momentarily, then compared it to love. "Look" he said, "I know why I love my mother. Nevertheless, if I list out the reasons, I am never satisfied with my answers. Any definition of love is certain to be incomplete. I know all these various and sundry reasons are why I love her, but I know there is more, even if I can't name what that something more is."

An existential mindset requires us to confront realities we would feel more comfortable ignoring—for example, the reality of death. US society is youth-obsessed, something we see in the media, the film industry, and the cosmetics industry—the latter of which rake in multi-billions of dollars. Look at plastic surgeon and cosmetic dental ads in the flight magazine next time you travel, and note how much of society focuses on appearance. None of that advertising, money, surgery, or denial can wipe

8   *Who Am I? The Power of Self-Discovery*

away the reality that death awaits us all. "He that dies pays all debts," Shakespeare wrote in *The Tempest*. Perhaps the primary work in human existence is to address effectively one's mortality and the anxiety involved in such contemplation—something that Yalom illustrates in his opus *Staring at the Sun* (2008). Whatever else, mortality inspires fear, denial, hope for some, and possibly represents the last great opportunity for growth in our lives. So when you consider your own demise, what are your thoughts, fears, and hopes?

Where Does This Leave You?

This initial chapter may seem perplexing for those readers contemplating entering a counseling program and those early in their program. Here is a piece of wisdom, or more accurately a tidbit of my experience. The counseling profession is a world shaded in gray, with less certainty than many find comfortable, and easy, precise answers are as scarce as warm Duluth January. Counseling a client caught between two opposing forces, both of which she finds appealing, can be fraught with challenges (more on this soon). As a counselor, I learned early on to role-play issues with clients during sessions as otherwise they often would not make necessary changes outside counseling. Here are some additional questions to entertain regarding the profession.

1. What matters most in your life? How congruent is your current behavior with what you say matters most? If this is a concern here, how might you bridge the chasm between what matters most and your current behavior?
2. When you have felt stuck on a particular issue, situation, or the like, how do you resolve this conflict?
3. If you were asked at a job interview (or likely somewhere else!) "What's the meaning of *your* life?" how would you answer?
4. How does the reality of death change your life? If you have not thought of it, I heartily recommend it. Counselors address mortality with clients regularly.
5. What are your core values? List at least ten. Now, how will these values inform and assist you as a counselor?

Lessons Learned

Perhaps the most unusual case I encountered as a counselor was in a university counseling center. An undergraduate came in one morning for counseling services. He was well groomed, an honors student, and had already been accepted to a very good university for graduate school. During the intake process, his scores on the Beck Depression Inventory-2 and the Beck Anxiety Inventory were low and the intake interview was unremarkable. Under "reason for the visit" he simply wrote, "Would prefer to discuss." Once counseling commenced, he recounted a fascinating tale of an encounter with aliens. At the conclusion of his story, he inquired, "So, do you believe me?" I paused briefly to consider his question. Frankly, no, I did not believe he actually met aliens, but decided to temporarily side-step the issue. "Look," I began, "people come in this office and tell me all kinds of things. It's often more important what they believe." He considered this momentarily, and then offered up another though. "Listen, I'm close with my parents. I told them about this and they are worried I might have schizophrenia or something. So, I said I'd come see you."

I was thinking of administering the Minnesota Multi-Phasic Inventory, second edition. The MMPI-2 is a lengthy test, assessing psychiatric and related disorders, with 567 items. The test and a referral to a psychiatrist were in order, but I decided to play the line out a little longer. I inquired about sexual abuse, but he denied abuse of any kind. He had already denied any hallucinations, delusions, and was well oriented to time, place, and person. His speech was fluid, coherent, and the content was absent any concerns save his story. I thought briefly of neurologist Oliver Sacks and one of his books. Knowing of little else, I pursued another line of inquiry: "Well, what you make of the experience?" He went on to say that he considered the encounter to have been positive and life changing. What had evidently changed for him was that previously he been a very rigid, emotionally cloistered person. If something did not fit into the scientific method, then he figured it was irrational and dismissed it. He smiled a very wide, natural smile. "Now, well it's like the experience has shattered that illusion and I feel liberated." "Well then," I continued, "what seems to be the problem?" "Look," he began, "if I were you and someone told me what I told you, I would think that person was looney. That's the problem. I mean, it's funny, as society would view me as ill when I actually feel better."

This was an odd moment where I felt torn. He did seem happy and quite stable, yet the professional in me was screaming, "Something's wrong!" "Alright, how else has this impacted your life?" He added that he felt less judgmental and critical of others and reported he had made a couple of friends where previously he had been isolated. I sat back and waited for some inspiration to come—an experience akin to waiting for Godot. Desperate as I was, I decided to try basic honesty. "Frankly, I do not know what to make of your story. I must tell you I am skeptical of alien visits. But regularly, students come through my door and speak of personal relationships with Jesus. Most such students are well oriented and usually struggling with stress or a relationship break-up." I did suggest him taking the MMPI-2, which he agreed to do. The results, however, came back with no particular cause for concern, with Scale 8 (Schizophrenia) and Scale 6 (Paranoia) well within the acceptable range.

"So, I'm not crazy, right?" He continued to be concerned about this. "Well, according to our intake interview, MMPI-2 and our session, you appear well-adjusted." He was still not quite satisfied. "But what do you make of my experience. I can tell you, I am not fabricating it." I shook my head. "No idea what to make. But what do you tell yourself about the experience?"

He smiled. "That it was a real gift. It's changed my life and opened me up to new ideas and possibilities and for the first time there's real meaning in my life."

We ended the session with the caveat that he could return should he feel anxious, depressed, or concerned about his mental state. I did repeat the possibility of his seeing a psychiatrist as a check, but, given his mood and cognitive state, I did not recommend a referral at that time. I never saw him in session again. While skeptical that he had actually encountered extraterrestrials, he seemed to be doing well on all fronts. What this client taught me was to remember to "keep that don't know

10 *Who Am I? The Power of Self-Discovery*

self," as the Buddhists say. The most important aspect of the session was not what I believed, but rather the impact the experience had on the client. Granted, we must do due diligence regarding assessment and intervention, but the more important part of counseling likely lies in keeping an open perspective and learning the lessons clients can teach us. I still do not know what to make of his incredible encounter of the third kind, but *my* belief was not what mattered, his was. I have retained a healthy sense of skepticism on such matters, but remain open to ways the unconventional may actually aid in therapy. In this unusual case, eschewing conventional belief systems was what led to his living more fully.

2 The Counseling Profession
Critical Information for Consideration

Anyone reading this text either is in the process of becoming a counselor (in a graduate counseling program), is interested in becoming a counselor, or already is a counselor. As a counselor, a counselor educator, an author of articles and books on counseling, and a person who has supervised counselors in the field and in training programs, I have had many opportunities to consider who is and *is not* appropriate for the profession. There will be a much more in-depth review of factors to consider in becoming a counselor in Chapter 3. This chapter addresses the counseling profession, how it differs from related mental health professions, the state of the profession, professional ethics, the U.S. Bureau of Labor's occupational outlook, benchmarks the profession has achieved, and remaining challenges. Naturally, this author's view is generally positive regarding the profession, having witnessed its significant growth, achievement of licensure in all 50 states and three territories (Washington, DC, Puerto Rico, and Guam), and gaining of insurance billing privileges. Despite all this success, there remain several unmet goals and challenges.

Professional Identity

The counseling profession is relatively new in comparison to its relatives— psychiatry, psychology, and social work. The counseling profession genesis goes back to 1952 when four separate organizations merged to form the American Personnel and Guidance Association (APGA). The APGA evolved into the profession now named the American Counseling Association (ACA), and is the largest and considered the profession's flagship organization. The ACA consists of 19 professional affiliate divisions (www.counseling.org/). Many mental health counselors, school counselors, addictions counselors, and rehabilitation counselors join both the ACA and their respective divisional affiliate (e.g., American Mental Health Counselors Association or AMHCA)—something encouraged in graduate counseling programs and by the ACA, and a practice encouraged in this and other texts by me.

A question the public, and certainly students in counseling programs, will ask is "How is counseling different from social work and psychology?" After all, all these professions also train professionals to counsel individuals. My own experience is the public does not understand the distinctions thus complicating the issues of professional identity. Professional counselors themselves often struggle to articulate the differences between counseling and related mental health professions. As counseling professionals, it is imperative we understand our identity as separate, and distinct from our colleagues in psychology and social work in particular (Healy & Hays, 2012). The counseling profession focuses primarily on the counseling relationship and encounter as its specialty. For psychology and social work, counseling is more an ancillary function (Remley & Herlihy, 2016). Clinical and counseling psychologists do provide counseling services as do clinical social workers, although their profession's primary mission is not counseling. Without question, as many mental health professions provide counseling services, the public continues to be confused between these disparate professions.

Professional identity can be a challenging concept to articulate, yet one vital to the viability and wellbeing of a profession. Think of well-known professions such as medicine, engineering, law, and accountancy—each of these is well understood, at least in general terms. Naturally, there are different types of physicians (surgeons, general practice, psychiatrists, etc.) and even accountants have variations. My experience, however, is that most adults understand what doctors, accountants, engineers, and CPAs do. Some researchers have argued that professional identity is a process as opposed to a specific outcome, and that counselors must frequently examine their identities to address emerging challenges (Brott & Myers, 1999; Hodges, 2019; Remley & Herlihy, 2016). Individual counselors must then be able to explain the philosophy undergirding the profession, professional practices, professional ethics, and scope of practice parameters, counselor training programs, licensure requirements, and outline differences between counseling and related occupations, to name some important responsibilities. Counselors with a strong professional identity often feel a sense of pride in being a member of their chosen profession (Remely & Herlihy, 2016).

While counseling was founded as a separate profession in 1952, it was only in 2010 that a definition of it was approved (Kaplan, Tarvydas, & Gladding, 2014). An ad hoc task force composed of delegates from major counseling organizations gathered in Pittsburgh at the ACA 2010 conference and approved the following definition of counseling:

> Counseling is a professional relationship that empowers diverse individuals, families, and groups to accomplish mental health, wellness, education, and career goals.
>
> (American Counseling Association, 2014, p. 20)

An operational definition provides illumination as to what counseling professionals actually do. While the definition of counseling is relatively brief, the nuances of counseling (e.g., professional divisions, research, ethics, training, etc.) would fill a lengthy book (or several texts). This chapter aims to provide clarity for the counseling profession and make it understandable to readers as well as the public. Knowledge and understanding of the counseling profession requires a brief foray into the philosophical underpinnings.

The Wellness Model of Counseling

The counseling profession developed out of a belief that the best method of assisting students and clients in resolving emotional, social, career, and relationship issues is the wellness model of mental health (Myers & Sweeney, 2005). Myers, Sweeney, and Witmer (2000) developed a comprehensive model of wellness that was specific to the counseling profession. The medical model has been the primary model that other mental health professions, such as psychiatry, psychology, and social work, have utilized to address emotional and mental health concerns. The medical model is an approach created by physicians for diagnosing and treating physical illnesses. In the medical model of treatment, diagnosis is the first step in assistance. Then, the professional sets about a treatment plan based upon that diagnosis to assist the patient to return to the level of functioning prior to the illness. The helping professional uses a scientific method, which is generally understood as evidence-based therapies, to help cure the afflicted person. The treatment plan is crafted as such, with measurable outcomes. As a cognitive-oriented counselor, I have done as such countless times myself.

Psychiatrists, who are physicians, utilize this approach, as do psychologists, nurse practitioners, and clinical social workers. All these professions matured while the medical model became the dominant approach and developed practice to align with that philosophy. Counselors, as previously mentioned, are a newer profession originally constructed on a different philosophy. Namely, the counseling profession subscribes to the wellness model of healing. The wellness model of counseling, furthermore, has solid research support as a viable treatment approach (Myers & Sweeney, 2005; Tagnoshi, Kontos, & Remley, 2008) and was championed by luminaries such as Carl Rogers (1951). The goal in the wellness model is for each person to achieve the most optimal mental and emotional health that is possible. In terms of a spectrum, on one end we have unhealthy, dysfunctional people, while on the other there exist healthy, fully functioning others. Fully functioning individuals likely approximate what Maslow called "self-actualized," which sits atop Maslow's Hierarchy of Needs (Maslow, 1968).

For clinical mental health counselors, and likely clinical rehabilitation counselors, addictions counselors, and others, wellness is at the core of their profession, although for these newer counseling affiliates, operations are more complex. A glance at the Council for the Accreditation of Counseling and Related Educational Programs (hereafter CACREP) for the clinical mental health counseling standards, however, suggests a very clinical focus (CACREP, 2016). The very name *Clinical* Mental Health Counseling, or *Clinical* Rehabilitation Counseling, and so forth, suggests a philosophy beyond the traditional wellness orientation. As a long-time mental health and addictions counselor, for third-party insurance and Medicaid reimbursement, a *DSM* diagnosis was required. Measurable treatment plans to address anxiety, depression, addiction, and so on, also are standard in clinical settings. Clinical mental health counselors, addictions counselors and clinical rehabilitation counselors are among the fastest-growing mental health professions in the USA (BLS, 2018–2028). So, as a graduate student and well into your profession,

14   *The Counseling Profession*

be grounded in a wellness-oriented profession, but be prepared to adapt to a dynamic, clinical focus. Given that the marketplace for clinical mental health counseling, addictions counseling, and clinical rehabilitation counseling is hospitals, outpatient clinics, and in- and outpatient addictions treatment, understanding the medical-model approach is an absolute necessity. You will notice signs of change, however. During my years in clinics, I cannot recall anyone mentioning the word *mindfulness*. Now, even in the country's most august hospitals, mindfulness is the term du jour in treatment. You will also hear much about the mind–body integration, and a recent training brochure I received regarding an upcoming training by a psychiatrist mentioned the word spirit. Change definitely is in the works!

A Brief History of the Counseling Profession

The counseling profession actually emerged relatively late in comparison to its colleagues of psychology and social work. Thus, the profession has had to "catch-up" to these respective related professions with regard to marketplace opportunities. The first half of the twentieth century witnessed several disparate organizations with some relationship to counseling, school guidance, advising, college student development, and so on. Then, in 1952, four different organizations met and agreed to merge, creating the American Personnel and Guidance Association (ACPA) evolving into what is now called the American Counseling Association (ACA) (Wrenn, 1962). The profession consisted of student affairs in college and university settings (e.g., counseling center, career services, dean of Students, etc.), P-12 schools as "guidance" workers, and in addictions treatment. In the late 1950s, the advent of the Cold War spurred Congress and President Eisenhower to implement the National Education Defense Act (NDEA). NDEA's primarily mandate was to stimulate the advancement of education in mathematics, science, and foreign languages, providing funding for school counselors (Wrenn, 1962). The Russian launch of Sputnik soon thereafter stimulated even more support for guidance professionals in schools, and the American School Counselor Association formed, furthering the professional identity of school counseling (Wrenn, 1962).

The counseling profession's early days (i.e., 1952–1960) were dominated by the influx of counselors in P-12 school settings and school counselors became fixtures in public school throughout the USA. Counselors continued in professional roles in community centers and in colleges, though arguably in less visible roles in comparison to their P-12 counterparts. School "guidance" counselors dominated the numbers in the broader counseling profession throughout most of the profession's history. Currently, however, clinical mental health counselors, addictions counselors, and clinical rehabilitation counselors are expanding at a much faster rate. In the near future, clinical mental health counselors will outnumber their school counseling colleagues, as evidenced by the U.S. Bureau of Labor Statistics for the CMHC and SC professions (2018–2028). In 1976, Virginia became the first state to grant licensure to counselors. The next four decades have witnessed all 50 states, Washington, DC, Puerto Rico, and Guam achieve counselor licensure (American Counseling Association, n.d.). The counseling profession's achieving licensure of all

The State of the Counseling Profession

Currently, the overall counseling profession is in a much stronger position than at any time in the past. The number of counselors has risen dramatically, with counselors, along with clinical social workers, dominating in community mental health settings, school counselors remaining stable in P-12 schools, and counselors becoming more common in private practice. While there are notable achievements, much work remains. Counselors were approved to be hired into Veterans Administration Medical Centers more than a decade ago, yet the actual number hired remains miniscule when compared to social workers. Counselors can bill Medicaid, but still cannot bill Medicare, which is a big constraint when it comes to providing treatment to elderly populations. Likely, the Medicare impediment is the largest hurdle the profession faces, and so the profession has targeted Medicare approval as the number one priority. The challenge to Medicare privileges is that both Houses of Congress must pass identical bills, which then go to the president to sign into law. Medicare approval bills have passed through both the U.S. House of Representatives and the U.S. Senate, though in separate years, and thus no such bill has gone to a president to sign into law. The counseling lobby continues to market Medicare to Congress on an annual basis. Eventually, a joint Medicare approval for counselor's bill will pass in Congress and be sent to the president to sign into law. I make this prediction given the growing numbers of counselors in agencies, private practices, and hospitals and numbers do make a difference—and will likely make the difference regarding Medicare reimbursement.

No doubt, a profession with a large number of members has a better chance of successfully lobbying elected officials attention. If we total the numbers of clinical mental health counselors, addictions counselors, school counselors, and clinical rehabilitation counselors, counselors number just above 700,000 (BLS, 2018–2028). According to the Bureau of Labour Statistics (BLS) figures, counselors actually outnumber social workers. The BLS figures can be fluid, meaning that some addictions counselors likely are social workers. Regardless, numbers certainly matter. Beyond Medicare billing privileges, some states have licensure laws that limit licensed counselors scope of practice. In New York, for example, diagnosis is not part of a Licensed Mental Health Counselor's scope of practice, thus limiting the profession in one of the most populous states. Despite the marketplace disadvantage, counselors are being hired into mental health and addictions jobs in record numbers. In my own program, hiring rates of our Clinical Mental Health Counseling graduates is virtually 100%. In point of fact, one large agency provider for mental health and addictions treatment regularly comes onto our campus to recruit counselors. They are proactive in recruitment due to a chronic shortage of therapists. Thus, business is good, despite the professional challenges. Thus, if a reader's questions is "Will I be able to get a job after graduation?" then the answer is "Yes, you have an excellent chance!" If the questions is, "What is the

16　*The Counseling Profession*

state of the counseling profession?" I would answer it in this manner: All 50 US states and three territories have achieved licensure, counselors are billing insurance in all states and three territories, counselors have been a fixture in P-12 schools for decades, billing Medicaid (in agencies), billing Tricare (military version of Medicare), are becoming as common as social workers in mental health agencies (some exceptions), and are one of the fastest-growing of all the mental health professions (BLS, 2018–2028). The evidence supports counselors as a viable, rapidly growing profession and one having gained a foothold in US society. As previously stated, however, work remains to be done.

Professional Goals Remaining

Naturally, while the counseling profession has made a quantum leap over the past two decades, there remains much work to be completed. Medicare reimbursement remains the top priority for the American Counseling Association and the profession at large. A close second likely is getting significant numbers of counselors hired into Veteran's Administration (VA) medical centers. Despite approval for employment over a decade ago, relatively few professional counselors have been hired at VA hospitals due to a lack of support within the VA. As previously mentioned, the profession must improve licensed counselors' scope of practice to include the critical issues of diagnosis. Licensed counselors have achieved this in most states, but in several, counselor licensure's scope of practice does not provide for a diagnosis. While counselors are very common in middle and high schools, there is a dearth of counselors serving elementary schools. Finally, the counseling profession has struggled with splintering between its major organizations. The American Counseling Association (hereafter ACA), American School Counselors Association (ACSA), American Mental Health Counselors Association (AMHCA), state counseling association, and so on, all compete with counselors for membership. Sadly, a high degree of, say, ASCA members do not join, say, the ACA. All mental health professions face this challenge of splintering, but none seems to have the membership disaffiliation struggles that are witnessed within the counseling profession. This latter intramural challenge may well prove the most difficult of all to solve.

As this text differs from standard, traditional, textbooks, I occasionally offer anecdotes from my own 30-plus years in the profession. Regarding professional memberships, I would strongly encourage all counselors to join the ACA, as it is the flagship organization for all counselors. All counselors should also join their counseling specialty organization (e.g., ASCA for school counselors, ARCA for clinical rehabilitation counselors, etc.), as well as their state counseling organization. Finally, counselors should keep a lifetime membership in their relevant professional counseling organizations (or for as long as one works in the profession). Keeping lifetime memberships in relevant counseling organizations helps the profession remain strong, promotes growth, helps with lobbying elected officials, and, most significantly, is the best way individual counselors can assist the profession in achieving marketplace parity.

Counselor Ethics: Cornerstone of the Profession

Professional ethics represent the cornerstone of the counseling profession. Likely, all professions have a code of ethics to provide a blueprint for members to follow. The American Counseling Association is the largest professional counseling organization and their code of ethics is the most comprehensive. The ACA revises their code on a periodic basis to adjust for societal, legal, and technological changes (Remley & Herlihy, 2016; Wheeler & Bertram, 2019). Ethical codes were crafted in order that professionals would have a guideline to follow when value judgments arise. An ethics code is, at best, a rough series of expectations and not a document that would have exact answers for every contingency. Perhaps one of the biggest frustrations I have noticed among beginning professional counselors and students in counselor education programs is the lack of absolute answers to ethical, legal, and moral questions. The foundation for ethical practice is based on knowledge of and adherence to the ACA Code of Ethics, although a best practice approach likely goes above mere adherence (Remley & Herlihy, 2016). Coming to understand that ethical practice involves following ethical standards, living a healthy, self-reflective professional lifestyle, and remaining informed regarding ongoing research and societal changes, is paramount. Let me give you an example from my own past.

When I began my own master's in counseling program in 1985, ours was the first counseling cohort required to take a course in Cross-Cultural Communication. At that time, the counseling profession was just beginning to acknowledge non-western cultural influences. Previously, the rugged individualist notion was the sole focus in the profession, mirroring white, euro-centric values (Lee, 2019). Our cohort of around 30 was overwhelmingly Caucasian, with one exception (from my memory). The following term, I was on my initial practicum in a small college counseling center. A Japanese-American student came to talk about her desire to become a teacher despite her parents' insistence that she should come into business with them. Naively, I inquired as to what might occur if she told her parents she wanted to be a teacher. I recall her eyes seemed to pop open! She explained that such a direct approach would be quite disrespectful in her culture and certainly in her family. Puzzled, I went to my supervisor, who was a very experienced counselor. He suggested I simply ask my client how she might work this issue out with her parents. He encouraged me to provide her a place to sort out the issue herself and cautioned against specific suggestions.

I was unsure whether the student would return, but she did, likely out of desperation. This time, I adapted in a Carl Rogers-like manner and asked how she might broach the issue with her very traditional parents. After spending the entire hour listening to her explain her grandparents formative years, who were both interned at a Japanese-American camp during World War I, she explained that addressing her mother first would be the first step. Then, after her mother spoke with her father, she could them discuss the matter with both. She did explain, however, she would follow her parents' desires over her own. She continued in counseling with me for several sessions to ready herself to talk with her mother. After speaking with her mother, she then met with both parents and fortunately her parents relented to her wishes.

18   *The Counseling Profession*

This simple experience from my distant past illustrates a simple, fundamental difference between a familial, collectivist culture and the individualist, western-oriented mindset still permeating much of US society. My career has provided me the opportunity to work alongside international students during my doctoral program, working with a multicultural clientele in public clinics, and on annual volunteer service projects in remote indigenous Australia and in South African orphanages. My advice: learn how to respect cultures that differ from your own. There will be value conflicts, especially with regard to gender and sexual orientation. The challenge is learning that respect does not imply agreement.

The Case of Leticia

Leticia is a recent graduate of a counseling program in California. She takes a job at a public mental health clinic in the greater Los Angeles area. The clinic serves a diverse population in east LA, including immigrants from a variety of African, Asian, and Middle-Eastern countries. Sawa, a Muslim woman from Senegal, studying at the local community college across the street presents for counseling. She discloses her spouse of two years has been physically abusive. She wants the abuse to stop, and has considered leaving her husband but feels trapped. "If I divorce my husband, my family will feel shamed and will shun me."

- How might Leticia might address this situation with Sawa?
- What are the challenges inherent in providing help?

Further Thoughts: There often is no easy answer when encountering cultural conflicts in the counseling encounter. You will have far more information to assist clients such as Sawa after studying the ACA Code of Ethics, and discussing ethical and legal concerns in classes and on your practicum and internships. Guidance from experienced supervisors and professors can make a big difference in your development as a counselor. First of all, in the scenario above, I suggest that Leticia should explore the options regarding her marriage. This could mean providing Sawa the opportunity to explore previously unthinkable possibilities (i.e., divorce), though without any pressure from the counselor. Leticia also needs to prepare Sawa for the consequences of any decision she makes. My experience is that many in Sawa's situation stay in an abusive marriage, although some elect to leave and face familial consequences.

Exercising Professional Judgment

Throughout their careers, counselors must exercise professional judgment in areas that are very difficult (like Leticia above). Counselors are accountable for making professional decisions regarding clients in a variety of situations regarding suicide probability, child and elder abuse, and the overarching, "what's in the best interest of the client?" issue. If a client believes harm resulted because of a professional decision made by a counselor, then the client might sue a counselor for malpractice

(Wheeler & Bertram, 2019). Consequently, when counselors exercise professional judgment, there remains a risk of an accusation of negligence. Here are a few of the types of potentially litigious issues requiring counselor vigilance:

- Addressing client lethality (danger to self and others)
- Determining how to prevent client suicide or harm to others
- Terminating counseling over a client's objections
- Setting ethical limits with a client expressing a romantic interest in you
- Rendering a diagnosis that may have negative implications for the client
- A terminally ill client in a state without physician-assisted suicide disclosing she will euthanize herself before the disease incapacitates her.

This chapter is merely the proverbial "snapshot" of professional ethics; you will need further guidance that can be found in the code of ethics (American Counseling Association, 2014), or through your ethics class, faculty, and onsite supervisors. Counselors must also obtain legal advice when legal issues arise in their practice as well as obtaining quality supervision and consultation. An attorney provides the counselor sound legal advice while a supervisor or consultant provides professional counseling input. While an attorney may be an expert on case law, he or she may not understand the socio-emotional vulnerability of your client.

The Case of Hiram

Hiram is a counselor in an interfaith suburban pastoral counseling center and has been licensed for five years. Hiram believes all life is scared and opposed abortion and capital punishment. Gerald, an elderly client, come in for counseling. Gerald discloses he has a terminal disease with less than six months left to live. Due to the additional emotional and physical suffering inherent in treatment, to say nothing of the financial cost and the impossibility of a cure, he states he plans to euthanize himself before the disease incapacitates him. He further says he has told no one else in his family and that counseling is to assist him in saying his goodbyes and putting his affairs in order. As Hiram practices in a state that does not provide physician-assisted suicide, the foreseeable-harm statute of the law regarding suicide applies. How should Hiram proceed?

- Naturally, he needs to seek legal advice from his attorney.
- He should review the ACA Code of Ethics regarding client harm and end-of-life decisions. (ACA, B.2.b).
- Perhaps the most complicated question is, "What's in the client's best interests?" The answer likely covers moral as much as legal and ethical issues. (ACA, I.2.a).
- What role does, or should, morality play in this scenario? The ACA Code of Ethics mandates tha values-based referrals are unethical (A.11.b). How does section of the Code of Ethics potentially complicate Hiram's approach with Gerald?

20   *The Counseling Profession*

A best practices approach would involve Hiram doing all the above as well as consulting with an experienced colleague. Realistically, he will need to assist Gerald in exploring euthanasia, the impact on family and close friends, and timelines. Remember, Gerald's stating he plans to euthanize himself carries no specific time-line, though with his illness, time is precious. Fortunately, most counselors never need to deal with issues such as Hiram's above, but *any* counselor potentially could. Therefore, it is critically important that you understand your ethical code, how legalities complicate treatment, and the role our personal morals play in addressing client issues. The following chapter will involve reflective questions to help deter-mine whether the counseling profession is a good "fit" for you.

Lessons Learned

My fellow graduate students and I were sitting together in the coffee shop section of the Memorial Union building at Oregon State University. From memory, it was the rough mid-way point of the fall term (OSU was on the quarter system). We were discussing the typical variety of subjects that graduate students usually discussed: classes, good and bad; professors, including our favorites and not so favored; work, as all held jobs; as well as the future job market. Interestingly, I recall this incident as it was the only time any of my circle discussed reasons for entering the counseling profession. There were four of us and we all mentioned the generic "I want to help people," "I find people's lives interesting," and "Counseling helped me and I want to help others." In reality, I somewhat dreaded addressing the issue of why I was in the counseling program. I entered the counseling program quite by accident. I took a graduate counseling course for teachers to assist me in my role as a resident director (RD) of a collegiate living group. I decided to apply for the program upon encour-agement from the instructor teaching the class. More significantly, my previous graduate program was not working out, so my decision to apply for the counseling program was a "Hail Mary" one (i.e., desperation).

As the discussion ensued, I became more anxious about my own shallow level of self-exploration and lack of investigation. Unfortunately, one of my friends remarked, "You've been quiet. What made you decide to be a counselor?" Taking a deep breath, I explained my poorly thought-out motivation. There was a momentary silence, as the trio looked at one another with raised eyebrows. Finally, another one broke the void by asking in a Reality Therapy manner, "Well, how's that working out for you?" Relieved, I was able to say that, quite by serendipity, the program and profession seemed a good fit.

Given that I entered the profession on a whim and was flying blind so to speak, I am indeed fortunate that things worked out for me as a counselor and, much later, as a counselor educator. Looking back, I would encourage *no one* to make their deci-sion in the default manner that I used. Frankly, my ambivalent approach was a meta-phor for my life at that point (aged 25). That is, I was riding in the passenger seat of my life, allowing others to take the wheel and drive me wherever they wished, all with my consent! This impromptu coffee klatch with my classmates shook me awake to the reality I needed to begin conscious planning. One of my professors was fond of saying, "If you don't know where you are headed, you are likely to end up in the wrong place." Chapter 10 of this text will address personal and career visioning and goal setting. I learned to begin regular self-reflection, set measurable goals, and seek guidance from those I respected. I hope all readers will choose to sit in the driver's seat of their life. That way, even if you do wind up in one of life's culs-de-sac, at least you made your own decision and can turn around and try another path. I would also opine that while I have made many, many mistakes in the past 35 years, at least they were my own mistakes and not those merely defaulted to others. This latter point of self-determination is of significant importance, albeit with cultural nuances.

3 Should I Become a Counselor?

To publish this text, Routledge required me to develop a prospectus. The prospectus includes sample chapters, estimated book length, target markets, and so on. Then, the company sent the prospectus to four professional counselors for review. One of the reviewers made the comment that a critical question for inclusion is, "Should I become a counselor?" I was in complete agreement with that reviewer and have even titled this chapter with the said suggestion. This chapter, then, will focus on requirements for becoming a counselor, reflective questions regarding reasons for becoming a counselor, and essential information regarding the counseling profession. Naturally, selecting a potential career is an inexact science at best. There are interest inventories such as the Strong Interest Inventory (SII) that assess interests across a wide range of potential careers, and aptitude tests such as the popular Armed Services Vocational Aptitude Battery (ASVAB). Likely, the best strategy is a combination of aptitude and interest assessment, combined with speaking with a professional counselor working in the field. Reviewing the U.S. Bureau of Labor Statistics online *Occupational Outlook Handbook* (OOH) for job projections is highly recommended as well (www.bls.gov/ooh). I would also recommend you utilize self-reflection for a deeper inquiry into your interest in the counseling profession. If need be, make use of a profession counselor to probe into reasons for becoming a counselor. Regarding this latter point, anyone interested in becoming a counselor should experience what it is like to be a client in counseling. You come to understand the nuances of counseling as a participant and develop empathy for clients.

Interest vs. Aptitude

Years ago, while working at a university counseling center, I was filling in part-time in the university's career center while they were short-staffed. I overheard one weary career counselor describe a challenging client in this way: "He has all the interest in being an engineer and none of the aptitude!" Sometimes the reverse can be true. A former student of mine, who was a pharmacist, left the profession to become, of all things, a counselor. When I inquired as to why she was leaving the pharmacy profession, she explained, "Pharmacy is a skill, but no longer an interest." The ideal makeup for any career would include both interest and aptitude among other qualities such as a good work ethic, ability to work with a wide variety of

Should I Become a Counselor? 23

people (e.g., those different in culture, ethnicity, political, etc.), and being an ethical professional.

Interest in a particular field is just what it implies. For example, anyone considering the counseling profession would certainly need to have a particular interest in working as a counselor. Such an interest would include the desire to assist people struggling with mental illness, relationship issues, career and vocational concerns, post-traumatic stress disorder (PTSD), and numerous additional emotional-social concerns. In over three decades of meeting with persons interested in becoming counselors, and in interviewing candidates, never have any espoused a disinterest in becoming counselors. (Readers will not be shocked by this revelation.) Essentially, everyone professing an interest in being a counselor has at least a basic level of interest. So, we have checked that box. The more complex consideration is that of aptitude.

Career aptitude is the potential to be facile in a given career. While career interest is relatively simple to assess, assessing career aptitude is far more difficult. Aptitude tests are evaluated with regard to predictive validity, or the extent to which success in whatever aptitude the test purports to measure can be predicted from the test results. Some aptitude tests are based on a generally standardized prior experience. An example is testing welders with a welding test. Other aptitude tests, like ASVAB, assess a variety of eight-ability scales such as Work Knowledge, Paragraph Comprehension, and Mathematics Knowledge among others. The ASVAB is administered and interpreted free of charge, by representatives of the Armed Services (U.S. Department of Defense, 2005). Military branches of service will use a recruit's ASVAB results to place that recruit into a particular job. The ASVAB, however, likely is not a good tool to assess suitable future counselors. So then, what are valid and reliable measures for determining potentially "good" counselors?

How Are Potential Counseling Candidates Selected?

While career interest inventories such as Strong Interest Inventory and aptitude assessments like ASVAB certainly have their place in the career field, assessing potential for future counselors is, in my 30-plus years, very inexact. To begin with, what exactly are the qualities a potential counselor should possess? Some qualities that come immediately to mind are empathy, healthy boundaries, ethical practice, healthy work ethic, personal resilience, a sense of humor, and good self-care. This is scarcely an exhaustive list, but one I try to cover when speaking with anyone interested in the profession. But, how have students interested in becoming counselors traditionally been selected?

Pursuant to the above paragraph, when applying to the graduate counseling program at Oregon State University, I was required to take the Graduate Record Examination (GRE), provide transcripts for review, and sit for an interview with select faculty members and graduate students. For the most part, this screening process has continued with marginal change. The weakness to this traditional formula is that the GRE is not a valid assessment for future counselors. The GRE does provide a basic snap-shot of academic aptitude, although norms on this test vary greatly

24 Should I Become a Counselor?

among institutions and departments (Hayes, 2017). Using GRE scores to predict success in graduate school is particularly difficult for many reasons. For example, applicants with low GPAs may be eliminated immediately, as undergraduate GPA and GRE scores are the primary criteria whereby applicants are selected for graduate school. Furthermore, as grades in graduate school often are restricted to A and B, GPAs can be inflated. Then again, the GPA and GRE likely are not assessing chief qualities for counselors. Neither the GRE nor most undergraduate courses assess the ability to relate to people, and neither do they assess empathy levels, tolerance for ambiguity, nor self-care. Perhaps the best criteria for predicting future success in any field is resilience, or what one scholar calls "grit" (Duckworth, Eichstaedt, & Ungar, 2015). Having spent countless hours in individual, group, and couples counseling regarding a wide range of mental health and development concerns, grit would be near the top of my admission list.

Graduate counseling programs are the "greenhouses" charged with developing future counselors. Needless to say, post-masters's experience in a school, agency, or hospital will likely be the more significant part of counselor identity and development, but the graduate years come first. The gatekeeping role of screening applicants for appropriateness to graduate programs is part of a counselor educator's professional ethics (American Counseling Association, 2014). From my experience, programs rely on individual or group interviews, transcript review, letters of recommendation, GRE scores (a less common requirement nowadays), or a written statement on why the applicant would make a good counselor. Once admitted to a graduate program in Clinical Mental Health Counseling, School Counseling, Rehabilitation Counseling, and so on, the faculty has two-to-three years to evaluate the student's appropriateness for the profession. Some students determine during their graduate program that a career as a counselor is not for them; others are dismissed from counseling programs. A few complete their program of study in a respective counseling area and then decide they will matriculate into a related career in student affairs (e.g., dean of students' office, academic advising, career center, etc.).

Decades ago, while enrolled in a graduate class on psychological assessment, the professor made the statement that despite the volume of assessments for psychopathology, addiction, student achievement, career, and so forth, the most accurate predictor of future behavior and success is previous behavior and success. He went on to say that even previous behavior was not a robust predictor either, citing achievement tests such as the SAT and ACT. My career of 30-plus years as a counselor and later as a professor supports my former professor's words. I can recall notable exceptions where formerly addicted clients achieved and maintained sobriety against great odds. I have further witnessed students who struggled academically during undergraduate and graduate years, but went on to become very successful counselors and counselor supervisors. Naturally, as one who is a great believer in assessment, experience has taught me assessment is no panacea and that I must make allowances for improvement and, certainly, resilience. To go further, I have witnessed academically gifted students whiz through undergraduate programs and subject area counseling courses, only to watch them stumble on field placement when confronted with clients' real-life issues. The bottom line in predicting success is that there are basic commonalities such as previous success and resilience, but predictive validity remains somewhat inexact. So, as is commonly mentioned in Zen Buddhism, "keep that don't know self."

Still, as I am writing this text to assist future counselors, counselor educators, and those possibly interested in the counseling profession, I feel an obligation to provide basic guidance on who *should* and *should not* become counselors. While the late Albert Ellis might be upset with my use of his favorite whipping word, "should," the term is most useful. I find self-reflection is one method of assessing interest and intent. I have developed the following list of questions to assist readers who are considering entering a counseling program to evaluate their motivations and suitability for the counseling profession. When you complete the assessment, ask yourself "What did I learn from this assessment?" "What could I improve upon?"

Reflective Questions for People Considering the Counseling Profession

If we wish to grow and mature as counselors, we must consider our motivations, intentions, and even our inner lives. I recommend you answer these questions as honestly as possible.

1. What motivates you to become a counselor? (Alternatively, "Why do you want to be a counselor?")
2. What qualities do you currently possess that would make you good at assisting people in need?
3. Consider a significant failure/setback you have experienced. What important lessons did failure teach you? How has learning from that setback helped transform your life?
4. Counselors often work with clients whose values may conflict with their own. How do you feel about counseling someone whose political, spiritual, and sexual values conflict with yours?
5. Pursuant to the previous question, the counseling profession maintains that values-based referrals are unethical. So, if a client considering gender reassignment comes to you for counseling, would you be able to "bracket off" your own values (if necessary) and counsel that client? Why or why not?
6. What would you most like to improve about yourself?
7. How well do you get along with people of a different culture, religion, ethnicity, sexual orientation, and political affiliation?
8. What type of a self-care practice do you have? Self-care could include a regular workout regimen, healthy diet, spiritual or mindfulness practice, family and friend supports, and so on.
9. If you were to ask someone who knows you well if the counseling profession was a good fit for you, what might that person say?
10. Why should a graduate counseling program admit you?

Attitude Assessment

Your attitude may well become your most important asset as a counselor or in any other capacity (Seligman, 2011). Take a moment to reflect on your attitude. Does your attitude communicate an openness to others? Do you enjoy new challenges? Do you begin your day with a sense of gratitude? When you complete the attitude assessment below, what do your answers suggest regarding your attitude? What changes might you wish to make?

Assess the current state of your attitude by answering the following set of questions. Indicate whether you primarily agree ("Yes") or disagree ("No") for each item:

1. I comfortable working with people of a different culture or religion.   Yes   No
2. When I have conflicts, it is usually the other person's fault.   Yes   No
3. I believe that most people can change.   Yes   No
4. I enjoy taking risks that increase my comfort zone.   Yes   No
5. Most people get ahead by personal connections, not work ethic or attitude.   Yes   No
6. I can respect people who disagree with me.   Yes   No
7. Each day I feel grateful for the joys in my life, however small.   Yes   No
8. When I face challenges and obstacles, I tell myself that this presents an Opportunity for personal growth.   Yes   No
9. When I have a disagreement with someone, I do my best to work out the issue in a respect manner.   Yes   No
10. People who know me well would say I generally have a positive attitude.   Yes   No

Lessons Learned

Just after completing my doctorate, I accepted a position as clinical director of a mental health clinic in the remote mountainous West. The clinic was conveniently located across the street from the local community college. Each semester, I taught one psychology class in the evening. My students were an amalgamation of traditional ages college students, older, non-traditional learners (the largest percentage of my classes), and even a few high school students in their junior and senior years. Early in my second semester, I posted an assignment whereby students were required to select an article from a professional counseling or psychology journal to critique. I provided a handout with several professional journals the community college library carried, and a sheet explaining the assignment parameters and expectations.

In the following class, everyone handed in their assignments. The student papers were typical for undergraduates, though with far more grade variation than is evidenced in graduate students. One critique in particular, however, stood out as the outlier. This student had selected an article in a tabloid periodical (I cannot recall if it was the *National Enquirer* or another). The article focused on the recent newborn of an African American and Caucasian parents. The article claimed the baby was born with polka dot skin, a result of miscegenation, and the author went on a racist and quite ill-informed rant regarding this case as evidence for resurrecting laws preventing interracial marriage and breeding. I was in equal parts shocked and angry at the article and the student for selecting it. Furthermore, even beyond the ignorant, racist tone, my student had neglected to critique a professional journal article. It seemed scarcely worth noting her paper was full of grammatical errors. She received an "F" for the grade, with me carefully explaining my rationale and requesting she see me to discuss the matter.

The following day, she came to see me in a huff. Furious at her grade, she gave me a private sermon on how she was soon to be an honor graduate of one of the local high schools and so forth. Keeping my cool—with difficulty—I remained silent until she was finished. I carefully reviewed the assignment parameters that were in the handout previously provided. I explained the assignment was to critique a professional journal article, and also offering that the article she reviewed was both racist and penned by someone totally lacking in medical knowledge. This approach had the effect of pouring gasoline on an already lit fire!

She seemed flabbergasted at my not considering the periodical was not a "professional" journal. I then opened the door to the views she had openly expressed, stating her views seemed focused on the racial superiority of whites. She replied that she had the right to her views, to which I regretfully agreed, though explained she was still required to follow the assignment instructions. I suggested we end the conversation and talk again when she felt calmer. She then stormed dramatically from my clinic office, leaving a trail of curious onlookers in her wake. That afternoon the psychology program chair called me regarding the matter. The student had complained to her and wanted me fired. I explained my rationale and the chair, who incidentally was married to an Asian man, became quite alarmed herself. Regardless, I agreed to meet with her and the student in the hope that this might be the teachable moment I recalled reading about in Parker Palmer's wonderful book on teaching (2007).

I was pleasantly surprised to see that the student came to the meeting acting contrite. She apologized for her outburst and asked if I would provide her a chance to redo the assignment. I agreed, though at a reduced grade. I did point out that while she had the right to her views—racist as they were— such views did not meet the standard of the class or the college, nor of the assignment. After the meeting ended, she redid the assignment using a standard journal and with far better editing. Her mood in class improved dramatically and she attended all classes and completed the term with a good grade. After the term concluded, she returned to my office, albeit in a calmer frame of mind.

She was applying to the community college's two-year addiction counseling program and asked me for a letter of recommendation. I was very torn between my belief in second chances and my concern regarding her previously held personal views. I explained this to her and finished by asking her this question: "If you were in my place, would you provide a letter of support? Why or why not?" She was briefly quiet, and then began to talk about her upbringing in a rural, environment, where the only person of color was a Latina cook. Her parents evidently held very traditional (a kind way of saying *racist*) views on race and how she never really had much opportunity to question those beliefs. She went on to say that being in our class, which had a number of Latino and Latina students, was the first time she had given serious thought to her parents' biased views. She pointed out she had made a couple of Latina friends from the class.

I explained she would have multicultural clients and asked whether she would be able to counsel them. "I have learned," she said, tears welling in her eyes. Despite my inclination to decline, I suggested she give me a couple of days to think the matter over. That afternoon, I sought counsel from a colleague. "Hector" (pseudonym) was a Latino and veteran substance abuse counselor at our clinic and a graduate of the community college's addiction counseling program. I explained the entire experience, her original racist paper, and then her turnabout in class and strong grade. Hector, a longtime resident of the rural area, had experienced his share of ugly bias. He was very thoughtful regarding the matter. "Look, you asked her a good question regarding if she was in your shoes. Ask her to write a letter explaining why she would say yes to a letter of recommendation." After more conversation, I agreed to consider this approach as it required her to further self-reflect on her views.

The following day, I sent her an email stating my conditions: she would need to write me a convincing letter. If her letter seemed genuine, I would write her that letter of recommendation. She replied she would get started on the letter. Two days later she hand-delivered it to the clinic office and asked to wait while I read it. In her thoughtful letter, she outlined her parents' very biased opinions, and then expressed how her original conflict with me led, ironically, to more egalitarian cultural views. She stated a willingness to support a student who had learned as she had. "But," she had written, "I understand you may not." Finished reading, I noted she was dressed professionally and looking at me with concern, awaiting my decision. "How do I know you have genuinely changed?" I inquired. She paused. "I suppose you would have to trust me," she admitted, with a serious look on her face.

She appeared genuine, and her performance and attitude shift in class had been impressive. Still, given her initial paper, I was hesitant. I then considered times in my own academic career when faculty had provided me second chances despite inconsistent academic performance. I recalled a graduate school professor personally calling the graduate admission office and telling them to accept me into the doctoral program despite my uneven academic past. Could I go out on a similar shaky limb? Between my head and heart, emotion won out. "I am going to write this letter on your honor that you have really changed," I said. "Thank you," she replied. "I won't let you down."

A year later, I accepted a job that took me halfway across the country and far from the clinic. I lost touch with my former student and never heard how her career plans turned out. I took a calculated risk based on her turnaround in class and the serious manner, which she seemed to have transformed her views. No one comes into this world selecting his or her parents, nor certainly their opinions. We do, however, have the option of independent thought and, as Murray Bowen would say, differentiating ourselves from our family of origin. My take-away lesson from this experience is that people can change provided they have the proper intrinsic motivation. My career, both as a counselor and a counselor educator has frequently involved me pondering other's second chances. I have written reports for judges, parole officers, child protection workers, as well as academic review boards, doctoral admissions committees, and potential employers. There always is some gamble involved, albeit more or less so depending on the person and issues involved. So, perhaps you would decide to grant a second chance, use sober reflection, consulting with someone you respect, speak with the person in question, and make an informed decision. Fortunately, many calculated risks work out, but be prepared should they not. I would also be less than forthright should I fail to mention times when my judgment was wrong and a parolee was arrested, someone relapsed after long-term sobriety, and the occasional student on whom I had gambled went on to fail. We live with both our success stories and those with a disappointing ending. Be prepared!

4 Becoming a Counselor
What's Involved?

The counseling profession has changed considerably since my entry to a master's counseling program over three decades ago. My first experience with a counselor was our own rural school counselor. He served grades 1–12, taught a high-school psychology class, and occasionally filled in as a science teacher. Originally certified as an agricultural and science teacher, he retrained as a school counselor during the early 1960s by taking summer classes at a university 90 minutes away. Much of his role centered on administering various tests such as the Iowa Test of Basic Skills (for eight years, ugh!), the PSAT, and the ACT. Unfortunately, behavioral issues typically went to the principal, where liberal use of paddling students with a board was the primary behavioral change technique. Needless to say, such were the dark ages of my educational past.

Over the decades, the roles of a counselor, whether in a school or community agency, has evolved. Changing demographics, social dynamics, along with licensure, have transformed the counseling profession (Lee, 2019). Society's change from the Caucasian nuclear families of the 1950s looks considerably different at present, with changing notions of what constitutes a family, increasing ethnic populations, and changing cultural norms and values (Lee, 2019). This sociocultural evolution has led to changes in counseling programs, particularly regarding curriculum, ethics, length of study, and those who become counselors. When I began my graduate studies in 1985, our cohort was the first required to take a multicultural counseling class. Fast-forwarding to the present, multiculturalism is generally infused throughout the curriculum, and at least one institution, the University of Malta, offers a master's degree in Multicultural Counseling.

While major changes have occurred within the profession of counseling regarding cultural, ethnicity, gender, LGBTQ issues, degrees offered (master's and doctorate in school, clinical mental health, clinical rehabilitation counseling, etc.), the process of becoming a counselor remains quite similar. First, those interested in becoming counselors must earn a baccalaureate degree (with rare exceptions), usually in psychology, though certainly not restricted to that discipline. (My own bachelor's degree was in English.) Then, the interested student enters a master's degree program in a counseling discipline (e.g., clinical mental health, school, career, etc.) and, after two or three years, graduates with a degree, then lands a job in an agency, school, hospital or another setting, and works for state licensure (or certification for school counselors in many states). The licensed or certified counselor then supervises newly minted counselors or counseling interns from a university program. The undergraduate to graduate school to counseling professional cycle continues, with new professionals coming into the field and experienced ones retiring.

Considerations

Although an exact number is difficult to sum, given the constant flux within higher education, the total number of counseling masters' program would likely be above 1,500. This includes one-faculty member programs in small colleges to large departments in major research universities that could approach 20 faculty members (master's and doctoral, with several different programs). Well-known virtual institutions, as well as traditional universities, offer entirely online counseling programs leading to degrees and license eligibility. Given all this variation in options, there are many factors to consider prior to matriculation into a particular counseling program. Here are some important considerations:

1. Is the program CACREP accredited? (Or is it Commision on Accreditation for Marriage and Family Therapy Education (COAMFT) accredited for Marriage and Family Therapy Programs or one of the respective accreditations for creative arts counseling programs?)
2. How many full-time faculty members does the program have? This is an issue of continuity as well as advising and mentoring. CACREP-accredited programs must have a minimum of three faculty members. Adjunct faculty, while dedicated, may have little time for advising.
3. What is the program's student-to-faculty ratio? Higher ratios likely mean less time for faculty to advise.
4. Is this a terminal master's program or does the department/program include a doctoral program in Counselor Education? A doctoral program might mean quicker matriculation to doctoral study.
5. Does the program offer paid graduate assistanceships? If so, how many?
6. What is the program's job-placement rate? If the faculty cannot tell you, you may wish to attend another program. Viable career mobility may be the most important consideration of all.
7. Most counseling programs are pluralistic in nature, meaning that they are nondiscriminatory regarding gender, minorities, LGBTQ people, religious orientation, veterans, and so on. However, make sure you ask, as a few institutions, particularly some in evangelical religious institutions may vary.
8. Does the institution offer on-campus housing? Some urban settings are very expensive and university housing is usually less costly, though offering less room.

Licensure: A Critical Credential

A critical concern for anyone entering a master's degree counseling program is ensuring that graduates of the program are license eligible in that state or territory,

32 Becoming a Counselor

or as in Canada and other countries, eligible for "Registration," an equivalent credential. When interviewing for admission, ask whether the said program's graduates are license eligible in that state or territory. The American Counseling Association publishes a helpful online document, *Licensure Requirements for Professional Counselors: A State-by-State Report* (American Counseling Association, 2016; www. counseling.org/docs/licensure/72903_excerpt_for_web.pdf). If you are considering a counseling program in, say, North Carolina, be "streetwise" and fact check what recruiters tell you. For example, there are numerous master's level programs in Clinical or Counseling Psychology. They may, in fact, provide good instruction and a solid educational foundation, but psychologist licensure is at the doctoral level in all but a few states. In Niagara University's Clinical Mental Health Counseling program, for example, we regularly get students holding a master's degree in Clinical, Counseling, or another psychology branch who completed a master's—and spent a lot of money—only to discover to their chagrin they were not license eligible in their desired state. By the way, one may reasonably question the ethics involved in offering a master's degree when the psychology profession maintains that the entry degree is a doctorate and state licensure is unavailable, apart from a few exceptions (e.g., School Psychology).

Many applicants and even graduate students are confused regarding the distinction between licensure and certification. This confusion is quite understandable, and one about which I was perplexed when I began my master's program over 30 years ago. State licensure actually is the *required* credential for billing insurance and moving into supervisory positions in agencies. Some addictions counseling positions still require only a bachelor's degree and the Certified Alcoholism and Substance Abuse Counselor (CASAC), and many states, such as New York, offer state certification as opposed to licensure for school counselors. Beyond schools, certification (usually national certification) is a voluntary credential. Counselor certification began when the profession created the National Board for Certified Counselors (NBCC; www.nbcc.org/) in 1982 (Stone, 1985). A Nationally Certified Counselor (NCC) is an individual who has met the requirements set down by NBCC. The profession established national certification when only a handful of states licensed counselors, in order to provide a unified national credential (Stone, 1985). To become an NVV, a counselor must complete a master's degree in counseling, have two years of post-master's experience, and pass the National Counselor Examination. The two years of post-master's experience is waived for graduates of CACREP-accredited programs.

Many licensed occupations also offer voluntary certification for specialists within that profession. The medical profession is a clear example. States license physicians, while specialization credentialing comes through a national organization (e.g., "Board Certified in Obstetrics"). Remley (1995) has argued that states should license counselors as generalists and the NBCC should certify counselors in specialty areas (e.g., Addictions). His position is that the role the NBCC plays in certifying counselors as specialists is vital to the success of the counseling profession. Remley further asserts that specialty designation should remain voluntary and be offered by a national organization such as the NBCC.

Becoming a Counselor   33

In addition to the NBCC, an affiliate, the Center for Credentialing and Education (CCE, 2014; www.cce-global.org), offers additional specialty certifications, including Approved Clinical Supervisor (ACS), Distance Certified Counselor (DCC), Global Career Development Facilitator (GCDF), Thinking for a Change Certified Facilitator (T4C-CF), Board Certified Coach (BCC), Educational and Vocational Guidance Practitioner (EVGP), and Human Services-Board Certified Practitioner (HS-BCP). Now, my experience is that graduate students and new counselors in the field, to say nothing of the general public, are often confused by the proliferation of credentials. Remember, state licensure is the most important credential for a professional counselor working in an agency, hospital, or in private practice. For school counselors, the important credential is state licensure for states that license school counselors, or state certification for those that do not license school counselors. For most counselors, certification is for a specialty area such as addictions, trauma, clinical supervision, and so forth. Many counselors hold a state license (e.g., Licensed Professional Counselor or LPC), and national certification (most commonly National Certified Counselor or NCC).

Additional national counselor certification also are popular. For example, the Credentialed Alcoholism and Substance Abuse Counselors (CASAC) credential is a national credential administered through individual states and territories. The CASAC credential was developed specially for the addictions profession to provide a standard credential for addictions/substance abuse counselors who lacked a master's degree and/or lacked credentials for state licensure. As the addictions counseling profession has moved towards the requirement of a master's degree, many counselors working in chemical dependency hold both the CASAC credential and a state license. Interestingly, CASAC, as opposed to licensure, has been the required degree in the addictions profession. This is the opposite of, say, Clinical Mental Health Counseling, where state license became the required credential. As the addictions profession moves to master's degree requirements, state licensure likely will become the required credential, while CASAC will be for specialty certification in addictions as per the Remley model.

License Portability Issues

In the USA, licensure is the purview of individual states and territories. In most states and territories, counselors must have a valid license before being allowed to practice counseling (Bergman, 2013). A major issue for all professions, given that state-to-state requirements in, say, teaching, medicine, and law can vary considerably, is licensure portability. This certainly has been no different for the counseling profession. Although CACREP accreditation has assisted with creating a national standard for accredited, most programs remain unaccredited (though CACREP accreditation has grown significantly in numbers, scope, and influence). This means counselor licensure requirements between states can vary considerably. Most states require 48 semester credit hours, while those having passed counselor licensure more recently require 60 semester credit hours, making portability difficult. A counselor holding counselor licensure in, say, New York (60 graduate credits) may have little

34 *Becoming a Counselor*

difficulty when relocating to a state requiring only 48 graduate credits. The reverse of this, however, involves much difficulty for the relocating counselor. At our CMHC program in New York, we have had experienced counselors with 48-credit degrees and licensed in another state, and many years' experience, required to complete three-to-four additional graduate courses in order to meet state requirements for licensure. The American Association of State Counseling Boards (AAASCB; www. aascb.org) is an organization working on making licensure easier for counselors. Part of their efforts involve working with counseling organizations (e.g., ACA, ASCA, AMHC, CACREP), lobbying legislators, and working towards more unifying licensure standards. The AASCB was a signatory of the very important Counseling 20/20 initiative, resulting in agreements regarding the definition of counseling, with the ACA being the flagship organization, CACREP the official accrediting organization, and so forth (Remley & Herlihy, 2016). Unfortunately, license portability for counselors remains very much a work in progress given varying standards. This unfortunate scenario will likely remain in place as licensure will continue to be the purview of states.

The "good" news regarding license portability is that it has improved somewhat. The most significant improvement was achieving counselor licensure in all 50 states and three territories. From Virginia being the first state to license counselors in 1976 to California in 2009, the counseling profession was remarkably successful, especially in light of opposition from established mental health professions (e.g., psychiatry, psychology, social work, etc.). Previously, when a licensed counselor holding a state license relocated to a state lacking licensure, finding a counseling-oriented job was very difficult. Now that all states and major territories have counselor licensure, AASCB, ACA, AMHCA, and other counseling organizations can focus efforts on more unified licensure. Unified standards between states and territories will help greatly with portability and ensure a strong, viable national profession.

Scope of Practice

Perhaps the most contentious issue between the counseling profession and that of related mental health disciplines is the scope of practice. The primary issues of disagreement are testing and diagnosis (Hayes, 2017; Wheeler & Bertram, 2019). Traditionally, the psychology and social work professions have maintained that counselors are not adequately prepared to use psychological assessments and diagnose. The counseling profession has fought these battles and in the vast majority of states and territories have won the right to use psychological tests (with some limitations), and diagnose using the *DSM* (Remley & Herlihy, 2016). For the most part, the counseling profession has been generally successful in defending scope of practice issues (Remley & Herlihy, 2016; Wheeler & Bertram, 2019). One likely can expect professional turf battles to continue given that counselors, psychologists, social workers, and so forth often overlap on the services provided with regard to counseling, assessment, and diagnosis.

Diagnosis is a significant economic issue for the mental health profession. Most insurance companies require mental health professionals to be qualified to diagnose in order to bill for counseling services. No doubt, psychologists and social workers have a stake in prohibiting counselors from providing diagnostic services, just as in previous eras the psychiatric profession attempted to limit psychologists and social workers. As with licensure, scope-of-practice issues involve the political process of lobby legislators to include diagnosis in counselor scope-of-practice rights. Most states have extended counselor scope of practice to include diagnosis and psychological assessment (Remley & Herlihy, 2016; Wheeler & Bertram, 2019). There are some states, however, where the issues of diagnosis remains unresolved and ongoing lobby efforts pro and con continue for the counseling profession.

The counseling profession has traveled a long distance with regard to diagnosing and treating mental disorders. Originally, the profession focused on a developmental counseling perspective that was in opposition to diagnosing using the DSM (Ivey & Ivey, 1999). Due to a changing marketplace, the counseling profession moved forward to include diagnosis in counselor education programs and in respective states professional scope of practice. Counselor preparation programs, particularly those in Clinical Mental Health Counseling and Clinical Rehabilitation Counseling, include diagnosis throughout the curriculum. Furthermore, CACREP-accredited counseling programs are required to include diagnosis in their curriculum, and the National Clinical Mental Health Counseling Examination (NCMHCE) tests counselor proficiency regarding diagnosis. The *Diagnostic and Statistical Manual of Mental Disorders*, fifth edition (2013), specifically mentions counselors as a profession qualified to diagnose: "The information is of value to all professionals associated with various aspects of mental health care including … counselors" (p. xii).

That the American Psychiatry Association (APA) agrees the DSM is important for counselors represents a significant step forward for the counseling profession. The counseling profession will need to continue to lobby legislators in those few states whose scope of practices does not specifically include counselors as having diagnostic rights. Given the profession has achieved this in most states, as well as licensure in all states and major territories, eventually counselors will have diagnostic rights in all states. Students in counseling programs should maintain professional memberships with ACA, ARCA, AMHCA, and so on, as well as their state organizations, as these organizations lobby legislators for professional practice rights, as this is essentially a political process. Once again, this is another reason professional membership is so important as the respective national counselor organizations (e.g., ACA, AMHCA, ASCA, etc.), as well as state affiliate organizations, lobby elected officials for scope-of-practice rights.

American Counseling Association

The American Counseling Association (ACA) is the largest counseling organization in the world and consists of 19 affiliate divisions and state branches that represent the counseling profession (ACA, n.d.). The ACA's roots go back to 1952 when the National Vocational Guidance Association (NVGA), the National Association of Guidance and Counselor Trainers (NAGCT), the Student Personnel Association for Teacher Education (SPATE), and the American College Personnel Association

36 Becoming a Counselor

(ACPA) merged to form the American Personnel and Guidance Association (APGA). The ACA consists of some 60,000 members and offers an annual national conference.

Student should join the ACA while in their graduate program and maintain active membership throughout their career as a counselor. All members receive a monthly magazine (*Counseling Today*), quarterly journal (*Journal of Counseling & Development*), reduced fees for the national conference, discounts on ACA publications, and monthly updates regarding news, professional development opportunities, and lobbying efforts in Washington, DC, among other benefits. Graduate students also receive liability insurance with purchase of membership, which is an asset, as CACREP-accredited programs require that students on placement have current liability insurance.

As previously stated, the ACA has 19 affiliate divisions. Members of the ACA may join one or more divisions in addition to ACA membership. Division members receive scholarly journals from divisions that publish them, newsletters, and information related to divisional matters. It is common for ACA members to hold membership in an additional division. For example, rehabilitation counselors often join both the ACA and the American Rehabilitation Counseling Association (ARCA), while mental health counselors would likely hold memberships of the ACA and the American Mental Health Counselors Association (AMHCA). Counseling faculty in universities frequently join the Association for Counselor Educators and Supervisors (ACES) in addition to the ACA.

Most states, plus the District of Columbia, Virgin Islands, Puerto Rico, Guam, Europe, and the Philippines have state ACA branches. Although these branches are chartered by the ACA, they operate as separate, independent organizations. Most branches hold annual or biannual conferences within their state. Many important issues, such as license and school counselor certification, are addressed at the state or territorial level. Furthermore, it is very important for counselors to know and be in contact with colleagues in their state or territory. The position among many counselor advocates is that counselors should hold ongoing memberships in ACA, and their respective organization (e.g., American Mental Health Counselors Association, American School Counselors Association, etc.), and their state or territorial organization (e.g., New York Mental Health Counselors Association) (Meany-Walen, Carnes-Holt, Minton, Purswell, & Pronchenko-Jain, 2013).

The following is a list of the important professional counseling organizations and their website addresses.

American Counseling Association (ACA)

Flagship division for all counselors. (www.counseling.org/)

American College Counseling Association (ACCA)

Counselors who work in community and technical college, college, and university settings. (www.collegecounseling.org)

Becoming a Counselor 37

American Mental Health Counselors Association (AMHCA)

AMHCA represents the primary professional organization for clinical mental health counselors. (www.amhca.org)

American Rehabilitation Counseling Association (ARCA)

ARCA represents the profession of clinical rehabilitation counseling, faculty, and graduate students. (www.arcaweb.org)

Association for Adult Development and Aging (AADA)

Counselors with a special interest in gerontology and those working with geriatric populations. (www.aadaweb.org)

Association for Assessment and Research in Counseling (AARC)

AARC promotes ethical, effective use of assessments in counseling and education. (www.theaaceonline.com)

Association for Child and Adolescent Counseling (ACAC)

ACAC represents counselors specializing in counseling children and adolescents. (www.acachild.com)

Association for Counselor Education and Supervision (ACES)

ACES represents college and university faculty teaching in graduate counseling programs, counselor supervisors, and counselors interested in supervision. (www.acesonline.net)

Association for Counselors and Educators in Government (ACEG)

Counselors employed in local, state, and federal governmental settings. (https://aws4.associationdatabase.com)

Association for Creativity in Counseling (ACC)

Counselors who have a special interest in creative approaches to counseling, such as art, music, or dance therapy. (www.creativecounselor.org)

The Association for Humanistic Counseling (AHC)

AHC is a professional organization for counselors interested in humanistic-oriented approaches. (http://afhc.camp9.org)

Association for Lesbian, Gay, Bisexual, and Transgender Issues in Counseling (ALGBTIC)

Counselors with a special interest in and providing counseling services to lesbian, gay, bisexual, and transgender clients. (www.albgtic.org)

Association for Multicultural Counseling and Development (AMCD)

AMCD strives to improve the understanding of multicultural issues in counseling. (http://multiculturalcounselingdevelopment.org)

Association for Specialists in Group Work (ASGW)

ASGW provides professional leadership in the field of group counseling in schools, agencies, inpatient and outpatient settings, etc.) (www.asgw.org)

Association for Spiritual, Ethical, and Religious Values in Counseling (ASERVIC)

ASERVIC is devoted to exploring spiritual, ethical and religious values in counseling and open to all regardless of spiritual orientation. (www.aservic.org)

Counselors for Social Justice (CSJ)

CSJ is committed to equality on a broad array of social and cultural issues in counseling. (https://counseling.csj.org)

International Association of Addictions and Offender Counselors (IAAOC)

IAAOC advocates for the development of effective practices in substance abuse counseling, counseling offenders, and counseling in correctional settings. (www.iaac.org)

International Association of Marriage and Family Counselors (IAMFC)

IAMFC is the professional organization focused on relationship counseling. (www.iamfc.org)

Military and Government Counseling Association (MCGA)

MCGA is dedicated to counseling issues and concerns in state, federal, and military settings. (http://acegonline.org)

National Career Development Association (NCDA)

NCDA's mission is to promote career counseling, advising, and development. (www.associationdatabase.com/aws/NCDA/pt/sp/Home_Page)
National Employment Counseling Association (NECA)
NECA's charge is professional leadership for counselors working with the unemployed and charged with job and career development. (www.employmentcounseling.org)

Additional Related Counseling Organizations

American School Counselors Association (ASCA)

ASCA promoted the profession of school counseling (P-12 grades, public and private secondary schools) for counselor education faculty, counselors in elementary, middle, and high schools. (www.schoolcounselor.org)

Council for the Accreditation of Counseling and Related Educational Programs (CACREP)

CACREP is the international accrediting organization for graduate counseling programs. CACREP accredits programs in Addictions Counseling, Clinical Mental Health Counseling, Clinical Rehabilitation Counseling, College Counseling, Counseling and Student Affairs, School Counseling, Marriage and Family Counseling, and doctoral programs in Counselor Education. CACREP also sponsors the International Registry of Counselor Education Programs (IRCEP) for counseling programs outside the USA. (www.cacrep.org)

International Association for Counselling (IAC)

IAC serves as the international counselling organization for counselors working across the globe. IAC membership is open to counselors in all countries. (www.iacsinc.org)

National Board for Certified Counselors, Inc. (NBCC)

NBCC serves as an independent credentialing organization credentialing organization for the counseling profession. Although US states and territories are responsible for licensing counselors, NBCC provides certification for specialty areas in counseling. NBCC offers certifications as National Certified Counselor (NCC), National Certified Clinical Mental Health Counselor (NCCMHC). NBCC also offers states the National Counselors Examination (NCE), and the National Clinical Mental Health Counselor Examination (NCMHCE) as licensure examinations. (www.nbcc.org)

40   *Becoming a Counselor*

Center for Credentialing and Education (CCE)

CCE is an affiliate of NBCC and provides a number of services. Most notably, CCE offers credentials such as Approved Clinical Supervisor (ACS), Board Certified Coach (BCC), Distance Certified Counselor (DCC), and Global Development Facilitator (GCDF), among others. (www.cce-global.org)

Websites of Expressive Arts Therapy Organizations

There are many professional creative therapeutic organizations. Readers may visit the websites listed for additional information on training, credentialing, and graduate programs.
American Art Therapy Association (AATA): www.arttherapy.org
American Dance Therapy Association (AADA): https://adta.org
American Music Therapy Association (AMTA): www.musictherapy.org
American Society of Group Psychotherapy and Psychodrama (ASGPP): www.asgpp.org
Center for Journal Therapy (CJT): www.journaltherapy.org
International Art Therapy (IAT): www.internationalarttherapy.org
International Expressive Arts Therapy Association (IETA): www.ieata.org
National Association for Drama Therapy (NADT): www.nadt.org
National Association for Poetry Therapy (NAPT): www.poetrytherapy.org

Bureau of Labor Statistics (BLS)

The Bureau of Labor Statistics (www.bls.gov) is part of the U.S. Bureau of Labor. The BLS publishes the online *Occupational Outlook Handbook* (www.bls.gov/ooh) tracking employment demand for counseling fields. Counselors and persons interested in counseling should check the BLS website for changes in occupational demand. The BLS updates career demand and professionals in the field on a regular basis, so regular perusal of their website is strongly encouraged.

Lessons Learned

After two decades as a practicing counselor, supervisor, and adjunct professor, I was recently new to my position as a full-time, tenure-track counselor educator. The state to which I had relocated, New York, lacked counselor licensure at the time. Our program in Mental Health Counseling was a three-year, intensive master's degree program with a hefty 1,000-hour field placement requirement. As a counseling professional who had run a county mental health clinic and a university counseling center, I felt ready to become a full-time counselor educator. Although I was excited to have finally joined the ranks of faculty in a tenure-track position after many years of teaching as an adjunct, I was quite unprepared for the realities beyond the classroom.

I began contacting agencies in our area in the hope of developing field placements and ran straight into closed doors. "Nope, sorry, we only take social work interns" was the almost universal refrain. Now, I had expected a fair amount of this, having run into it previously in county clinics and university counseling services. Still, I expected to have some degree of success developing partnerships with treatment agencies. One curt director of an area clinic told me frankly, "Your profession will need to achieve licensure to get grads hired and you will never become licensed in this state." The next sound I heard was the buzzing of a hung-up phone. I replaced the receiver, leaned back in my chair and considered my options. I had just left a secure job running a university counseling center and moved across the country on a gamble. Suddenly, it looked as if I had placed a "bad" bet. Unsure what to do, I went to speak with an older colleague.

Sam was a long-time faculty member who had spent several years as a high school counselor in New York State. "Look," he said, "our enrollment in the school counseling program is huge, so you won't lose your job. Honestly, you won't have much success with that program [Mental Health Counseling]. Focus on the school program, get whatever trickle of students you can in the mental health program and don't worry about it." I should point out that our school counseling program was as over-enrolled as the mental health one was under-enrolled.

Sam gave me sound advice. The prudent course was to put 90% of energy into the established school counseling program as the payoff was there. As a career mental health counselor, however, I found this scenario troublesome. Certainly, I wanted our school program to continue with healthy enrollments and for graduates to find employment. Fortunately, all was going well with the school counseling program as the enrollment was huge. Enrollment in the mental health counseling program was an anemic seven students! Likely, the only reasons the university did not cut the program were, first, the school counseling program was so large and, second, the administration did not seem to know we had a graduate Mental Health Counseling graduate program. So much for flying under the radar of the provost's office.

I enjoyed teaching students in the School Counseling program, but longed to improve the situation for the less than a minyan of persons enrolled in the Mental Health Counseling program. Nothing I tried—calling, emailing, asking to meet in person—helped. Discouraged, I was ready to hoist the white flag and surrender all efforts. Soon thereafter, I received an unexpected call. Our dean of students called to inform me that his wife was a clinical supervisor at a local agency that treated children and adolescents. She had just become aware of our mental health counseling program and wanted to meet. Excited, I took the information and called her and we set up a meeting at her agency. I discovered she also was a graduate of a mental health counseling program and, according to her, probably the only such in the entire area. She agreed to sign a Memorandum of Understanding (MOU) to take our interns at her agency. She then gave me some helpful advice: "Listen, you will have an uphill battle for a long time. Now, addiction treatment agencies are under a different state regulatory agency and require only a CASAC (Credentialed Alcoholism and Substance Abuse Counselor). Gear your program towards substance abuse and you will have a lot more luck."

Finally, an opening and a viable strategy were in sight. On contacting the person she suggested at the identified agency, I received a warm reception. Yes, we could meet. I met with the contact at his agency and we signed an MOU as well. He explained, "We have a revolving door of openings due to burn out, retirement, counselors quitting their jobs, and such. Tough gig, you know." I did know, after having filled in as an addiction counselor during my years in community agencies. I informed all students in the Mental Health Counseling program that we would focus our placements on addiction treatment agencies. The students were a tougher sell, as practically none wanted to work in the substance field. Reasons cited were low pay, tough clientele, relapse rates, and a profession many saw as the stepchild of the mental health profession. As reality set in, most of our students began accepting placements in substance abuse treatment clinics, with a few going to the previously mentioned agency treating children.

The great result was that 100% of our small class of Mental Health Counseling graduates found employment. All but one or two were hired into addiction treatment. The word spread that we had an intensive program that led to a guaranteed job. Soon, eight students became 16 students, and then 30 students. The only downside was that the administration got wind of our success and began taking a closer look at our program. Our dean of the College of Education counseled me, "Just focus on your job placement and significant growth, we can market that." Regardless, flying unnoticed by the administration had been more comfortable than the possibility of someone in higher authority actively tracking our successes and setbacks.

Occupational life continued as it was for a couple of years, until one morning I received an email from the state organization with the shocking news that both houses of the State legislature had passed a counselor licensure law and the Republican governor had actually signed it. The only people who might have been more surprised than myself possibly were the social workers and psychologists who had empathically asserted that counselors would never become licensed in New York State. "When pigs fly," had been one critic's statement. Well, perhaps there were some flying porcine types within our borders as counselor licensure actually passed against stiff opposition!

What I learned from this challenging situation is that what has been may, and likely will, change. The counseling profession has now achieved licensure in all 50 states and three territories. Improvements regarding scope-of-practice issues and Medicare reimbursement remain, but these are reachable goals. My advice to anyone reading this text is to seek out and listen to counsel from counselors, social workers, psychologists, and other mental health professionals' voices, but keep an open mind regarding change. My prediction is the counseling profession will achieve parity with our mental health colleagues. This is because the number of professional counselors is roughly equal to that of social workers (using BLS figures), and graduates of counseling programs have had significant success in becoming hired by agencies, as well as schools.

5 Counseling
A Broad Profession in the Twenty-First Century

The counseling profession has matured considerably since its official founding in 1952. In a previous era, the profession primarily focused on training counselors for careers in schools, vocational-guidance centers, and college student personnel; the profession is now significantly broader and larger than in previous times (Gladding, 2018). While school counselors remain the largest of the counseling specialties, clinical mental health counselors will likely surpass them as the largest subset of counselors (BLS, 2018–2028). Addictions counselors is now emerging as a master's level profession after decades as a baccalaureate-level or less profession, and counselors are becoming more common in correctional settings and in hospitals. This chapter will highlight the various types of counseling and include guidance activities regarding which type of counseling profession best suits a reader's needs. Naturally, many if not most readers of the text will already be enrolled in a graduate counseling program (Clinical Mental Health Counseling, School Counseling, Clinical Rehabilitation Counseling, etc.). Nevertheless, the information in this chapter could be even more relevant as you may have questions as to whether you are in the program that best fits your skills and interests. It is also worth mentioning that some counseling-oriented professions may not yet exist. Online counseling has grown and developed into a specialty field and few would have imagined this in the recent past.

Common Specialty Areas of Counseling

School Counseling

School counseling has traditionally been the largest of the counseling professions. School counseling received a boost from the federal government during the late 1950s with the passage of the National Defense Education Act (NDEA) (Gladding, 2018). The goal of the legislation was to promote postsecondary education and specifically to assist the country's educational system to meet technical and scientific demands. Specifically, the federal government desired a strategic, comprehensive method to identify promising scientific and engineering types of students during junior high and high school. Of particular concern was the ability to compete with the Soviet Union in technical and scientific areas (Gladding, 2018). With the

44   *Counseling*

launch of the Soviet satellite Sputnik, the USA had fallen behind in the space race. The National Defense Education Act (NDEA) provided federal funds for training school guidance professionals (i.e., counselors). Because of NDEA, the counseling profession received a large increase in teachers interested in retraining as school guidance professionals. School counselors today work in primary through high school settings. With strong national numbers overall at 324,500 (BLS, 2018–2028), school counselors have traditionally been the largest of the counseling professions. School counselors work in public and private P-12 educational settings, although many elementary schools still lack counselors (Gladding, 2018). Traditionally, school counselors were required by respective states to have served as teachers for a prescribed period of time (often a minimum of two years) before being certified as counselors. Currently, most states have either changed this requirement of alternate created pathways for non-teachers to become certified as counselors. The American School Counselor Association (ASCA) is the flagship organization for the school counseling profession. The ASCA was until recently an affiliate of the American Counseling Association (ACA), though it now operates as a separate professional counseling organization. Most graduate school counseling programs are two years in length, with a 48-semester credit hour requirement for the master's degree.

The occupational outlook for school counselors varies depending on the particular region of the country, with the Sun Belt (e.g., California to Florida) having the fastest-growing job market (BLS, 2018–2028). Many in the profession speak of a large wave of school counselor openings due to retirements, though this can be difficult to predict. The BLS currently projects school counselor occupational demand at a rate of 8%, which is considered to be faster than average nationwide. Job market demand will vary considerably due to the region of the country, with urban versus suburban versus rural settings. Likely, the best advice for any aspiring school counselor is to be flexible about location regarding the job market. Thus, a newly minted school counseling professional may need to work in an inner city setting for a few years, where the educational, social, and economic conditions are less than ideal. Having made the previous statement, I would argue that urban schools have the greatest need and many counselors may find the challenges rewarding. Likewise, some new counselors will relocate to rural or remote areas of the country, moving far from family and friends, at least for a few years. My personal experience is that few graduate students are interested in hearing that they may not land a job in a well-paying, high-achieving suburban school in a desirable geographic location. The reality is that most beginning school counselors will need to look well beyond the area of their ideal job choice.

The role of the school counselor has likewise evolved from its "guidance" infancy. School counselors perform a variety of professional roles, including career and vocational testing, career and academic counseling and advising, personal counseling, serving on multidisciplinary school task forces, and running SAT/ACT test preparation, among other duties. Current median salary figures for school counselors are among the highest in the profession at $56,310 (BLS, 2018–2028) and most school counselors work on ten-month contracts, though variation exists. Be aware, of course, that schools can vary considerably and underfunded, urban or rural schools may offer the most immediate opportunity.

Clinical Mental Health Counseling

Clinical Mental Health Counseling has become one of the fastest growing of the counseling professions with a current projected 22% growth rate and a median salary at $44,630 (BLS, 2018–2028). Clinical Mental Health Counseling is a relatively new profession, with Virginia passing the first counselor licensure law in 1976 (American Counseling Association, 2016). CMHC programs began as community counseling programs and were usually 48-semester credit hour programs and two years in length. Currently, as CACREP accreditation has strengthened, CMHC programs are 60-semester graduate credits and typically three years in length. As counselors are now licensed in all 50 states and three territories, Clinical Mental Health Counselors have likewise seen their numbers grow considerably (BLS, 2018–2028). Clinical Mental Health Counselors work in community agencies, addiction treatment (inpatient and outpatient), psychiatric centers (inpatient and outpatient), and multidisciplinary health clinics among others. Some Clinical Mental Health Counselors even work in P-12 school settings, though some states have yet to credential CMHC's for school settings (e.g., New York State). Without question, through the growing focus on trauma and addiction (e.g., opioids, alcohol, tobacco, etc.), the CMHC profession promises strong growth potential.

Addictions Counseling

The profession of Addictions Counseling (also called Substance Abuse Counseling or Chemical Dependency Counseling) has been undergoing significant changes in recent years. Originally, addictions counselors were principally composed of former addicts in long-term sobriety. Few held an advanced degree and many lacked any college education. Many if not most addictions counselors' model was the 12-step, Alcoholics Anonymous (AA), peer-led, spiritual model of recovery. Although the addictions counseling profession has evolved since its early years in the 1930s, 12-step-type recovery groups such as AA remain popular in addictions treatment (Juhnke & Hagedorn, 2013). Nevertheless, addictions counseling is moving towards a more standard level of education with the profession having developed advanced degrees in addictions counseling. The CACREP now offers accreditation for graduate programs in Addictions Counseling. Addictions counselors can become state licensed in all states, usually, however, as Licensed Professional Counselors (LPC) or Licensed Mental Health Counselors (LMHC) (American Counseling Association, 2016).

Originally, addictions counselors worked towards the Credentialed Alcoholism and Substance Abuse Counselor (CASAC), as licensure was generally not an option. As the addictions profession has matured, formalized training programs have become common at community colleges (two-year associates degrees), with undergraduate (BA/BS) and graduate programs (MA/MS). Unlike in previous decades

46   Counseling

where an addictions counselor almost was required to prove she or he was a former addict in successful recovery, such a bias has become greatly reduced (Juhnke & Hagedorn, 2013). The job market for addictions counselors remains one of the strongest of any mental health profession with a 22% growth rate and a median salary of $44,630 (BLS, 2018–2028). Now while the growth rate is strong, BLS has recently combined Substance Abuse Counselors with Mental Health Counselors, so salaries will vary even more than usual. Due to a plethora of addictive substances and the public's awareness of addictions issues and treatment, the job market for addictions counselors is unlikely to subside anytime soon.

My own experience as a mental health/addictions counselor and counselor educator is that frequently addictions treatment providers have trouble retaining addictions counselors and regularly contact my colleagues and me looking for potential counselors to hire. Just recently, an area organization concerned with the opioid epidemic contacted my colleagues and me to meet and discuss how area treatment providers might retain and recruit counselors. Weekly, if not daily, local, regional, and national media report on drug addiction, overdoses, healthcare costs, and deaths due to addiction. Thus, when someone asks me "What's the most promising mental health profession to go into?" I always suggest addictions counseling and administration. Several graduates of our Clinical Mental Health Counseling program have become addictions counselors, moved into administrative roles running clinics, and even into higher-level management. Management level counselors will earn a higher salary given increasing responsibilities, but also will have more challenges with staff, given a supervisory role. So, readers looking for a challenging career with a strong job placement market and the ability to advance would be wise to consider the addictions field.

Now, have just completed the previous paragraph, prudence requires giving the cautionary "other" side to a career in the addictions field. First, addictions counseling is very difficult. While I cannot conceive of any easy counseling occupation, counseling addicts, many of them long-term addicts struggling with multiple substances, with some being violent offenders and having served time in jail or prison, holding generally less education, and poor occupational history, to say nothing of high trauma rates (i.e., PTSD), addictions counseling is *really* tough work. Much of an addictions counselor's caseload is composed of mandated clients (DiClemente, 2003; Prochaska, Norcross, & DiClemente, 2013). This means the average court-mandated client has little motivation for change (Prochaska, Norcross, & DiClemente, 2013).

Clinical Rehabilitation Counseling

Clinical rehabilitation counseling remains a popular counseling specialty area. Occupational projections have remained steady growing at a rate of 10%, meaning faster than most careers, though a median salary of $35,630, lower than their school and mental health colleagues (BLS, 2018–2028). Clinical rehabilitation counselors traditionally worked in vocational rehabilitation centers as well as hospitals. Many graduate rehabilitation counseling programs specialize in areas such as assisting the

Counseling 47

deaf and hard of hearing, visually impaired, intellectually disabled, chronic injury clients, and so on. Without question, there is great need for clinical rehabilitation counselors given the numerous disabilities from which many children and adults suffer.

Most states license rehabilitation counselors through the standard Licensed Professional Counselor (LPC) or Licensed Clinical Mental Health Counselor (LMHC) process. This means clinical rehabilitation counselors can work in community agencies in a variety of roles as well as in vocational rehabilitation agencies. Working with military veterans would appear to be a natural place for clinical rehabilitation counselors to find employment. VA Medical Centers have been very slow to open up employment to counselors, likely due to social workers being the traditional mental health profession staffing the VA. Like clinical mental health counselors, clinical rehabilitation counselors will eventually find a niche in the VA, although this job avenue continues to be very slow in developing. Clinical rehabilitation counselors interested in working with veterans may find employment in community-based clinics serving veterans, such as in residential-based addictions treatment. No doubt, counselors who are military veterans will have a better chance of being hired into the VA or other clinics specializing in treatment veterans for PTSD, substance abuse, depression, and other mental health concerns.

One of the changes in the clinical rehabilitation counseling profession is that the Commission on Rehabilitation Education (CORE) has now merged with CACREP, meaning Clinical Rehabilitation Counseling is now a CACREP-accredited counseling specialty area. The inclusion of clinical rehabilitation under the CACREP accrediting organization means CACREP influence has become stronger and more consolidated. Clinical rehabilitation counseling arguably has a stronger lobby as a result of the merger (as does the CACREP). Likely, clinical rehabilitation counseling programs will increase, though perhaps not in the dramatic manner that clinical mental health counseling has witnessed.

Trauma Counseling

Trauma counseling is a relatively new field composed of numerous different professional treatment counselors, psychologists, social workers, and psychiatrists. Some stand-alone graduate master's degree programs in Trauma Counseling exist, though typically social workers and clinical mental health counselors, addictions counselors, and clinical rehabilitation counselors provide the majority of counseling to trauma survivors. Graduate certificate programs in trauma counseling have become far more common, and I have noticed numerous ones advertised through social media. My own trauma counseling certificate program was very intensive and took me three years to complete (due to my teaching schedule and international work).

Trauma recovery has become very popular in the mental health field. Five different therapeutic approaches tend to dominate: Prolonged Exposure, EMDR, Dialectical Behavior Therapy (DBT), Trauma Focused CBT, and most recently, Acceptance and Commitment Therapy (ACT). These five approaches focus on holistic mind and body (and sometimes "spirit") care for trauma survivors (Levers,

48   *Counseling*

2012). Treatment involves focusing on cognitions, behaviors, body work (e.g., yoga, massage, acupuncture, etc.), mindfulness such as breath work, meditation, healing visualization, among others (Evans, 2012). A large part of trauma counseling is assisting survivors to address ongoing concerns such as flashbacks, panic attacks, negative thoughts, nightmares, and so forth (Curran, 2013).

Clients suffering from PTSD due to sexual abuse, combat experience, or other first responder roles (police, fire fighters, paramedics, etc.), automobile accidents, among other ways, often will self-medicate using alcohol, opioids, and other drugs to dull the emotional and physical pain caused by trauma. Marsha Linehan, developer of DBT, advises clinicians to tell PTSD sufferers that they are having a normal reaction to an abnormal experience (Linehan, 1993). Essentially, Linehan suggests informing PTSD sufferers that flashbacks, anger, nightmares, and panic episodes are the body and mind's natural method of getting the individual's attention and saying essentially, *Deal with me!* (italics mine). The important part of Linehan's focus is that the environment (or perpetrator) is the issue, and symptoms essentially exist to teach us to reach out for professional help. Framed in this more holistic manner, clients suffering from PTSD may be more amenable to therapeutic intervention.

Pastoral Counseling

In this section, a distinction will be made between pastoral counseling, which is a broad multifaith profession and, say, "Christian" counseling, which typically is narrower in scope. The American Pastoral Counseling Association (AAPC) is a well-respected organization with an ethical code requiring members to practice non-discrimination towards clients of other religious faiths and those of none. AAPC ethical standards also affirm non-discrimination towards LGBTQ persons. Pastoral counselors often receive clerical training as well as professional counseling training either at a seminary, yeshiva, or other religious educational body, or at a traditional postgraduate program housed in a college or university.

Pastoral counseling conducted in a church, mosque, or synagogue, for example, may be distinct from that in a community-based pastoral counseling center. In the former, the pastoral counselor may be counseling a parishioner and thus a dual relationship exists. The operative question herein being which role dominates: that of being the religious leader or that of the counselor? Pastoral counselors trained in in AAPC-accredited counseling programs or centers, the individual's emotional and spiritual wellbeing are primary, not the adherence to a particular religious faith or dogma. Regardless, having worked in two pastoral counseling centers, a dynamic tension between spiritual issues and a mental health focus certainly exists.

Pastoral counselors are not as numerous as clinical mental health counselors, school counselors, and addiction counselors, though pastoral counselors may work in these counseling areas, especially in parochial schools, and addictions treatment clinics. The number of pastoral counselors employed in the USA is difficult to discern, as the BLS (www.bls.gov/) does not track the pastoral counseling profession. A website named Indeed (2017) cites more than 20,000 pastoral counselors in the USA. Persons interested in pastoral counseling as a profession should visit the AAPC website to access a list of accredited graduate programs. Pastoral counselors will need to be well versed in the typical mental health issues (in *DSM-5*) such as anxiety, depression, addiction, and so on, but also existential concerns such as life meaning, death anxiety, and spiritual concerns. Many pastoral centers will also expect to employ liturgically trained counseling professionals who will have an additional graduate degree or more in divinity, a particular field of theology, or a similar degree.

Counseling in Correctional Settings

Counselors working in jails and prisons are a more recent addition to the counseling profession. Correctional facilities employ counselors to address issues of addiction, sexual offender treatment, PTSD, and a wide range of mental health disorders. Addiction treatment is of primary focus, as relapse to a previous drug is a significant contributing factor in recidivism (Butzin et al., 2006). Many addictions and clinical mental health counselors find employment in jails, prisons, and detention facilities. The standard master's degree in a counseling field is required, and often corrections facilities prefer to hire experienced counselors who already hold a license. Salary and benefits tend to be very competitive within the field as incentives to recruit counselors into correctional settings. Federal and state prisons hiring counselors likely will offer a higher salary and benefit package as opposed to a county jail.

Turnover can be high, depending on the type of facility (county, state, federal), size of institution, how well staffed it is, and its population (minimum vs. maximum security). The best part of counseling in a correctional setting, other than potential pay and benefits, is being in a profession that enjoys a challenge. One study suggested 26% of inmates may suffer from mental illness and addiction (Gonzalez & Connell, 2014). Correctional facilities likely are more punitive than therapeutic in nature, and likely will challenge counselors, especially more progressive ones. Counselors with a background in addictions counseling, and who have a law enforcement background, likely have an advantage in being employed in jails and prisons.

Counseling in the Military

Due to recent congressional legislation, whereby counselors now work in VA Medical Centers and bill TRICARE, the military is becoming a market slowly opening to counselors (Hodges, 2019). Career opportunities in the military are still restricted for counselors as the armed forces currently recognize only psychologists and clinical social workers for active duty. Now, counselors do serve veterans in a variety of ways. Many private mental health and addictions treatment contractors provide trauma and addiction recovery. In the area where I reside, a large healthcare organization hires counselors to staff inpatient and outpatient treatment for veterans. The Department of Veterans Affairs recently opened four regional crisis-line centers. Veterans can call a toll-free number and speak with a professional counselor for crisis counseling and intervention.

Although the military is a large, top-down, bureaucratic monolith and changes very slowly, little doubt remains that counselors will be a significant part of mental

50   *Counseling*

healthcare provision in the future. Although the VA/military job market is a mere trickle at present, with licensure in all 50 US states and three territories, TRICARE billing privileges, and approval to work in VA Medical Centers, change is happening. Former veterans are the most natural types to counsel veterans and, as previously mentioned, have a better chance of being hired at VA Medical Centers.

Creative Arts Counseling

Numerous creative arts counseling professionals now find work in schools, hospitals, and private practices (Hodges, 2019). Creative arts therapy professions include art therapists, music therapists, play therapists, dance and movement therapists, and animal-assisted therapists among others. The occupational outlook is difficult to discern, as the Bureau of Labor Statistics does not track creative arts therapy professions. The best resource for readers interested in one of the creative arts fields, is to visit the various professional websites (e.g., American Art Therapy Association, American Dance Therapy Association, Association for Play Therapy, etc.).

Each professional website includes membership information, education, training, and credentialing requirements, ethical codes, and convention and conference information.

Here is a list of professional creative arts therapy organizations and their websites: American Art Therapy Association ((http://adta.org)
American Dance Therapy Association (http://adta.org)
American Music Therapy Association (www.musictherapy.org)
Association for Play Therapy (www.a4pt.org)
International Society for Animal Assisted Therapy (www.aat-isatt.org)
North American Drama Therapy Association (www.nadta.org)

Adventure Based Counseling (ABC)

Adventure based counseling is a creative approach to counseling and personal growth utilizing challenge courses, trust exercises, and the natural environment in therapeutic ways. I have positioned adventure based counseling, often called adventure based therapy, as separate from the creative arts counseling approaches due to the fact it emerged separately from the therapeutic professions and that it differs significantly from, say, art therapy, dance therapy, and the others. Adventure based counseling was an outgrowth of the recreational therapy profession. More recently, counseling and the broader mental health professions (psychology, social work, psychiatry, etc.) have taken adventure approaches and molded them to address social deviance in adolescents, for personal growth, to foster team work among co-workers, and improve self-confidence through challenging fears (Garst, Schneider, & Baker, 2001).

Adventure based counseling typically involves structured activities, for example, taking a group of 10–12 adolescent offenders on a 7–10-day hike through the Adirondack Mountains, the Rockies, Sonora Desert, or another beautiful naturalistic setting. During such an excursion, the co-counselors (or co-leaders) will create trust exercises whereby each youth may have a partner to assist each other preparing meals, during long hikes, and pairing them in sharing exercises. Frequently, an outdoor experience would involve daily use of structured group therapy to address personal growth issues or peer conflicts (Marmarosh, Holtz, & Schottenbauer, 2005). Groups are often run after meals (e.g., breakfast, lunch, dinner), with each member giving and receiving feedback. Groups may also be call on an ad-hoc basis during the day should the need arise—something quite common in ABC. For example, conflict is very common during intensive outdoor experience, and verbal and even physical altercations may occur. When such an event happens, groups are called, with the group members required to confront the perpetrators. Typically, adventure based therapy with adolescents will involve a level system, whereby participants on higher levels earn more privileges. There is a non-level, sometimes called "Risk" or another name indicating concern. Participants on Risk have lost all privileges and may be assigned additional work details, early bedtime, and restricted from certain activities. Participants may get off Risk and back on the level system through evidencing prosocial behavior. Group members vote to put participants on Risk and also to remove group members from Risk.

Adventure based counseling has many additional variations. Persons struggling from depression, anxiety (e.g., PTSD, GAD, etc.), addiction, and those simply seeking personal growth experiences may join an adventure based therapy exercise. In one case, while living in Oregon, I recall a counselor leading growth excursions through the Cascade Mountains on three-to-seven-day hikes. Daily group therapy was a staple, as were trust exercises, daily chores, and self-disclosure. One trust exercise involves pairing up with a partner. One partner would be blindfolded and led on the hike by the other. The dyads would hike for extended periods, such as one or two hours, and then switch roles. Other trust exercises involved partners assisting each other hiking on steep, narrow cliffs, or simple tasks like setting up a tent together, or preparing a meal for the entire group. Group members kept daily journals and were encouraged to share their successes and challenges during group therapy. Each member would also share three personal "gratitudes" during the evening.

Business and education have incorporated adventure based therapy into trainings. In lieu of a trek through bucolic wilderness settings such as, say, Rocky Mountain National Park, they may contract with a local challenge course. Challenge courses often involve climbing to heights (while roped into a partner), low ropes challenge which resembles a spider's web, climbing walls, zip lines, blindfold trust walks, trust falls (into a partner's arms), and so on. Some challenge courses are set in rural parks and include kayaking with a partner (challenging if you have never kayaked), hide-and-seek, and so forth. The critical components are learning to transcend fears, increase self-confidence, and develop healthy attachments with others on whom they learn to depend. Group sharing for personal growth (if not therapy in business and educational groups) is a common component of adventure challenge courses (Forgan & Jones, 2002). Participants may be assigned to write a three-to-five-page paper detailing their experience, what they have learned, and growth they have made during the challenge experience. Often, there will be a debriefing session

52 Counseling

after the adventure based trek is completed so as to encourage self-reflection on lessons learned and improvements gained as well as a structured, formal ending of the experience.

Genetic Counseling

Genetic counseling is one of the newest of the medical-mental health professions and one of the fastest growing in the country with 27% growth expected, and a median salary of $80,370 (BLS, 2018–2028). While total numbers of professional genetic counselors remain small (around 3,000 genetic counselors) (BLS, 2018–2028), the profession is likely to grow significantly in the coming decade. Although genetic counseling is separate from the established counseling profession, I am including it in this book due to the number of inquiries that have come to me in the past decade. Having profiled genetic counseling in my text *101 Careers in Counseling* (2nd ed.) (2019), it simply makes sense to continue discussing this separate, though related profession. A genetic counseling curriculum is a blending of bioinformatics with coursework in counselor education. The Accreditation Council for Genetic Counseling (http://gceducation.org/Pages/Accredited-Programs.aspx) website lists 41 accredited genetic counseling programs in the USA with an additional four in process. The website lists four in Canada as well, so the number of genetic counseling training programs is limited though gradually expanding. Again, it is likely the future will evidence a significant increase in graduate genetic counseling programs due to an increased focus on heredity factors related to diseases. STEM-type careers in the sciences already are expanding at an accelerated rate and the genetic counseling profession seems poised to benefit from this expansion.

Given the rapidly expanding field of genetics medicine, technology, and information, genetic counselors work in a wide variety of settings (National Society of Genetic Counselors, n.d.). Many genetic counselors work in research hospitals providing genetic testing, interpreting genetic test results, and writing opinions regarding the results. This information is used for the genetic counselors or physicians in advising patients of their genetic markers and potential disease risks. Other genetic counselors work in medical clinics providing face-to-face counseling to patients, or via the phone, or video conferencing.

Becoming a genetic counselor requires completion of a master's degree in genetic counseling from an accredited program. Admission to genetic counseling programs are quite competitive and the curriculum, a blending of biological sciences and traditional counseling skills, is rigorous. An intensive clinical internship in a clinic or hospital under supervision from a credentialed genetic counselor is required as well. After completing an accredited program, graduates must pass a state examination to become certified (some states license genetic counselors). Readers interested in the field of genetic counseling should refer to the National Society of Genetic Counselors (www.nsgc.org/). From my perspective, the genetic counseling profession would appear to be well positioned from an increasing high-technological future. Professional ethics in the genetic counseling field would be of critical importance given the issues involved, such as preventive surgeries (e.g., mastectomies), the potential for aborting a fetus given genetic markers for major diseases, and possible genetically engineered human body parts at a future date. An exciting field, though one fraught with ethical concerns.

Counselor as Professional Coach

Professional coaching has become very popular across a broad range of professions. From an internet search, I have found professional coaching in fields as diverse as business, engineering, and counseling, including graduate certificate programs and even master's degrees in professional coaching. I have further noticed a large number of counselors, social workers, and psychologists advertising their coaching services alongside their counseling and assessment services.

When I first came across the term "professional coach," I was confused because, given my athletic background, coaching involved some type of sport. When the field became popularized, it was clear that professional coaching was a multidisciplinary, hybrid profession. Professional coaches seem to work in their select field (or related fields), providing mentoring, advising, and training. While many of the skills involved are similar to those in counseling, professional coaching is not a mental health profession. Many counselors and related mental health professionals certainly provide professional coaching services, but focus, orientation, and expectations are different from counseling.

Regarding training and credentialing, there is no particular degree nor credential required to provide coaching services. Anyone can advertise themselves as a professional coach to the general public. However, several organizations offer information and credentialing in professional coaching. The International Coach Federation (ICF), the Association for Professional Executive Coaching and Supervision (APECS), and the American Coaching Association (ACA) are just a few. Credentialing in coaching is offered through organizations such as the Center for Credentialing and Education (www.cce.org), an affiliate of the National Board for Certified Counselors (www.nbcc.org), as well as the Institute for Life Coaching (www.lifecoachtraining.com).

While many unanswered questions remain regarding the field of professional coaching, no doubt it has become a very lucrative occupation (LaRosa, 2018). You should, however, consider some questions before plunging ahead into the coaching profession. For example: What training, experience, and credentialing is actually necessary? Who will provide you supervision? What code of ethics covers counselors providing coaching? (The American Counseling Association? A professional coaching organization?) What is the duty and standard of care in professional coaching? Finally, what precisely is your interest in, and motivation for, becoming a professional coach? I recommend that you should carefully consider these and other questions. No doubt, professional coaching has become very profitable, at least for some. You would also want to weigh out the risks involved with coaching, as whenever there is money to be made, risk management seems to increase exponentially.

How Do I Know Which Counseling Profession Is Right for Me?

Most graduate counseling applicants and students I have interviewed and taught during the past 30 years seldom articulate any confusion regarding their counseling focus area (e.g., clinical mental health vs. marriage and family). Nevertheless, as this text represents a wide-angle view of the profession, it seems prudent to include a section on counseling specialty areas. Many applicants come to the interview with at least a basic idea of the program for which they are applying, whether school counseling, clinical rehabilitation counseling, or clinical mental health counseling. Yet, my experience is that once in the counseling program of interest, some discover it to be a poor fit. Now, this is natural, as selecting a graduate program of study is scarcely an exact science. When considering how the median age of my students has gotten younger over the past three decades, the selection process becomes even more imprecise. Still, I would maintain there are some basic questions to consider regarding selecting a graduate counseling program or specialty area. Consider the questions in the following section.

Relevant Questions to Consider Regarding Selecting a Counseling Program

1. Why are you interested in a particular counseling field? What specifically interests you about, say, clinical mental health counseling, school counseling, marriage and family counseling, and so on?
2. Have you ever spoken with a counselor in your interest area about their career? If you have, what did that person tell you about the field? How do your interests match up with the job? (If you have not spoken with a counselor in your interest area, you would likely find that conversation enlightening and helpful.)
3. What specifically interests you about working in the counseling profession?
4. Given that many entry-level counseling jobs are in inner-city schools, addiction treatment centers, and even in remote communities, would you be willing to consider these options?
5. Initially, you may be forced to work with clients you do not like or are uncomfortable in counseling. How do you feel about working with sex offenders, addicts, abusive men, gang members, or clients or students with several behavioral and/or intellectual challenges?
6. Given that counseling caseloads can be full and that the majority of clients are struggling with academic concerns, mental illness, PTSD, addictions, self-injurious behaviors, suicidal ideation, and so on, the work can be very stressful and burnout is an ever present concern. On a scale of 1–10, with 10 high, how effective is your self-care plan? If it is below 6 you may wish to consider how to improve it. If you lack a self-care plan, you will certainly need one as a counselor.
7. If you were to ask a trusted friend or mentor—one who would provide honest answers and not merely tell you what you want to hear—whether they consider you a good candidate for a counseling program, what might that person (or persons) tell you?

8. Self-reflection is a critical part of effective counseling practice as well as a healthy life. Therefore, what natural skills and abilities do you possess that would assist you in becoming an effective counselor?
9. The field of counseling requires addressing conflict between students and teachers, clients and various authority, between family members, and occasionally between you and the client. On a scale of 1–10 with 1 low and 10 high, what is your comfort level in addressing conflict? Why would you give yourself this particular score? How could you improve your score?
10. Developing resilience will be a necessity as a professional counselor, given challenging issues and clients, and the demands placed on a counselor. On a scale of 1–10, with 10 high, how resilient are you in working through challenges and personal and professional disappointments? How might you improve your resilience?

Recommended Reading

Bureau of Labor Statistics (2016–2026). *The occupational outlook handbook*. U.S Department of Labor. Washington, DC: Bureau of Labor Statistics.
Hodges, S. (2019). *101 careers in counseling* (2nd ed.). New York: Springer.

Lessons Learned

"I want to be a counselor," the late-thirty-something man, sitting across my desk from me, stated. Now, an interested person coming to speak with me about our graduate counseling program and the profession is scarcely novel. What made the encounter interesting and unusual was the person interested. I will call him "Paul" (pseudonym). Paul had had a very difficult life to say the least. As an indigent, urban, African American born to a drug-addicted mother who was unsure who Paul's father was, he had many of the wrong statistics working against him. Growing up in a blighted inner-city, with gang activity all around him, trouble found him very early in life. He matriculated into a gang, and was mentored in the finer nuances of theft, drug production and distribution, and the ubiquitous cycle of violence gang brotherhood requires. Unsurprisingly, the legal system eventually took charge of his life, and he served a brief stretch in prison.

As state prisons are replete with sub-rosa gangs, one would have expected more trouble with insidious gang activity on the inside, resulting in a longer sentence, and then, upon release, the resumption of old habits and a quick return to a correctional environment. For the first time in his life, however, he met someone who made a positive impact on his life. During prison, he began studying for his GED—mostly to while away his sentence in the hope it would lead to an early release. It was during one of his classes that he made a connection with a middle-aged woman who taught at the prison. As Paul had always been an indifferent student at best, he was initially skeptical that education could have any real impact on his life. Yet, he found he liked and respected this tough, no-nonsense, middle-aged Caucasian woman who equally cajoled and encouraged her students.

56   Counseling

Despite misgivings, he approached her after class to discuss his life and current situation and this led to regular meetings between them. She began to mentor Paul, noticing he had a facility for academic work—something neither he nor anyone else had ever contemplated. "Look Paul," she said one day, "take a look around you in this prison. How many college grads you figure are incarcerated here?" He shook his head, not knowing. "None Paul. Hey, a few *are* in other prisons, but not many. Now, how many high school drop-outs you figure we got here?" He had a pretty good idea about that simply by looking at the full GED study classes. "Bottom line Paul, you need a new plan if you want to stay out of prison. You and I need to discuss and figure out a future for you. One that doesn't involve gang activity."

Over time, he began to use the library to explore career options. Taking the Self-directed Search (SDS) career interest inventory, he began to realize his interest in human behavioral matters. Borrowing an outdated psychology text, he discovered Freud, Rogers, Skinner, Beck, and many others. He decided that perhaps being a psychologist would be a good option. Then, much to his dismay, he found he would need a decade or more of formal education! Just the idea of the local community college was daunting enough, to say nothing of a doctorate. He discussed the matter with his teacher who counseled him to pursue his interests at the community college. "Take it one step at a time," she advised. "There are other related careers that require less education, like counseling." He looked further into the matter, and found the community college had an Associate's degree in Addictions Counseling that was only two years long. Two years seemed possible and the community college seemed friendlier, especially to ex-convicts with spotty educational backgrounds.

During his incarceration, he completed his GED, and then, with the help of a state-funded program, he began taking courses offered through a community college. Focused and academically motivated for the first time in his life, he threw himself into his studies with a previously lacking hunger. Prior to his parole, he completed several college courses, with a B or above grade in all. He was admitted into the Addictions Counseling program and though he struggled in some classes, he graduated and eventually landed a job as an Addictions Counselor. He completed his CASAC credential, and progressed in the field. Yet, he wanted more responsibility. A colleague advised him, "You will need a bachelor's and then a master's degree in counseling in order to get a license. Without a master's you won't get a license. Without a license, you will hit a career ceiling."

Thus, Paul enrolled in the local state college and majored in psychology. This time, he had more struggles. Unlike prison where he had unlimited time to study, his case load at the treatment center was overflowing! Many of his clients were ex-convicts like himself, and needed much mentoring and guidance to remain sober and out of prison. Often exhausted, he missed classes, failed some courses, and took several years to graduate with his baccalaureate. Although he met the goal of a college degree (the first in his entire family), his grades were marginal. Graduate school seemed hopelessly beyond reach and he found himself discouraged. A co-worker, however, happened to tell him that one of his relatives went to a local small college with a counseling program. "They have a history of taking chances on people, especially those working in the addictions field," the relative counseled.

"Hey, give it a shot. What do ya have to lose, right?" Reluctantly, Paul agreed, though with misgivings.

So now Paul, former gang member, high school drop-out, ex-convict, then addictions counselor and now college graduate, had made his winding journey to my cramped office in a former men's dormitory. He was perhaps the most honest applicant I had ever had. "Hey, I realize my background and grades are not the best. But I know how to reach people … ya know, those like me. I can't promise top grades, but I will work very hard." Indeed, his letters of reference from his supervisors at the clinic backed him up. After consultation with my colleagues (he did have very low grades), we admitted him on probation. Determined to prove himself, Paul worked very hard, skipped no classes, got help with his writing, and took any and all of the proactive measures he could. Still, he struggled academically. He spoke of quitting the program, but a couple of fellow students, a colleague at work, and myself encouraged him to keep at it. He took a year longer, but finally he graduated with his master's degree, another first in his family. Paul would eventually pass the state licensure examination and years later become a supervisor.

The Pauls of the world are not the people that higher education historically tends to favor as students. In fact, many if not most faculty members would prefer to work with privileged, wealthier, more academically prepared students and not those like Paul (e.g., GED, ex-convict, gang-banger, and economically poor). The lesson the Pauls of my world have reminded me is that it is the broken, the addict, the violence survivor, the overlooked, the misunderstood, the disappointing student, and the ex-convict who compose most of the people we serve. Who besides the Pauls who inhabited that dangerous and damaged world are best prepared to help those on Maslow's lowest step? Can we really imagine that the light, bright, white, suburbanites make the best candidates to become counselors? As a white person, I have nothing per se against "my people." Nevertheless, the strongest correlation with grades and SAT/ACT/GRE scores is family income (Reardon, 2011) meaning that white (and Asian Americans) dominate. As a professor, I continue to be astonished that many very privileged faculty colleagues across various disciplines, some of whom graduated from Ivy League-type institutions, are unaware of the socioeconomic DMZ running between the inner cities and the leafy suburbs. I am pleased to have *all* hard-working students regardless of pedigree, background, culture, and so forth. The Pauls of the academic world, however, are a rare species, and significant under-represented in graduate counseling programs. We need more of those who have transcended poverty's escape velocity and beaten long odds, as the school of hard knocks has prepared them well to understand and overcome hopelessness and failure.

I have often wondered as I provided counseling, consultation, training, and coaching across the USA and overseas in South African orphanages and in remote indigenous Outback schools, if I would ever be half the counselor Paul became. I really wonder how much that PhD is worth when measured against the odds he beat.

6 Mindfulness and Wellbeing

The past decade has witnessed a plethora of books, trainings, workshops, and even graduate-level counseling courses in mindfulness-based counseling. There are even standard, evidenced-based therapeutic approaches that incorporate mindfulness into treatment. These disparate approaches are Dialectic Behavioral Therapy (DBT; Linehan, 2014), Mindfulness-based Cognitive Therapy (MBCT; Williams, Teasdale, & Segal, 2007), and Acceptance and Commitment Therapy (ACT; Hayes, Strosahl, & Wilson, 2012) to cite a few. It seems many of the training flyers I receive through the postal service and over email carry the word "mindfulness" somewhere in the title or description. I have noticed trainings for mindfulness-based school counseling, the mindfulness-based classroom management, mindfulness as a treatment for grief, loss, and trauma, and so forth. Just as I was commencing this chapter, a colleague in Australia contacted me about designing a mindfulness-based certification program for the teachers, counsellors, psychologists and administrators in her remote Northern Territory schools. Readers should scarcely be surprised that mindfulness has become a ubiquitous term with regard to all things related to mental health, health, education, yoga, and so forth.

What Is Mindfulness?

Most significantly, we should clarify precisely what we mean when talking about mindfulness. In point of fact, when I query my graduate students and participants in my workshops regarding the term "mindfulness," they seem to have two reactions. First, they are interested in the term and using it in whatever counseling or teaching they are doing, and second, they do not know how to define the term. In mindfulness meditations I have led, I define and explain what I mean by mindfulness and how it is embedded in out meditation. Kabit-Zinn suggests mindfulness is awareness arising through paying purposeful attention in the present moment, without judgment though with wisdom (Kabit-Zinn, 2013).

The nonjudgmental aspect of mindfulness requires that we adopt radical acceptance of ourselves as humans (Brach, 2003), meaning that we understand and embrace our fullest humanity. Doing so does not mean that it is acceptable to be irresponsible or hurtful to others. In fact, radical self-acceptance requires adopting a more peaceful way of life in our relationships with family, friends, colleagues, clients, students, other creatures, and the environment (Brach, 2003). What radical self-acceptance could mean for counselors, especially counselor in training, is that we accept and learn from our "bad" sessions with clients without beating ourselves up with negative self-talk. In fact, as you begin to live and practice more mindfully, your self-talk likely will become more kind, gentle, and less critical and possibly carry with it more curiosity. Readers might well be wondering, "Okay, just how could I become more mindful and practice radical self-acceptance?" That is a good question and the answer has many avenues of possibilities.

Mindfulness in Daily Life

A mindfulness lifestyle and practice for counselors and counselors in training can be quite simple; in fact, I would recommend keeping one's practice simple. More than two decades ago when I was on the path to becoming a monk, my spiritual director, a psychologist in his former secular life, recommended that in addition to daily meditation that I incorporate daily "gratitudes" into my life. "Each morning, start by acknowledging three things you are grateful about. This will help ground you, especially on the days you do not feel grateful." While I had some skepticism regarding the utility of this assignment, nevertheless I began incorporating this suggestion into my daily meditations. To my surprise and delight, my former mentor was right. Every day, I begin by acknowledging my health, my best friend, and a fulfilling career (and I keep going …). On my "down" days, acknowledging my "gratitudes" helps provide a stronger sense of meaning and purpose. Kabit-Zinn (2013) essentially makes the same point that by acknowledging feelings of gratitude we are putting wisdom into action. While the nature of wisdom could be debated, my experience personally and professionally is that acknowledging feelings of gratitude does seem a wise practice.

Meditation is quite popular in counseling and psychology circles in contemporary times. It has even found its way into corporate America, albeit in more progressive companies, especially on the west coast. I have led meditation sessions on three continents, in colleges and universities, public and Catholic schools, in the Australian Outback, mountains of South Africa, Central America, and even in my backyard of western New York. Meditation is possibly one of the most important daily practices people can engage in to help them manage a dynamic, overly busy life dominated by touch screens (Hahn, 2016). One meditation retreat I assisted with required we collect phones and other high-technology devices, as we had observed participants literally dashing out between sessions to check email, text messages, calls, the internet, and so on. Participants were not temporarily withdrawing from busy society and their jobs—they brought them into the retreat! Many would report a sense of initial anxiety at surrendering their attachment to work, news, email, and social media. Through practice in disengaging from these external, and at times unnecessary, connections most participants found being off-line liberating. One college president exclaimed, how she felt through meditation and separation from her phone, that she could make healthier, less ego-driven decisions. So, power-down through meditation and a recess from your phone.

60 Mindfulness and Wellbeing

One of the best suggestions regarding letting go of attachments came from my reading Mark Epstein's seminal book *Thoughts Without a Thinker: Psychotherapy from a Buddhist Perspective* (1992). While many ideas Epstein introduced regarding mindful counseling practice were valuable, there was one in particular that stood apart. I was running a university counseling center and constantly juggling clients, supervision, teaching, serving on committees, and making all-campus presentations. Epstein wrote that he would often see seven or eight patients in a single day. Sometimes, with more demanding sessions, he found he carried challenges from one session into the next, making therapeutic success difficult. His answer was that he had to find at least 60 seconds of meditation where he visualized letting go of any unresolved issues prior to beginning the next session. Although skeptical initially, I found this suggestion made a significant positive impact in my counseling practice, and also in my teaching, supervision, and conference presentations. Basically, our attachments may bring about anxiety in us due to our desire to possess something such as love, approval, success, and so forth. Now within healthy limits, there is certainly nothing wrong with love and success. There is little doubt, however, that we can hold onto relationships in unhealthy ways and we may do much emotional damage to ourselves when we have not achieved what we desire. Thus, as we release our desires, we can then become more objective in relationships and live more simply and with less anxiety.

Another mindfulness-based practice I have discovered is that of listening to guided meditations. There are many helpful, free, online meditations that can be easily downloaded onto a smart phone, laptop, or other such device. My favorite time to practice is in the early morning at home, or sitting in my office before anyone else arrives and listening to a guided meditation while staring through my third-story window. The critical factor for me appears to be a slowing down of my thoughts, leading to a reduced heart rate, relaxation of my limbs, neck, chest, and feet, and an overall sensation of warmth throughout my body. The guided meditations seem to leave me feeling relaxed in a way similar to aerobic exercise—something the medical profession has recently discovered (Young, 2011).

Clearly, mindfulness, as expressed through attitude, presence, meditation, breath work, and so forth is an important component of a healthy lifestyle (Brown & Ryan, 2003). Professional counselors and counselors in training can benefit from mindfulness-based stress reduction, meditation, as it may assist them in managing the multiple demands of providing clinical work (Baer, 2003). Given that mindfulness training has become ubiquitous in society, as well as in contemporary therapeutic approaches (Kabit-Zinn, 2013; Linehan, 2014), perhaps assessing mindfulness is a worthy idea. Several mindfulness scales have been developed, including the Mindful Attention Awareness Scale (MAAS; Brown & Ryan, 2003), the Toronto Mindfulness Scale (Lau et al., 2006), the Cognitive and Affective Mindfulness Scale (CAMS; Feldman, Hayes, Kumar, Greeson, & Laurenceau, 2006) to cite a few. For purposes of operationalizing mindfulness, the Mindful Attention Awareness Scale (Brown & Ryan, 2003) is offered as an example.

The Mindful Attention Awareness Scale (MAAS)

The MAAS is a 15-item scale designed to assess a core characteristic of mindfulness, namely, a receptive state of mind in which attention, informed by a sensitive awareness of what is occurring in the present, simply observes what is taking place.

Instructions: Below is a collection of statements about your everyday experience. Using the 1–6 scale below, please indicate how frequently or infrequently you currently have each experience. Please answer according to what really reflects you experience rather than what you think your experience should be. Please treat each item separately from every other item.

1	2	3	4	5	6
Almost Always	Very frequently	Somewhat frequently	Somewhat infrequently	Very infrequently	Almost never

___ 1. I could be experiencing some emotion and not be conscious of it until sometime later.

___ 2. I could break or spill things because of carelessness, not paying attention, or thinking of something else.

___ 3. I find it difficult to stay focused on what's happening in the present.

___ 4. I tend to walk quickly to get to where I'm going without paying attention to what I experience along the way.

___ 5. I tend not to notice feelings of physical tension or discomfort until they really grab my attention.

___ 6. I forget a person's name as soon as I've been told it for the first time.

___ 7. It seems I am "running on automatic" without much awareness of what I'm doing.

___ 8. I rush through activities without being really attentive to them.

___ 9. I get so focused on the goal I want to achieve that I lose touch with what I'm doing right now to get there.

___ 10. I do jobs or tasks automatically, without being aware of what I'm doing.

___ 11. I find myself listening to someone with one ear, doing something else at the same time.

___ 12. I drive places on "automatic pilot" and then wonder why I went there.

___ 13. I find myself preoccupied with the future or the past.

___ 14. I find myself doing things without paying attention.

___ 15. I snack without being aware that I'm eating.

Scoring: To score the MAAS, simply compute a mean (average) of the 15 items. (K.W. Brown & R.M. Ryan (2003). The benefits of being present: Mindfulness and its role in psychological well-being. *Journal of Personality and Social Psychology, 84*, 822–848. Reprinted by authors' permission.)

Now, the MAAS focuses more on trait factors as opposed to state factors of mindfulness. One suggestion would be to use the MAAS, or another mindfulness

62 *Mindfulness and Wellbeing*

scale (e.g., Toronto Mindfulness Scale, Cognitive and Affective Mindfulness Scale, etc.) as a means of periodic assessment prior to a mindfulness practice, during that practice, and a post-test after an extended period of meditation, present awareness, breath work, and so on. Note how your scores change on particular items on the MAAS. The important aspect of mindfulness is cultivating an awareness of the present moment without judging yourself on any particular item. A second suggestion is the use of mindfulness scales such as the MAAS, Toronto Mindfulness Scale, and others to help become more fully present in your personal life and with the clients you counsel. Mindfulness also is part of a healthy, holistic lifestyle as temporarily detaching from our responsibilities reduces anxiety (Kabit-Zinn, 2013). I have included the Dimensions of a Healthy Lifestyle (DHL) below for a more wide-angle assessment of personal health and mindfulness.

The DHL is more of a "temperature taking" exercise to see how you are functioning at the present time across a broad range of lifestyle. The DHS uses a 1–10 rating scale and is intended to be used as a checklist. So, answer each question in a "where you are" mode as opposed to how you believe you "should" be on the scale. Then, if you find yourself deficient, remember not to be self-critical. If you feel a need to improve in a given area, remember that incremental improvement may be healthier and more realistic than major improvement. During your time on field placement, my suggestion is that you review your scores monthly. If you are a professional counselor in the field, the same monthly recommendation applies as well (perhaps taking the DHL monthly for up to six months).

Dimensions of a Healthy Lifestyle (DHL)

Spirituality/Religious Life
My spiritual/religious life provides a sense of purpose and helps me address
  major life challenges.
(Note: An alternate phrasing for nonspiritual/nonreligious people might be:
  "My sense of life meaning/purpose provides fulfillment and helps me address
  the challenges in my life.")

1   2   3   4   5   6   7   8   9   10

(1 = *no help at all*; 10 = *strongly helps*)
If your score was less than five, how could you improve your situation?

Mindfulness:
I live with in purposeful awareness of the present moment, and with a
  nonjudgmental mindset regarding my life. I use meditation, breath work, and
  daily affirmations to lead a more meaningful life.

1   2   3   4   5   6   7   8   9   10

Personal Vision
"I have a clear vision in my personal, spiritual, and professional life."

1   2   3   4   5   6   7   8   9   10

(1 = *No vision*; 10 = *I have a clear vision*)
If you do not have a clear personal, spiritual, or professional vision, how could
you develop one? Visioning is a key component to success in all these areas.

Self -Worth
"I feel worthwhile as a human being and have a strong sense of self-acceptance.
Although I am not perfect, I feel generally good about myself."

1   2   3   4   5   6   7   8   9   10

(1 = *I am worthless*; 10 = *My self-worth is very strong*)
If you are experiencing low self-esteem, how could you begin to feel better about
yourself? What actions could you take to begin to feel more self-confident?

Goal Setting
"I feel self-confident about setting and meeting goals and demands in my life."

1   2   3   4   5   6   7   8   9   10

(1 = *I lack confidence in my ability to meet demands and the goals I set*; 10 = *I feel
very confident in setting, planning, and meeting goals and demands*)
If you lack clear goals in your life, how could you begin to create some
clear goals?

Rational Thinking
"I believe I perceive my life and life situations in a rational manner. I seldom
engage in overly negative thinking."

1   2   3   4   5   6   7   8   9   10

(1 = *I frequently engage in irrational thinking*; 10 = *I am very rational in my beliefs*)
If you have rated yourself as frequently engaging in irrational beliefs (e.g., "I
am a loser," "I am worthless," "No one could ever love me," etc.), how could
you begin to think in a more rational manner? (Or, if you are unsure as to
whether your beliefs are rational, you might consider asking someone you
trust for feedback.)

Emotional Understanding and Regulation
"I am in touch with my emotions and am able to express the full range
of emotions appropriate to the situation. I also am not governed by my
emotions."

1   2   3   4   5   6   7   8   9   10

64 *Mindfulness and Wellbeing*

(*1 = I am not able to regulate my emotions and often express emotions inappropriate to the situation; 10 = I am able to regulate my emotions and experience emotions appropriate to the situation*)

If you find you are not experiencing an appropriate range of emotions, or you find you are too often ruled by your emotions, how could you begin to change this? Remember, you will have "negative" emotions, so the task is to regulate them appropriately.

Resilience

"I am a resilient person, and able to analyze, synthesize, and make a plan to deal with challenges and projects that come my way."

1   2   3   4   5   6   7   8   9   10

(*1 = I do not feel resilient; 10 = I am very confident in my resiliency*)

If you do not feel resilient (or you are not as resilient as you would like) or do not have the ability to resolve difficulties in your life, what could you do to begin to develop more resilience? (Note: If you feel stuck on strategizing with this component, perhaps begin by making a list of ways you feel resilient. Or, ask someone who knows you well to list ways they see you as being resilient.)

Sense of Humor

"I possess a healthy, appropriate sense of humor that helps me deal with the stresses of life."

1   2   3   4   5   6   7   8   9   10

(*1 = I have no sense of humor; 10 = I have a healthy sense of humor*)

If you do not feel your sense of humor is either strongly developed, appropriate, or provides an effective release of stress, what could you change to improve the situation?

Fitness or Recreation

"I have a regular weekly fitness/recreational routine that helps me stay physically and emotionally fit."

1   2   3   4   5   6   7   8   9   10

(*1 = I have no activity routine; 10 = I have an active physical/recreational routine*)

If you do not have a regular weekly fitness routine, what could you do to change this? (Remember, you do not need to become a marathoner, competitive cyclist, swimmer, or dancer. It is simply about developing a regular routine of 20 minutes a day, at least 3 days a week.)

Healthy Diet

"I regularly eat a balanced diet, including healthy vegetables and fruits."

(Note: Healthy is not meant to imply you *never* eat unhealthy foods because that's not realistic. In fact, sometimes it is good for the psyche to eat ice cream, cookies, and so forth. Just don't do it too often. Rather, it is about eating unhealthy food in moderation.)

1   2   3   4   5   6   7   8   9   10

(1 = *My diet is unbalanced and unhealthy*; 10 = *My diet is balanced and healthy*)

If your diet is unhealthy (eating high-fat food, "junk" food, fast food too often), how could you begin to eat a healthier diet? (For in-depth help, you may wish to consult a dietician.)

Mindful Living

"I maintain a mindful lifestyle by not abusing alcohol or other drugs, by wearing a seat belt, having regular medical exams, and by refraining from high-risk activities (e.g., casual sex, binge drinking, binge eating, restricting food, etc.)."

1   2   3   4   5   6   7   8   9   10

(1 = *I do not live a healthy, mindful life*; 10 = *I maintain a healthy, mindful lifestyle*)

If you find you are not living a healthy, mindful life, what steps could you take to change this?

Managing Stress and Anxiety

"Through my diet, workout routine, friendships, and so forth, I have the ability to manage stress and anxiety. When I find I am unable to manage the stress and anxiety in my life, I check in with close friends and family or if the need arises, I see a counselor."

1   2   3   4   5   6   7   8   9   10

(1 = *I am regularly unable to manage the stress and anxiety in my life*; 10 = *I am able to manage the stress and anxiety in my life*)

If you find you regularly have difficulty managing the stress and anxiety in your life, how could you begin to manage that stress and anxiety better?

Sense of Self

"I feel that my self-identity is strong and well developed."

1   2   3   4   5   6   7   8   9   10

(1 = *My sense of self is incongruent with who I am because I try too hard to be who others want me to be*; 10 = *My sense of self is very congruent with who I am*)

Some people struggle with their own identity for various reasons, such as enmeshment with family, codependence with a loved one, low self-esteem, and so forth. If you find you are struggling with an inability to develop your own identity, what are some options for exploration? (Options that would reduce your struggle or help you resolve your personal identity struggles.)

Connection to Family or Culture

"I feel a strong connection to my family or culture."

1   2   3   4   5   6   7   8   9   10

(1 = *I feel no connection to my family or culture*; 10 = *I feel a strong and healthy connection to my family and culture*)

In the event you feel no connection to your family or culture, what would you say accounts for this? Also, how could you begin to make stronger connections to your family and culture?

Career/Vocational Development

"I feel a sense of satisfaction in the career I am pursuing." (e.g., mental health counselor, school counselor, rehabilitation counselor, etc.)

1   2   3   4   5   6   7   8   9   10

(1 = *No satisfaction*; 10 = *Maximum satisfaction*)

If your chosen career does not provide personal challenge and satisfaction for you, what steps could you take to create more fulfillment and satisfaction? (Or, if you are unemployed, how could your job search become more fulfilling? Or, how could this period of unemployment be more productive?)

Hobbies

"My hobbies help me relax and provide a sense of enjoyment."

1   2   3   4   5   6   7   8   9   10

(1 = *I have no hobbies or they provide no sense of enjoyment or relaxation*; 10 = *My hobbies are a pure joy*)

If you lack hobbies or outside interests from work, how could you create some fulfilling pursuits?

Social Life

"I have healthy relationships that provide me a sense of emotional connection and help make life more rewarding."

1   2   3   4   5   6   7   8   9   10

(1 = *I have no significant relationships, they are shallow, or provide little in the way of emotional connection*; 10 = *I have healthy and fulfilling relationships and they are an important part of my life*)

If you lack significant personal connections or your relationships do not provide you a sense of emotional connection, how could you begin to address this? (Or, how could you begin to create fulfilling relationships?)

Intimacy

"Intimacy, or love, is a central part of my life and my relationship with my spouse/partner provides the grounding, intimacy, and close connection I need. (Note: Intimacy could involve sexual intimacy or even a close, nonsexual relationship)."

1   2   3   4   5   6   7   8   9   10

(1 = *Intimacy is largely absent from my life*; 10 = *Intimacy is a large part of my life and provides me with great satisfaction*)

If intimacy seems absent from your life, or seems unhealthy or unfulfilling, what do you need to do to change this situation?

Mindfulness and Wellbeing   67

Follow-up Questions Regarding Your DHL Score and Self-Care:
Regarding these dimensions, which do you appear to be strongest on? Weakest?
How could you improve your strengths and build upon your weak areas?
What action could you take to improve your self-care? What supports do you
need to create a healthier lifestyle? If you are unsure how to create a healthy
self-care lifestyle, who could you ask for help? (i.e., your doctor, counselor, a
nutritionist, your spiritual leader, family member, friend, etc.)
(Reprinted from S. Hodges, *The Counseling Practicum and Internship Manual: A Resource for Graduate Counseling Students*, third edition. New York: Springer, 2020. Reproduced with the permission of Springer Publishing Company, LLC.)

Lessons Learned

December 25, 1992, was a day I never can forget. Undoubtedly, it was the worst day of my life. It was not the particular day per se, but rather the type of year that was the principal problem. I had experienced the death of my grandmother, who along with my previously deceased grandfather, had raised me and four of my siblings. My marriage had also ended abruptly. I was struggling in my doctoral program and seriously wondering whether I would be able to finish my degree. Living on a graduate stipend, I was barely scraping by with regard to rent, food, and other requirements. Finally, I was all alone and far from close family and seemingly devoid of strong relationships. Depression, that subtle predator forever at the periphery of my consciousness, greeted me upon waking that Christmas morning. No welcome gift as one can imagine!

I felt little cause for celebration that day and wondered just how I would pull myself out of this dark, foreboding valley. I had learned that when in doubt, consider what has worked previously. I flicked on my portable cassette player and began listening to Enya, one of my favorite musical artists. As she sang in her hauntingly melodic manner, I recalled Viktor Frankl's iconic wisdom. That is, everything can be taken from a person except one thing: to choose one's attitude in any given set of circumstances. As Enya sang in Gaelic, I sat up from my Navy surplus cot and pondered what significance Logotherapy had for my situation. The principles of Logotherapy sounded good, as meaning seemed to have abandoned my life. But, as I recalled, my regular running routine always seemed to lift my mood. Wearily, and with scant motivation, I rose, dressed in my running clothes, made coffee, ate a snack, and hoped motivation would return.

After some two hours of coffee, followed by light stretching, I braved the external world. Despite fatigue, I jogged for nearly two hours—albeit quite slowly. After showering and eating a light lunch, I did feel a slight mood improvement. I recalled that regular aerobic exercise had proven a valid ancillary treatment for depression (along with medication and counseling). My further experience was that a purposeful day and week also seemed to help. In fact, when I was busy between work and classes, I seemed to be most fulfilled. Feeling mildly inspired, I sat down and made a schedule for the holiday break. Each day, I would either run or take a long

68 *Mindfulness and Wellbeing*

walk. But that still left a lot of unstructured time. One can only run and walk so much. How might I fill in the daytime portions? At night I could watch films or read, but I felt a need to be productive during daylight hours. Basically, I was in search of a purpose.

Several years earlier, I had started writing a fiction novel. After one week of barely scratching my notebook, I gave up. Seven years later, almost to the day, I picked up that same notebook and began creating a cast of characters, the setting, timeline, and so forth. That Christmas day, I worked at my desk for eight hours! The next day the same, and the day after that. My daily rituals of running and writing became as regular as a Trappist monk obeying the canonical hours. Two weeks then flew past and a new academic term commenced with me feeling a renewed sense of purpose.

I finished that book, after some 350 pages. I have yet to publish it, though that seems less important at this point. What was so critical was my need for meaning and purpose during an arduous, transitional period of my life. It was meaning and clear purpose, illustrated by running and the creation aspect of writing fiction that became my salvation. My depression lifted, though I had *much* work to do regarding recent grief, academic, and life-meaning issues. Nevertheless, my mood improved significantly and people in my life, such as friends, colleagues, and even my professors, noticed. I returned to my meditation practice, a practice that had lapsed during my tumultuous year. The daily meditations helped lift my mood significantly as well.

The most important lesson I learned in those dark, waning days of 1992, was that schedules meant responsibility and responsibility meant purpose and provided much needed meaning. My running routines, often through hilly woodlands in western Oregon, got me out into fresh, cold air and seemed to lighten my heavy mood. More than schedules and rising serotonin levels, however, the creative process involved in crafting a work of fiction provided the greatest "lift". During the past 26 years since I have authored and published numerous essays, articles, poetry, textbooks, and novels. The genesis of my productivity was rising from that hard, narrow cot during a dark winter morning and thus liberating a dormant capacity. Life still happens of course, as loved ones die, friendships end, and marriages have their ebb and flow. The consistency in my life has been meditation, running, creation through writing, and fortunately love.

One person's pathway to meaning and purpose may be an existential desert to another. Readers of this text must discover their own pathway to meaning, purpose, and hope. My way and my journey may not work for you as we are different people, representing cultural variations, gender differences, varying emotional needs, spiritual variations, and different socioeconomic constraints. What I have discovered through my work in distant lands with different cultures, however, is that meaning and purpose are universal. That cold, dark, lonely Christmas morning was, ironically, my vehicle towards renewal and rediscovery of meaning, purpose, and joy. Somehow when in the dark valley of grief, depression, perhaps even despair, we must slowly begin the slow, arduous trek upward. Fortunately, I was able to find my vehicle of transformation. You will need to find yours.

7 Groups, Couples, and Family Counseling

While working on my master's degree, one of my classes was treated to a guest lecture from an alumnus working in the field. She informed us that diversification could be very beneficial for our future careers as community and school counselors. She mentioned the need for ongoing training, now a requirement to keep a license, though back in the mid-1980s it was more of a personal commitment to stay occupationally relevant. She mentioned various training and credential possibilities that could be helpful, including skills such as mediation, art therapy training, and training in supervision and in counseling couples. I was interested in more training in the use of art in counseling, and perhaps mediation. But the thought of counseling couples was totally unappealing. Moreover, I understood marriage and family therapy to be a completely different field requiring a separate advanced degree.

I put little additional thought into the matter until the following term when taking the one course in family counseling. Each class required role-plays in couples and family counseling. I enjoyed the role-plays and some of the couples' counseling scenarios were quite humorous. Still, I remained uninterested in further training and supervision to counsel couples. (I certainly was not interested in counseling whole families.) As luck or fate might have it, the following term, a young couple came to see me at the counseling center. Because they were seeking relationship help, I explained the need to refer them to the director, who had training and experience in that area. Unfortunately, the director had a waiting list three weeks long! I reiterated that I had had a single class on couples and no experience. I further brought up the issue of ethics and not practicing beyond my scope of competence. The young couple seemed dismayed. "But, what if you just listen and give us feedback?" the female partner said. "You could … coach us." There was a pause as I considered her suggestion. "Look, it's you or no one," she added. Feeling caught between ethical parameters and their desperation, I "punted" and explained the need to discuss the matter with my supervisor, the director.

The director listened carefully, then suggested I simply act as a resource and help them with their communication. Then, when his schedule allowed, I could refer them. He also said he would provide tips on our lunch break (in his office). Feeling relieved, though still not confident, I agreed. A few days later, the couple returned. In the meantime, I had pulled resources together that might help the couple with their communication challenges. It seemed they were unofficially engaged and

70 *Groups, Couples, and Family Counseling*

excited about the prospect of marriage. The concern was that they had difficulty in working through conflict. Explaining that this was common, my spiel was that my role was to be a communication facilitator and not a couple's counselor. I went on to add that our conversations would, nevertheless, remain confidential and that when the director had an opening in a few weeks, I would make a referral. This all seemed acceptable to the couple.

The initial session went very well, partially due to the couple's willingness to disclose issues of conflict. My approach was listening and providing observations. I also added homework in the way of the "Simple dialogue." My instructions were for the couple to set aside a 15-minute period whereby one partner would talk, while the other just attended in silence. The caveat being the "talker" could not blame the listener, but was to acknowledge emotions and thoughts. For example, "I felt hurt when you didn't ask how my Calculus test went," Or, "I felt validated when I you brought me a cup of coffee during my afternoon break." This basic couple's communication 101 seemed to work rather well.

After only two sessions, the couple voiced that they would like to continue with me for a few more sessions as opposed to taking the referral to the director. The director agreed, although he suggested that should the couple return, they should try to schedule with him. I certainly agreed to that. After two more sessions, they felt confident to discontinue with my facilitation, although they planned to continue with the simple dialogue and had registered for a premarital retreat led by an experienced marriage and family counselor. Happy in my fledging success, though relieved to see the couple finish, I returned to providing individual and group counseling. Soon thereafter, however, another couple came to see me. I repeated the process, and simply provided communication feedback, the simple dialogue, staffed with my supervisor, and read texts by Jay Haley and others for more ideas. I also spoke regularly with the director, who was full of ideas.

For the next year, I would have a steady drip of couples—married, cohabitating, just dating—on my case load. I continued to simply be a facilitator, and used the simple dialogue of caring days (unsolicited small acts of kindness for the other partner). When I graduated, I gave no thought to couples work for a few years. During my final year of graduate school, however, I had a year-long internship in a pastoral counseling center. My supervisor, a social worker with extended training in couples therapy, required me to assist him in providing co-counseling to couples. He provided a crash course in the Solution-focused model, and we spent the academic year seeing couples (along with individual and group therapy). One Friday per month, we had a social-training event with other therapists seeing couples and families. Everyone present was a supervisor (except me of course) and was able to offer valuable insights and helpful training. I was learning much but still viewed myself correctly as a counselor providing individual and group counseling.

After graduation, I was hired to run a county mental health clinic in a remote region of the state. I provided individual counseling in addition to my administrative duties. Then, a few couples began to trickle into the clinic. I found none of the clinical staff had training or experience with couples. After conversations with my supervisor and a couple of calls from local ministers, I agreed that we needed to provide counseling services for couples. Unfortunately, I was the lone member of the clinical staff with any real training and experience in counseling couples. However, I did not feel ethically competent to counsel couples without more training and supervision. So, the executive director, my boss, agreed to pay for me to receive additional training and supervision in relationship counseling. I found a semi-retired licensed marriage and family counselor some 30 miles away to provide me supervision. I further attended regional trainings in couples counseling, and carried a case load of one or two couples per week, finding the work fulfilling and enjoyable. I continued counseling couples when I directed a university counseling center and worked in another pastoral counseling center. Naturally, I continued with continuing education training on couples counseling from established relationship counselors in divergent forms of Solution-focused Family Therapy and Systemic Family Therapy, and I have found such differences between these respective schools of thought most enlightening.

What I get from my experience is that life happens and the vows we take, such as, "I will never …" often are made without ample forethought. So much of my career has involved me working in areas and with clinical populations I could never have imagined (e.g., domestic violence, sex offenders, trauma work, overseas in orphanages and remote indigenous Australia, etc.). In the words of that famous film spy character, "Never say never." Every time I have uttered such words or even committed such to thought, life, serendipity, karma or something seems to provide just what I wanted to avoid.

Continuing the narrative, part of my foci in this chapter is to get readers considering how they can branch out beyond traditional, individual-oriented counseling into group and relationship (i.e., couples and family work). So that I am not misunderstood, you will need more training and supervision should you wish to counsel couples and families (Gladding, 2019). Additional training would include additional postgraduate coursework, ongoing supervision, and continuing education (CE) in couples and family counseling. Some of you may wish to earn a second degree in marriage and family counseling/therapy. Granted, it is not always easy to earn a second master's. Most significantly, you need more training. In the Buffalo-Niagara Falls area, one outpatient clinic serving high-needs referrals from an inner-city middle school, offers hands-on training in family counseling. The model is Solution-focused with teams working behind the two-way mirror to assist an individual or counseling team in the actual session. The said clinic also offers trainings, as well as weekly individual and group supervision. This type of arrangement is an ideal one for training, experience, and supervision.

Group counseling is far more natural for counselors, especially those working in addictions treatment settings. In fact, group counseling tends to be the preferred method of treatment for addictions, given the need for support, and historic 12-step programs (DiClemente, 2003). Many if not most counselors-in-training will receive hands-on group experience during their practicum-internship experience. My own experience, in over 30 years in the profession, is that graduate students are more anxious about providing group than individual counseling. This seems natural to me, as in individual counseling one can focus on one person's experience, and build

72   *Groups, Couples, and Family Counseling*

a treatment plan around that client's particular needs. Add seven to nine additional people to the therapeutic mix, however, and you have numerous experiences, stories, values, opinions, and so forth. Then, the issue of which member should get most time, how to address clients who monopolize the "airspace," those who are silent, and inter-client conflicts with the group and counseling becomes far more complex.

So, regarding group counseling, I default to my own experiences in the field. Upon completion of my master's degree, I transitioned from a university counseling center, with educated, mostly motivated adults who were working to realize professional goals as educators, business owners, medical professionals, among other professions to an in-patient psychiatric facility treating children and adolescents. At the university center, most clients showed up for individual counseling, with me co-facilitating a group with another graduate student, and the outlier couples. At the psychiatric center, however, the treatment focus was very different than my previous experiences. Working the 3:00–11:00 p.m. shift, we held group sessions immediately after school (and a similar time during summer break), then another before bedtime, with ad hoc groups called whenever needed. (Additional groups were *always* needed!)

Unlike orderly, outpatient treatment at the university center, treatment at the psychiatric center was sometimes chaotic and occasionally rowdy. My first week on the job, an adolescent threatened a staff member, and the "restraint" team was called. Two burly men showed up, rolled the errant kid into a ball, taped his ankles and wrists behind him, and then quickly carted him off to a juvenile detention facility an hour away. As a young, idealistic counselor, freshly minted, I could scarcely believe what I had witnessed. The scene of a violent, screaming adolescent being held down by two large, strong men conjured up images of a popular Jack Nicholson film! We quickly pulled the other adolescents into group, and debriefed the incident. Given that practically all the kids in the psychiatric center had been traumatized to begin with, I marveled at their ability to be therapeutic after witnessing such a disturbing spectacle.

Fortunately, such restraints were outliers—although they occasionally occurred. The psychiatric center did provide me in-depth, intensive training in co-facilitating groups. My shift partner, a veteran of nearly a decade, was an outstanding group facilitator. She was almost as tough on me as she was on the adolescents, but she also did encourage me. The day she let me lead a group was one of the most significant intrinsic rewards in my professional career!

So, what I am saying to readers, not very subtly, is that experience, along with quality supervision, will be your best teachers. Regardless of whether you received much group or couples training in your program, and many of you will not (or did not), this does not mean you cannot get it in the field. Many students whom my colleagues and I have trained over 30 years complain they will not be prepared for the workplace because they did not get enough training in some area. I explain the practicum-internship experience (1,000 hours over four semesters in our program) is the backbone. We go on to elaborate that their education will continue throughout their careers. One graduate of our School Counseling program completed her entire internship in an affluent public, suburban high school. Then, she landed a job in an inner-city high school, serving children of immigrant and low-income families. Fortunately, her school partnered with a local clinic and utilized graduate student help in upskilling the treatment teams (school counselors, school psychologists, and school social workers) in group and family therapy. Family therapy usually involved a single-parent mother or grandmother attending with the student for the purpose of helping the student succeed in school (i.e., preventing drop-out, addressing drug use, gang recruitment, violence, teen sexuality, etc.). Despite almost quitting several times during her first year, she persevered, eventually becoming experienced in group and family counseling using the Solution-focused Brief model.

Thus, I expect that through my narratives to have established readers in counselor-in-training programs must be open to postgraduate experiences that complete and deepen their therapeutic skill. Give such realities then, what additional education, training, and resilience are needed to grow and flourish in group and marriage and family counseling? I have already addressed the need for ongoing education (course work, CEs, etc.), supervision, and experience. More than anything, resilience is a function of attitude (Duckworth et al., 2007). Therefore, more important than any skill (other than professional ethics), you will need to develop true "grit" for the workplace. Most readers will not graduate and matriculate to cushy suburban P-12 schools, ease into well-funded university counseling centers, nor find work in affluent hospitals and agencies. Most likely, you will begin your career in under-resourced, urban schools, or in agencies serving a high-needs population in blighted urban areas, or in rural America with few additional resources in the community for support or referral. So, be prepared, develop a strong self-care practice, and do not get too discouraged.

Challenges in Couples and Family Counseling

The rationale for working with families as opposed to individuals has strong support with regard to the reality that we all exist in multiple, often interlocking systems (Gladding, 2019). My professional experience has been that many mental health, addiction, abuse and neglect issues in individuals, have their genesis in their families of origin. Families provide interconnectedness among members, with actions impacting the entire system. For example, a child bullying school-age peers may well have learned such behavior at home through viewing his father's abusive behavior. The same can certainly be said of children growing in in a family of substance abuse, school drop-outs, and multigenerational unemployment. Much like a blood test the doctor takes during a patient's annual physical, family case history can serve a similar function in counseling. I have also found genograms and family maps helpful to both the client and myself with regard to understanding family dynamics regarding addiction, PTSD, and high school drop-out rates, as well as in individual and collective resilience (e.g., college degrees, long-term work history, financial independence, etc.).

Another compelling rationale for couples and family therapy is that it tends to be effective, at least to some degree. In a meta-analysis of over 250 studies on family and couples therapy, various theoretical approaches to family and couples counseling

74 *Groups, Couples, and Family Counseling*

were superior to no counseling at all and no study indicated negative or destructive effects (Pinsof & Wynne, 1995). Some indication suggested couples and family therapy had a positive impact in treating serious disorders such as schizophrenia, depression in married women, adult obesity, anorexia, childhood conduct disorders, various addictions, to cite some. While family and couples therapy was not sufficient to treat these disorders, "it significantly enhances the treatment packages for these disorders" (Pinsof & Wynne, 1995, p. 2).

Finally, couples and family therapy has been viewed as effective by overwhelming percentages of participants (Gladding, 2019). In a survey, Doherty and Simmons (1996) found that some 97% of clients rate the marriage and family counseling they received as good to excellent. An equally large percentage of clients reported that the services they received from marriage and family therapists helped them deal more effectively with the issues in their relationships and their life. These robust positive percentages are very rare in counseling and therapeutic studies, and other studies positive results more in line with conventional counseling success rates (Grande, 2017). Regardless, most participants rate couples and family counseling as effective. More surprisingly, is the reality many of these couples—married or partnered—do split up after therapy has concluded (Gladding, 2019; Grande, 2017).

So, given that growing up in some type of family (e.g., nuclear, single-parent, LGBT, blended, foster, etc.) exhibits such a powerful influence on an individual, more training and skill in couples and family therapy are strongly encouraged for anyone working in the mental health field. I would even advocate that school counselors get additional training in family counseling as so many school children's lives are complicated by family dynamics of domestic abuse, addiction, and divorce. Many years ago, I recall the director of Juvenile Justice, where I lived and worked, expressing that whenever he encountered a youth in the legal system, he had learned to tell himself the child's behavior was likely symptomatic of some family dysfunction.

There have been numerous historical high water marks in the history of family therapy. Chief among these was the founding of the American Association of Marriage Counseling (AAMC) in 1942. Luther Groves, who was instrumental in the AAMC's founding, authored the seminal text on the subject, titled simply *Marriage* in 1933. Later important theoretical influencers were Gregory Bateson, Milton Erickson, Carl Whitaker, Murray Bowen, Jay Haley, Virginia Satir, Salvador Munchin, among others. The AAMC grew and evolved into the American Association for Marriage and Family Therapy in 1977. The International Association for Marriage and Family Counseling (IAMFC) was established in the late 1980s and is affiliated with the American Counseling Association (ACA) and the Council for the Accreditation of Counseling and Related Educational Programs (CACREP). The AAMFT remains the largest professional organization representing couples and family therapists and publishes the *Journal of Marital and Family Therapy*, while the IAMFC publishes *The Family Journal*.

Unquestionably, the term "family" has evolved significantly since the founding of AAMFC in the early 1940s. While post-World War II definitions of family centered on male-dominated, intact, nuclear families, current views include numerous family types such as blended, single-parent, unmarried partners, gay and lesbian couples and families, and so forth. Popular approaches to family and couples counseling include Bowen Family Systems, Experiential Therapy, Structural Family Therapy, Strategic Family Therapy, Feminist Family Therapy, Narrative Family Therapy, and Solution-Focused Family Therapy among others (Gladding, 2019).

As one who became involved in couples and family counseling (albeit initially unwillingly), there are many different challenges therein as opposed to group and individual counseling. In my experience, couples and family counseling is significantly different to individual and groups counseling. In family and couples counseling, you are dealing with more than one person, and unlike group counseling, the couple or family in question have a direct relationship with one another (i.e., family members). These respective family members form a unit, may produce children, and provide a source of emotional support and intimacy. Certainly, clients in individual counseling and members in group counseling exist in various systems as well, though not in the same family system. Thus, the issues of a collective, close personal relationship makes couples and family counseling very different from other types of counseling. Family roles may be clear and well defined, too diffuse, or overly rigid. For those of you training to become family counselors, you will already know this. For graduate students in clinical mental health, school counseling and other tracks, this may be novel to you. As case studies breathe life into abstract discussions, consider the following case study below.

The Case of James and Sarah

James and Sarah come to the Healthy Way Agency for couples counseling. They have been married for two years and have no children. Ciara, a recent graduate of a marriage and family counseling program, conducts the intake, informed consent, and interview. The couple appears to be having "communication problems" as both Sarah and James espouse. Before the couple leaves, Ciara sets an appointment for the following week. The next one arrives and James comes to the session alone, as Sarah has been held up at work. James asks for the session anyway, stating he could use any insights Ciara might have. During the session, James discloses that he has been having an affair with a female co-worker. "You're not going to tell Sarah, are you? Please don't tell her! Our conversation today is just between us, right?" Ciara is very conflicted as to how to proceed. She wants to honor James' request, but also feels a responsibility to Sarah and their relationship. How do you think Ciara should proceed? If you were Ciara's supervisor, what would recommend?

Now, anyone who has completed a master's in counseling program should be aware of proper informed consent. Having made this statement, I can attest that in 30 years of clinical work, more than 20 years of supervision in several US states and overseas I am aware of numerous issues similar to the Case of James and Sarah. When it comes to legal and ethical issues, legal experts will go back to review the counselor's informed consent (Wheeler & Bertram, 2019; Remley & Herlihy, 2016). So, what is critical is that which you covered during informed consent. Makes sure you cover it well.

76   *Groups, Couples, and Family Counseling*

Now, as per ACA ethics (American Counseling Association, 2014) and those of the International Association of Marriage and Family Counselors (2017), Ciara should have informed both spouses of the guidelines of the therapeutic relationship. It is hoped that she explained the therapeutic relationship was with both parties, not an individual. The question then immediately arises as to whether she erred in counseling James alone. Now, many couple's counselors I have known would sometimes see each marital partner alone to gather information that might not be obtained otherwise. Unfortunately, this raises the possibility of encountering what James dropped on Ciara. Then the sticky issue is who holds confidentiality: is it strictly with the couple? Can each claim, as James has done, that Ciara cannot share his "secret" with Sarah? Unfortunately, we do not know for certain what Ciara told Sarah and James during informed consent, though any such agency would make lines of confidentiality explicit! If Ciara has not made such lines clear, the agency's legal counsel would need to offer an opinion. In the meantime, Sarah likely would need to explain to James that she would not divulge the affair and that James is responsible for divulging any such secrets to Sarah.

Now, the Case of James and Sarah is a classic example of what sets couples counseling apart from individual and group counseling. During my career, I have had many clients disclose affairs in individual and even group counseling, though without the complication of a spouse or partner also being involved in our sessions. Furthermore, there will be other complications in couples and family counseling that may be absent in individual and group encounters. This is especially true in family counseling as marital, developmental, generational and cultural issues may conflict. Consider the following case study.

The Case of the Faraday Family

Ahmed and Jehan Faraday and their adult son Amir present to the Spectrum Cultural Center for counseling. The Faradays are a highly educated, financially successfully family. Their counselor is Abdul, who is a Muslim, though born and raised in the San Francisco Bay area. The Faradays immigrated to the area 25 years ago from the India. The Faradays are a Muslim family with a 21-year-old daughter at a university and a son Amir, who is 24 and in medical school. Ahmed is an orthopedic surgeon and Jehan is a professor of mathematics at a local university. The reason for seeking counseling is over conflicts with Amir. After the intake when the first session begins, Ahmed and Jehan state they need Abdul to inform Amir he must obey his parents' wishes and marry the Muslim woman they and the woman's parents have agreed upon. Amir, who was born and raised in the USA, is adamant at being able to select the person he wants to marry and refuses his parents demand. How would you suggest Abdul proceed? What are the various cultural and ethical issues he must negotiate?

The Case of the Faradays is a classic example where a pluralistic counseling profession may come into conflict with more traditional-minded people. Abdul's role as an ethically practicing counselor is very clear. Amir is a competent adult—in fact a medical student—with the right to self-determination. Ahmed and Jehan, however, may likely see Abdul as acting culturally insensitive and betraying his culture merely by doing his job. Now, this is not unique to non-western cultures, as many majority culture families often disagree with the counseling profession, especially with regard to issues of gender, LGBTQ, adult children, and so forth. So, while Abdul's ethical responsibility is clear, how he might proceed with honoring Amir's ethical and legal rights while simultaneously not alienating Ahmed and Jehan is not. As one who has worked extensively in non-western countries and cultures, such a situation is very delicate for the counselor.

Abdul would be wise to explain his professional role (e.g., role of the counselor, ethical practice, etc.) while noting Ahmed and Jehan's concerns, as Ahmed's practice is governed by the professional ethics of the American Medical Association (AMA) and Jehan's university has a standard of conduct. He might thereafter suggest they have a conversation regarding their conflict with Amir. Ahmed and Jehan clearly work alongside westerners in their professional roles as surgeon and professor. He would be wise to provide Amir the opportunity to address his desire to his parents as he may believe they do not trust his judgment. If nothing is gained, providing the family the opportunity to address concerns and conflicts could help lessen the conflict. It is fair to say, however, that not all conflicts, cultural and otherwise, are resolved to everyone's satisfaction.

The Case of Laura and James

Laura and James are a married, mid-twenties couple, who are members of an evangelical Christian church in a rural community. Their counselor is Ruth, an experienced counselor working at the Good Works Pastoral Counseling Center. Ruth is a licensed counselor as well as a minister at a local, progressive, Christian church. Laura and James are professional people in the small community, and their parents are devout members of the church they attend. Recently, however, they have begun to have serious doubts regarding their church's teaching regarding homosexuality being a sin, gender roles, and several firmly held tenets of their faith. They wish to discuss whether remaining with their church is in their best interest, especially now that Laura recently discovered she is pregnant. Laura then drops a bombshell statement, explaining, "Our families will shun us if we leave the church. See, we are taught to always obey our parents as that was God's law. What can we do? We came to you because we know you are a minister as well as a good counselor." Ruth listens intently, though she feels her anger building towards a church that would be so rigid and put such demands upon its members. Ruth also is married to another woman, who is an attorney in the region.

Having been the counselor in a very similar situation many years ago, I understand the feelings of the couple and the counselor. Regardless of Ruth's views about her client's church, she must ethically bracket off her own values to focus on her client's (American Counseling Association, 2014). After eight very intense counseling sessions, filled with much processing and venting of anger, the young couple make the very difficult decision to leave their church despite what that decision entails.

78 *Groups, Couples, and Family Counseling*

The following Monday, a large group of protestors carry an angry, hate-filled sign in red lettering, picket the Good Works Pastoral Counseling Center, demanding Ruth be fired for "Making Laura and James Leave their Church," with some carrying signs condemning Ruth to Hell for her sexual orientation, and they block the entrance to the center chanting, "Drive her out of town!" at Ruth. How should Ruth proceed in order to protect herself from personal and professional harm? Given this is a rural community and likely very conservative, what additional issues might that entail? If Ruth sought you out for advice, how might you advise her? Finally, if you were on the Pastoral Center's Board of Directors, what action might you take to protect Ruth, the rest of the staff, the center, and the clients it serves?

Couples and family counseling is an eminently rewarding, albeit often complex and challenging profession. The Case of Laura and James illustrates the type of issues a counselor must consider and help prepare clients to address. Issues such as in the Case of Ahmed and Jehan and that of Laura and James certainly can arise in individual or group counseling as well. The important point is to assist couples and family members in sorting out the pressing issues during the session. At times, as in the latter situation, living and practicing in a rural community can make ethical practice more complex than that in urban centers. Counseling situations that could be challenging in more progressive urban or suburban settings can be downright volatile in rural ones. Laura and James' plight, as well as that of Ruth, underlines the necessity of supportive family, friends, and colleagues. Unfortunately for the couple, they may have no family left. This could be potentially devastating when the reality settles in. Ruth herself needs much personal and professional support as well. Sadly, every day there are people going through what Laura, James, and Ruth experienced in this case study.

The Need for Continuing Education

Given that most state licensure laws and national certification require continuing education to maintain a license to practice, career-long education will be a reality for all counselors. Continuing education (CE as it is often called) is part of what professional organizations such as ACA, ASCA, ARCA, as well as the state affiliate of these national organizations, provide at conferences and through electronic means. Private, independent organizations also provide CE, either in person or via the internet. As I was writing this chapter, I received a brochure advertising mindfulness-based couples therapy. Professional organizations' conferences, as well as those offered by private organizations provide important training and networking opportunities for counselors at all stages of their career to deepen in their knowledge, skills, and dispositions regarding the topic at hand. Many clinics now provide training to their staff, with some even offering outsiders the opportunity to participate in the training as well. In fact, one of the large mental health corporations in my area offers regular training for employees (e.g., counselors, social workers, psychologists, nurses, and even administrative staff) as well as graduate interns. Employees and interns may participate without charge. This is a handy service option, saving the employee much time and money for training. Organizations also are more likely to retain staff as professional training is a significant benefit to staff. So remember when you become a supervisor, clinical director, or CEO, to provide CE training for your staff as it is likely to pay off therapeutically and financially.

Another valid reason for continuing education beyond the "have to" requirement is to remain current in your professional practice. We all have likely encountered professionals in numerous fields who seem badly out of date regarding current practices. During my time of running clinics, I would meet the odd clinician who disclosed not having read a journal article or book in some years. The ACA code of ethics mandates remaining current in practice through ongoing training, coursework, attending conferences, or by another legitimate means (American Counseling Association, 2014). My own experience is that most counselors are conscientious about continued education for their own improvement as well as maintaining their right to practice.

Another reason to be active in ongoing training and education is when you wish to develop a specialty area in the field. I have mentioned this in previous chapters including this one. As I mentioned, when circumstances demanded I acquire more training in couples and family counseling, I received two years of supervision, coursework, attended professional training courses, watched professional videos, read books in the field, and so forth. In essence, there was a period of several years where I was essentially a "student" long after my formal degree work ceased. What I am saying—perhaps in a long-winded fashion—is that you will need to follow a similar path for your own career. In my case, I never intended to counsel couples or families; the situation simply arose. Likely, such a situation will occur in your career and you may wind up pursuing training in a counseling specialty area you never previously considered.

The Future: Addressing Trauma in All Forms

Early in my career, back in the mid-1980s, I realized most of my clients were suffering from some type of trauma. Now, not all would necessarily have met criteria for PTSD, but many continued to repeat the same self-defeating patterns by romantic involvements with verbally, physically, and even sexually abusive partners and through self-medication with alcohol and other drugs. Unfortunately, there was not the recognition of trauma treatment that came two decades later. Researchers such as Bessel Van der Kolk, Marsha Linehan, Stewart Chen Hayes, and many others revolutionized the field of trauma treatment. Linehan's Dialectical Behavioral Therapy (DBT) model was the first one I studied. I was drawn to BDT, as Linehan's approach to treating women with Borderline Personality Disorder (BPD) was a non-blaming approach I found refreshing (Linehan, 1987). I had been counseling women with the BPD diagnosis, all of whom were traumatized, many from childhood sexual abuse. I was finding little empathy or sympathy for these clients. Some in the mental health community appeared to view BPD suffers as "drama queens who do not need nor benefit from therapy" (Heller, 2014, p. 1).

During a state mental health conference during the mid-1990s, I attended a session on treating BPD clients, presented by an Ivy League-trained psychiatrist.

80 Groups, Couples, and Family Counseling

I had sat in one a previous session of his on depression and been favorably impressed. I was very shocked, however, when during his workshop on BPD he opined that his method of treatment was to inform the BPD client, "You have a personality disorder. You likely have fired all previous clinicians and will eventually fire me." Now, his words did match some of my own clients, but I was most distressed to hear him stating such to a client. After all, as one of my BPD clients disclosed, "if your therapist does not have faith in you, who will?" Indeed, this is a worthwhile question. I was alarmed at the psychiatrist's statement, but lacked the moral courage to confront him in such a public forum. Contrast that deterministic, and insensitive verbiage to Linehan's approach that goes something like (italics mine): *You are having a normal reaction to an abnormal experience. Of course you are angry* (Linehan, 1987; 1993). When I began to use Linehan's approach of understanding and respect, my therapy sessions went much better. Admittedly, my clients with BPD were very challenging, labile, and experts at finding my emotional triggers (I hid my emotions well). Still, when I learned to focus on the trauma, I had more luck in engaging with the client.

Regarding therapeutic approaches to trauma treatment, counselors and other clinicians have their favorite approaches. In my area, and seemingly nationally, DBT, EMDR, ACT, and Trauma-Focused CBT, all which seem to have a *mindfulness* base of late, appear to be the treatments of choice. Several graduates of the counseling program I teach in have become DBT team leaders, credentialed in EMDR and ACT or a cognitive approach addressing trauma recovery. Naturally, leaders in all these approaches will promote their approach as the preferred treatment of choice. My own review of the literature is all seem to have promising efficacy, at least to some extent and thus my recommendation would be for counselors to focus on one of these approaches. A counselor's place of employment may be the deciding factor on which approach to take, as in western New York, I have noticed ads for ACT Team Leader, or seeking experienced EMDR or DBT therapists, and the like. Naturally, it is very possible, even likely that another approach or at least a variation of the aforementioned approaches will emerge and become popularized in the manner of DBT, EMDR, ACT, and so forth. In the meantime, the recommendation here is to focus on one of these.

Lessons Learned

The last decade of my life and career has involved me going overseas to volunteer in South African orphanages and in remote, indigenous schools and communities in Australia's Northern Territory. I offer many services, including trainings on working with traumatized youth, preventing vicarious trauma, self-care, among others, as well as provide consultation to therapeutic staff, one-to-one coaching/consultation for teachers, child-care workers, social workers and community elders and even offer counseling on request. Generally, I spend between four and six weeks overseas, living in remote areas of Australia or orphanage grounds in South Africa.

In June and part of July 2015, I spent five weeks in the Kwa-Zulu Natal region of South Africa. During this time, I volunteered providing trainings on trauma

Groups, Couples, and Family Counseling 81

treatment, suicide prevention, self-care, and other related topics in five orphanages and three schools, delivered 22 presentations, keynoted a conference, and provided a lot of consultations and co-therapy with social workers. Feeling exhausted at this point, I was winding down and looking forward to returning home to New York. The director of the final orphanage I visited had asked if I could co-facilitate a meeting with a 17-year-old girl and her estranged family. I agreed, provided the social worker was agreeable. The social worker was quite eager to have me in the session, explaining that the family, which were an aunt and uncle (the girl's father had died of HIV+ and her mother's whereabouts were unknown). The aunt and uncle were planning to tell their niece they would be unable to take her into their home when she turned 18 in six months' time and was released from the orphanage. She went on to explain that this particular girl, "Harmony" (pseudonym), would understandably be very hurt. The social worker further explained Harmony was an excellent student and had even won a scholarship at a university, which was rare for a child raised in an orphanage. Evidently, the aunt and uncle had several children and were raising additional nieces and nephews and were stretched perilously thin. Harmony had been looking forward to living at her aunt and uncle's home on university holidays. Now, she would be homeless when school wasn't in sessions as she was too old for the orphanage.

Harmony was an adolescent female who had defied considerable odds. She had been taken from her drug-addicted mother, while her father, who had earlier abandoned the family, had died of HIV+ related causes. Her extended family had been unable to care for her and thus she ended up at the orphanage while in grade school. She was a very bright, articulate child, respected by her peers, teachers, and orphanage staff. She had given the introduction of me at a general assembly when I had arrived at the orphanage, and had sought me out thereafter. Harmony herself had evidently suggested I be included at the family meeting with her aunt and uncle. This was unusual, although I had previously participated in a couple of such meetings at other orphanages.

The meeting came and true to the social worker's prediction, the news was a huge disappointment to Harmony. In fact, the session was more counseling session than anything else, with me as the de facto family counselor due to my experience in such. After the session, the social and worker and I continued a one-hour debrief session with Harmony as she was in crisis (though not suicidal). At the conclusion of the meeting, she requested a follow-up session with me the following day, which went as well as it could have gone. In fact, I met with her each day that week. On my final day at the orphanage, the social worker pulled me aside. "Harmony wants to meet with both of us together. Do you have the time?" I did and that afternoon after school, we met with Harmony in the social worker's office.

"I have a question for uncle," Harmony began. "Aunt" and "uncle" are used as terms of respect when addressing elders in the orphanage system. "You are a kind man, educated man and I understand you and your wife have no children." I nodded. "Well, I was wondering if you might consider adopting an African girl." Both the social worker and I immediately went into shock. Neither of us had foreseen this heavy question coming. We had expected Harmony to continue to address

82　Groups, Couples, and Family Counseling

the topic of her aftercare plan now that it no longer involved any family. So caught off-guard, I could not articulate any words in response to her weighty question. After I recovered, I explained that while I thought highly of her, mentioning her strong scholarship, leadership activities (campus prefect, captain of netball team, school awards, etc.), and resilience, my wife and I would not be able to adopt her. Whereupon, she began sobbing and voicing "nobody loves me."

None of my counseling education and training—master's or doctoral program—experience, nor my own intuition, was of much guidance. For a change, the ethical code seemed like empty rhetoric, and all answers I might conjure up sounded like frivolous excuses from a privileged westerner. I have had to give a lot of difficult feedback to clients over the 25 years of counseling and consulting work. None of those difficult, sometimes painful, situations impacted me as much as this meeting with Harmony. How do you adequately explain to an orphan child that you cannot adopt her? Repetition of the national laws, ethical codes, and personal circumstances scarcely seemed sufficient answers.

The social worker and I did the best we could to salvage the situation, reminding her of how much progress she had made, her scholarship to the university, and the future impact she could have on children such as herself (she planned to study medicine in the hope of becoming a pediatrician). None of our interventions seemed a sufficient salve to soothe her raw emotions. I apologized to Harmony, explaining I was sorry to have contributed to her grief. The session ended soon thereafter, with the social worker scheduling a follow-up with her the next day. When Harmony left the office, the social worker called Harmony's housemother over and we informed her of the news. "Gracie" (pseudonym), an experienced housemother, vowed to watch Harmony and promised to contact the social worker in the event of a health and safety issue. She further promised to check in with Harmony daily for the next week.

Harmony did ask for me to say goodbye to her, and in the presence of Gracie and the social worker hugged me, rivers of tears rolling down her face. That last image of her has haunted me since. While counseling clients, whether as individuals, couples or family, or groups, with children, adolescents, and adults, sometimes our best efforts boomerang back on us in the most excruciating manner. Ethically, and realistically, I had made the "correct" decision in turning down Harmony's request for adoption. Doing the *right* thing, however, did not leave anyone, most particularly me, feeling very good. What I learned, or more accurately *relearned*, is that I will hurt people in my professional role, even when striving to act in the client's best interest. More to the point, *what's in the client's best interest* certainly can be a topic for debate. In this case with Harmony, I followed the relevant laws and professional ethics, to say nothing of what was reasonable. Whether I did what was in Harmony's best interest, however, is something I am far less sanguine about.

Finally, one must ask, "What actually is in the client's best interest?" and "How do we determine what is in their best interest?" Usually, I have found it a matter of reviewing professional ethics, relevant laws and/or assessing the pros and cons of a given situation. In fact, as a counselor, counselor educator, and a concerned individual, an Occam's razor approach, or the most simple solution usually is the correct one, typically guides my decision-making process. No question, of course, that ethics and legalities should be the first considerations. There is, however, that occasional moral issue that supersedes all ethical codes. In my experience with Harmony, I passed on the professional ethics section of her issue, though may have failed miserably on the greater moral imperative. In practicing the self-compassion aspect of a mindfulness-based approach and lifestyle, I try to refrain from self-judgment in this and other difficult situations I have experienced. Mostly I am a realist and understand my influence will be quite limited to education and counseling. But I see her sometimes, especially when confronted with the faces of neglected and wounded children seeking more than temporary support.

8 Emotional Intelligence
The Most Critical Component for Counselors

American society has long been focused on standardized test scores. Many states, such as New York have created high stakes tests to augment P-12 education. Furthermore, IQ scores, SAT scores, and ACT scores have long held a lofty status in US society. In fact, the latter tests, achievement-orient tests such as the SAT and ACT, have become a multi-billion dollar industry, the status of which, however, has recently been challenged with many colleges and universities opting for "test free" admission. Meanwhile, popular publications, such as *U.S. News & World Report*, publish an annual issue on the best colleges in the country, much of which is based on standardized test scores of students. Interestingly, several years ago I did some iso-called best colleges and discovered that all these institutions were very rich (Hodges, 2002). Furthermore, students at our most elite colleges are among the most privileged in the world, with family median incomes well above the norm. So, the belief that all children in the country have an equal opportunity for educational, vocational, and economic self-actualization is essentially a modern-day fairy tale. So then, should we just throw up our collective hands and shrug off social determinism for family wealth? Of course not, but what additional factor or factors can defray socioeconomic pedigree? According to Daniel Goleman (2005) what actually matters most, more than IQ, SAT/ACT scores, more than money, and even greater than academic pedigree, is emotional intelligence.

Emotional intelligence has been defined as the ability to recognize, understand, and manage our own emotions as well as to recognize, understand, and influence the emotions of others (Goleman, 2005). While I favor Goleman's definition of EQ, I wish to take it a step further and add the concept of resilience. Let me digress to illustrate the point. For many years, our school counselor was a crusty farmer who had begun his career teaching agriculture in our remote, small-town school in the Ozarks. He eventually retrained as a school counselor and even developed a psychology class, which he taught until his death. I recall that during one particular class we were reading and discussing the concept of intelligence, and what factors make up intelligence. As high school juniors and seniors we eventually brought the conversation around to the ACT were scheduled to take very soon. At some point during the discussion, our teacher stated that while he was a believer in assessment, he was skeptical that test scores, be they Stanford-Binet or SAT, were a good measure of future success. This opinion was a real surprise to members of our class, as this very teacher and school counselor had been assessing us since grade school. "There are better methods of evaluation," he went on to opine.

So, if there were better methods of evaluation, what specifically were those methods, someone inquired. He went on to express that he had come to believe there was what he termed a "magic ten percent." This august group—the magic ten—might not have the highest SAT or ACT scores, nor an IQ score two standard deviations above the mean. He went on to say that the magic ten were resilient, creative types who would find a way to conquer any obstacle put in their path. "If I could develop an assessment that would identify such types, I would be a very rich man," he stated. A classmate inquired, "What defines this group of people?" He replied, "They are people who are always telling themselves 'I can' as opposed to 'I can't' or 'I won't.' Essentially, they succeeded because they believed they could and continued to work at success and achieving their goals even when such appeared hopeless."

I had for a long time sought positive attention from the counselor. He was constantly singing the praises of successful graduates our school has produced: a national merit scholar; a graduate who had become a successful engineer; and most especially my valedictorian elder brother, whom he seemed to hold at the pinnacle of success. Then there were the students like myself. Average-oriented intellectually, as well as athletically, adolescents with marginal future prospects regarding societal advancement. I had been taught that education was a means both of social mobility and personal development. What happens, however, when your academic experiences, to say nothing of standardized test scores, suggest meager future prospects? I also recalled this same counselor explaining that only some 10% of a graduating class would matriculate to college. Of that small group, the attrition rate was nearly 90%! The odds were too crushing to contemplate.

As one of these socially and academically awkward students, my psychology teacher's/school counselor's message resonated with me. I so badly wanted to believe in self-efficacy despite very little tangible evidence that success seemed part of my future. Thus, I continued spelunking through my senior year, finishing as I started, with mixed academic results. This same school counselor, with the transforming words, ironically often seemed to harbor little else but criticism for me. Even when I earned an A grade in his psychology class, he muttered that it likely should be an A minus. This gifted teacher and innovative man seemed to be just one more elder in a long line to view me as another of the masses heading into an occupational brick wall. Certainly, he had reasons to think the way he did. There was little fanfare about me. One classmate, in what seemed an effort to cheer me up stated: "You know, you're not the smartest fellow, but you're a really nice guy," he opined much to my sad astonishment. Likely, he was just echoing the party line as never would I have been picked as most likely to succeed.

My P-12 career culminated as did most of my generations with a high school diploma. As it was in small towns like mine, the entire town turned out for the ceremony. On that hot, humid, stifling graduation evening in our school's overcrowded gymnasium the class of 1978 marched in and out of school history. After the ceremony, as our class of 53 were saying goodbyes to family, friends, and teachers,

86   *Emotional Intelligence*

I noticed the school counselor walking straight towards me, with what seemed to be malice in his eyes. Lines of well-wishers and graduates parted as if the man were Moses himself. "What have I done now?" I wondered anxiously. "Listen," he began, "You haven't had it easy, and I know I've been hard on you. But you have persevered through a lot. I believe you will graduate from college and become a success." Then he embraced me, saying, "I think you're one of the magic ten." Nothing in my young, arduous life, thus far, had ever sounded so sweet and encouraging. That this counselor and educator I had so respected, whose attention I so vainly craved, had actually lavished high praise on me, was the most positive surprise my ears had heard. His timely words were the best award I could have earned. "Remember, keep telling yourself 'I can, and I will,' he counseled."

Fast-forwarding more than four decades, there is plenty of research that resilience is a better indicator of future success than standardized test scores (Duckworth, 2016). My school counselor and teacher was well ahead of his time with regard to promoting this idea of resilience in youth. Now, he did not have the most progressive methods in instilling such, but he did get me and others to think differently about predicting achievement. Essentially, he was suggesting that attitude, as evidenced by self-talk, was far more important than GPA or ACT/SAT or IQ. That late May evening of 1978, I strolled from the building with my shoulders square, ready to commence my journey. The life pathway has indeed been long—full of challenges, struggles, and intrinsic rewards. I think of my former educator and counselor and his magic ten. I so wanted to show him my college diploma, and far more my master's and doctoral degrees. But just a few months after graduation, he collapsed and died while herding cows on his farm. But I remember this man, far more than any of the long line of teachers, professors, and supervisors in my life. I learned of personal and vocational persistence, of grit, and the power of belief in oneself. I remember, I believe!

Emotional intelligence (EQ for short) has become a cause célèbre in the past decade. Daniel Goleman has written a best-selling book on the subject, illustrating that EQ may be more important than IQ (Goleman, 1995). The significant point to remember here is that EQ and IQ need not be distinct. Furthermore, anyone can improve their emotional intelligence through mindful self-reflection, regular practice, and through becoming more emotionally regulated. After all, as counselors challenge their clients to make more rational and informed decisions, especially when under duress, it becomes incumbent upon us to model what we profess.

Emotional Intelligence Defined

The first issue for consideration is, what is emotional intelligence? To paraphrase Goleman, EQ is the capacity to be aware of, manage, and express one's emotions, and to handle interpersonal relationships judiciously and empathetically (Goleman, 1995). Without question, counselors must develop and use EQ skills during their job if they are to be successful. As a 30-year veteran, I can specifically think back to my experiences of counseling mandated clients (e.g., sex offenders, domestic batters, addicts, etc.), many of whom challenged me on a variety of levels. The ability to remain emotionally regulated, or grounded, and stay clear-headed during moments of stress was a key ingredient in successful therapy. I must also say that whenever I failed to make use of good EQ, and became argumentative with clients, I regretted it 100% of the time. Fortunately, most of the time I was able to manage my emotions, revise my self-talk, and be able to remain therapeutic, even when the client was not interested in my doing so.

Making Use of EQ

Now that we have defined emotional intelligence, and made reference to when it may be needed, when are some specific times that EQ is required? Based on my experience as a counselor, clinical director, and professor, I would say the following times should be on the list: giving and receiving feedback; managing and revising negative self-talk; dealing with challenging clients, colleagues, supervisors and supervisees; managing setbacks and failures; and during personal and societal transition. In addition, EQ is of vital importance during moments of conflict when we are most likely to regress and make reactive statements that we wish we could withdraw. So, the operative question then becomes how can I develop emotional intelligence so that I manage my cognitions and emotions before they manage me? The following is a case-study illustration of EQ.

The Case of Caitlin

Caitlin recently graduated from a counselor education program and is working in a community agency in a large inner city. She grew up in a middle-class family with parents who were social justice advocates, and in her undergraduate and graduate years of study she performed extensive volunteer work. She especially adhered to the ACA code of ethics, and is a tireless advocate for multiculturalism and pluralism. She enjoys her job providing counseling to a diverse clientele of individuals and groups, and strongly believes she is making a small difference. One day, however, she overhears an older, long-time colleague making disparaging comments about transgender people. She is bothered by this and approaches the colleague to address the issue. Her colleague is dismissive and states, "Look, you are born either male or female. That's how God and nature expect it to be. We need to help them become one of the other."

Caitlin can hear her angry self-talk shouting in her head and her blood pressure suddenly increases exponentially. She is frustrated and angry any counselor would express such a narrow-minded, unethical attitude. She wonders how she should address the issue with her colleague without simply venting her anger at her coworker. If you were advising Caitlin, what would be an emotionally intelligent approach to addressing this conflict?

Discussion

No doubt, many counselors would be as angry as Caitlin in the above situation. Having spent many years in community mental health settings in rural and even

88 *Emotional Intelligence*

remote areas, I am not naive, however, about the fact that some do not share Caitlin's colleague's sentiments. Nevertheless, Caitlin needs to respond in a manner that addresses the issues regarding client wellbeing, and the counselor imposing his values onto the client. Likely, Caitlin may need to briefly calm herself through exercise, meditation and discussing the matter with a trusted colleague before addressing the conflict. With preparation, she is more likely to regulate her emotions during the meeting, as her colleague may refuse to recognize his bias, ethical perspective notwithstanding. Finally, should her colleague continue to be dismissive of transgender persons, she may need to discuss the matter with a trusted colleague, and then meet with her supervisor. Nevertheless, the manner in which she addresses this ethical issue is as important as the issue itself.

When Hope and Fear Come into Conflict

Caitlin's feelings of emotional turmoil are not unusual for anyone. From prehistoric times, the fight, flight, or freeze response has become imprinted in our human DNA, a vestige continuing through into these modern (postmodern?) times. Deep inside her amygdala and hippocampus, the region of the brain that regulates emotion, a struggle for control occurs. Caitlin's initial urge is to lash out verbally at her unenlightened colleague, but her prefrontal cortex, a more rational brain lobe wins out, and she makes the more informed decision to take a brief time out before addressing the issue with her colleague. Now, the issue still remains, but she can make a plan on how to strategize dealing with an unethical colleague. During her initial confrontation with her colleague, it is likely that Caitlin's self-talk became very angry or fearful. Whenever stressful situations occur, the amygdala send out messages that release cortisol, which stimulates the fight–flight–freeze mechanism. When that occurs, negative self-talk tends to follow. Consequently, theorists such as Albert Ellis trained their clients to focus on monitoring and revising self-talk. When people learn to challenge unhealthy, fearful, self-defeating self-talk, they are likely to make more rational, informed decisions (Ellis, 2004a). A rational, informed approach is what Caitlin needs in this situation with her colleague.

Now, having mentioned the founder of Rational Emotive Behavior Therapy (REBT), it is important to emphasize that Ellis did not call his approach emotional intelligence, as likely he preferred to focus on the cognitive aspect. Ellis frequently stated however that cognition and emotion were strongly correlated, meaning that rational, healthy cognition usually resulted in more healthy emotionality (1999; 2004a). Moreover, a large part of emotional intelligence requires the ability to "catch" and evaluate negative self-talk before it influences behavior. In fact, Goleman (1995) posits self-talk as a staple of good emotional intelligence and wellbeing. Blending Ellis and Goleman, one might well consider that the litmus test of good EQ comes when the counselor (or anyone else) is triggered by an act in the workplace, an argument at home, or an enraged driver. Clearly, regulating self-talk in such challenging situations is a critical part of good EQ, as well as healthy living. As self-talk is vital to our emotional and even physical health, let us examine how we can begin to target and improve it.

Self-talk: The Canary in the Mine and the Mind

During my grade school years, we learned that miners used to take canaries down into the mines with them. If the canaries passed out, the miners knew poisonous gases were leaking and that they would need to get back to the surface, or else they might die. From this historical vignette came the popular expression *the canary in the mine* to address any situation of potential risk. Likewise, self-talk is the essential "canary" that prevents psycho-emotional self-destruction. Over 25 years of providing counseling and training in a variety of settings—community mental health, residential psychiatric, university counseling services, remote indigenous schools and communities, and orphanages—I have been witness to numerous children, adolescents, and adults exclaiming, "I had no choice!" with regard to unleashing verbal and even physical assaults upon third parties. In essence, my first task of any treatment plan with such clients is to teach them that, indeed, they do have a choice. Unquestionably, many of the clients I served had been traumatized physically, sexually, and emotionally (often all three) and were unregulated emotionally and lashed out due to being triggered. One of the first things I would teach them was to notice their self-talk. With the vast majority of wounded clients, their self-talk was very angry, violent, and self-destructive. Such is understandable given their traumatization. To live a healthier, happier, more fulfilling life, however, requires successful trauma treatment. An ongoing facet of efficacious treatment is good self-regulation, aided by realistic, healthy self-talk.

One of my favorite sayings regarding arresting self-talk in order to self-reflect and manage thoughts and behaviors is what is called the Three Cs: Catch it–Challenge it–Change it. "Catch it" means catching the negative self-talk ("I'm a loser!"); "Challenge it" is to ask, "What's the evidence that I'm a loser? Given I have an advanced degree and have held a long-term job, likely not true"; and "Change it" means saying the revised, healthier statement such as, "I am a very capable person." The Three Cs are a staple of cognitive therapy and of good emotional regulation and EQ. Now, as I favor the cognitive approaches to therapy, I will frequently make mention of Ellis, Aaron and Judy Beck, Donald Meichenbaum, and others. However, a counselor need not be a practitioner of one of the cognitive approaches to use the Three Cs. In fact, counselors using any approach could make use of this simple, though effective technique to assist clients they serve. In point of fact, I make use of the Three Cs on an almost daily basis. The Three Cs are another example of a solid, effective EQ type of intervention. The Three Cs can be illustrated by the following example:

Client: I still keep hearing myself saying, "You suck as a teacher!"
Counselor: That sounds pretty harsh. Yet, you said before you work hard and seem to be making a difference with some of the students in your classes.
Client: Yeah, but not all.
Counselor: Well, few of us reach everyone. Nevertheless, here's a suggestion. Whenever you think, "I suck," I would like you to catch that word, and challenge it with the evidence.

90   *Emotional Intelligence*

Client: What evidence?

Counselor: You said earlier you seemed to be making a difference with some students, right?

Client: Sure … but not all.

Counselor: Okay, so the evidence is you are having success with some students. That seems to contradict the message of "I suck!" So, you catch the "I suck", challenge it with the evidence you are reaching some students, and change the message to something more accurate like, "I am successful with some students." How does this sound?

Client: Well, frankly it sounds too easy. Really, is that all it takes to feel better?

Counselor: Yes, it's fairly easy to catch, challenge and change the self-talk. The difficulty is you have to do it every day for the remainder of your life. (Pause) Just as I must do. That does make a difference.

Client: You?

Counselor: Yes, me. My self-talk can be negative as well. The Three Cs have made a big difference in my mood and behavior. See, we begin to believe what we tell ourselves. So, let's be realistic, though kind and accurate with ourselves.

Client: I'm willing to try. How many times a day do I have to do this?

Counselor: Let's start with five times a day. So, track with a notebook of or computer. We'll talk about how that goes in our next session.

One week later:

Counselor: Alright, I gave you the homework exercise of Catch-it, Challenge-it, and Change-it. How did it go?

Client: Honestly it felt very unnatural at first, especially the first couple of days. Thereafter, I began to feel better. So, it seemed to work, at least somewhat.

Counselor: Good that you felt better. Now remember, the longer you get in the habit of using the Three Cs, the more natural it becomes and the better you will feel.

Client: I will keep at it. You know, it's pretty simple.

Counselor: Likely it works because it is simple.

The Three Cs and challenging and revising negative self-talk are what Ellis (1999) illustrated as a staple of REBT. The client in the above situation is correct, as the process can seem too easy. However, as I used to tell clients and in my workshops, the difficulty is using the Three Cs model on an everyday basis. As one who has struggled with negative self-talk since childhood, I can verify that the model works very well provided you continue to work it. As a long-distance runner of 45 years (albeit a slow one!), there is no point at which I can stop running and expect to remain a fit runner. I must do it regularly. The same goes for healthy self-talk and healthy self-talk is strongly correlated to adaptive behavior as well (Ellis, 1999). My former high school counselor was always fond of saying: "If you believe you can succeed, you are right, at least to some extent. If you believe you can't succeed, you

Emotional Intelligence   91

are certainly right as well." So, for good EQ, daily revision of your self-talk are necessary. No question, as my high school counselor and Dr Ellis agreed, self-talk and belief will become a self-fulfilling prophecy. So, the more relevant questions is not, do you wish to succeed, but rather, are you willing to do the internal work (i.e., the Three Cs) necessary to make working towards your goals achievable. Basically, if you believe success is impossible, why put forth any effort. If you believe success is possible, you are much more likely to put in the effort and make the necessary sacrifices.

Self-talk, Goal Setting, and Measuring Progress

So, as a professional counselor or a counselor-in-training, you must come to understand the value of the internal messages you give to yourself (i.e., self-talk) and the value or revising that self-talk—what Ellis called cognitive restructuring (Ellis, 2000). As we have covered thus far, self-talk is the beginning step towards emotional wellbeing and good emotional intelligence. As previous have illustrated, good emotional and mental wellbeing is more a matter of ongoing practice than ever reaching a terminal point of self-actualization. This is no criticism of Maslow (1968), and on the contrary, healthy self-talk is a vestige of the self-actualized person. My own belief backed by experience in the field is that EQ, self-actualization (to an extent anyway), is more the fruit of regular, daily discipline (e.g., the Three Cs). Likely, the self-actualized person practices healthy self-talk, exhibits good emotional regulation and possesses strong EQ.

When I was beginning my master's program in Community Counseling, we studied the humanistic and existential approaches to counseling and psychotherapy. During those years, such approaches were solidly how I aligned myself therapeutically, especially with Rogers' Client-Centered Therapy (Rogers, 1951). I believed then, and still now, that genuineness, empathy, and positive regard were key ingredients to establishing the therapeutic alliance. While I gradually moved over into a cognitive approach, I have continued to use Roger's therapeutic building blocks to establish therapeutic rapport, and, to the extent possible, in my teaching and consulting. Furthermore, I firmly believe in Frankl's (1969) assertion that meaning in life is the most important ingredient in developing a fulfilling life. This can be evidenced in Beck's research on suicide prevention, as he has established that pessimism is the best predictor of suicide intention (Beck & Steer, 1987). Conversely, the best antidote against depression and suicide is likely that of optimism or hope (Beck & Steer, 1987; Seligman, 2011). So, to conclude this paragraph: emotional intelligence is manifest in optimistic, rational thinking, in realistic self-talk, part of cognitive restructuring, embedded in learned optimism, and the natural result of all is a belief that life has meaning. This meaning may vary across cultures and spiritual and religious orientations, but all have some concept of meaning in life as important. To venture into social constructivism, perhaps existing meaning is the meaning the individual ascribes to a particular experience or onto their life as a whole.

Now, while I am a firm believer that choice, meaning, EQ, self-actualization, and so on are important, my struggle with existential and humanistic language lies in

92   Emotional Intelligence

the difficulty in quantification and specificity. The following statements below are to assist you in clarifying your EQ-type strengths. As counselors provide mental health treatment, advocacy, and guidance to people grappling with anxiety, depression PTSD, addiction, and so forth, it is essential they have a good self-care plan which begins with a clear understanding of their resilience.

Acknowledging Resilience

1. How do you keep yourself motivated and working in the face of disappointment?

   _____

   _____

   _____

   _____

2. Everyone faces fears during their lifetime. Consider a time when you showed courage in the face of something or someone frightening. How and when did you show courage?

   _____

   _____

   _____

3. When you receive critical feedback, how do you manage and respond?

   _____

   _____

   _____

4. When negative thoughts and self-talk enter your head, how do you address them?

   _____

   _____

   _____

5. How do you deal with failure when you experience it?

   _____

   _____

   _____

6. How do you maintain a positive outlook?

   _____

   _____

   _____

Emotional Intelligence   93

7. If a close friend were asked about your strongest asset, what answer would that friend likely give?

_____

_____

_____

8. Regarding the previous question, what answer would you like a friend to give regarding your strengths?

_____

_____

_____

9. What accomplishment are you most proud of and why?

_____

_____

_____

10. What is the most important action you take on a daily basis?

_____

_____

_____

_____

Self-talk Exercises

A critical component of EQ and good mental and emotional health involves regularly evaluating and reframing negative self-statements. The following is an exercise for consideration.

There are ten negative statements listed. You will revise each into a more positive, realistic statement. Remember, a realistic statement involves challenging a negative thought or statement by saying: "What's the evidence for _____?" Then, crafting a more realistic self-talk message. See the example that follows.

Example of Self-talk Revision

Her negative self-talk: Yun-Mi says to herself: "I fail at everything!"
Her revised and realistic self-talk message: "Well, I have been successful at some things such as graduating from college, my counseling program and getting this job."
Conclusion: "Okay I'm human and have my successes and setbacks."

Yun-Mi's revised message and conclusion seem more accurate than her initial negative message. Ask yourself how often you have made negative overgeneralizations

94   *Emotional Intelligence*

like Yun-Mi above. We all have and will continue to do so. Thus, the need for the Three Cs and related work. Consider the following:

1. "I suck at everything!'
   Revised message:

   _____

2. "I'm a total failure!"
   Revised message:

   _____

3. "I can't seem to do anything right!"
   Revised message:

   _____

4. "I feel like an imposter and undeserving of my job/career/education."
   Revised message:

   _____

5. "Nobody likes me."
   Revised message:

   _____

6. "I am ugly."
   Revised message:

   _____

7. "No one will ever want to hire me."
   Revised message:

   _____

8. "No one will ever love me."
   Revised message:

   _____

9. "My life is meaningless."
   Revised message:

   _____

10. "I can't survive the death of my spouse/partner/child.
    Revised message:

    _____

Reminder: Most of the above revisions are easy to revise into a healthier message. Item numbers 8 through 10 will be more challenging, as such is realistic as well. My own experience is that negative, even seemingly hopeless self-statements can be revised to something more hopeful. In some 25 years of counseling across numerous cultures, I have worked with clients to revise painful self-talk. I can say that all informed me self-talk revision was helpful, even if they were still in grief. "It doesn't cure my grief, but it does help make it lighter," admitted a woman whose son had been killed in his teens. Her statement did not come easy, and it fact we spent around four months together in grief counseling. Nothing was "fixed," her late son did not return, and there would always be an emptiness in her life in the wake of his untimely death. But, the grief did become less, or at least *lighter*.

The Miraculous Question

Steve de Shazer and his spouse and colleague Insoo Kim-Berg created what has come to be known as the *Miracle Question* (de Shazer, 1994). Now for my own purposes, I have chosen to refer to my version of *The Miraculous Question* (apologies to de Shazer and Kim-Berg). The focus of this question is to gauge one's level of optimism. The second part of this question is how to begin to create what you would want, or to assist your clients in doing so.

The Miraculous Question: Okay, so while you were sleeping, something miraculous occurred and an issue or decision you were struggling with was resolved. So, upon waking what will be different about your life now that this issue has been resolved? What might family and close friends notice being different about you? So, how can you begin to create this miraculous situation? What steps could you begin taking today?

The steps can be small, baby steps even. The important point is to visualize the career and life you want and then to begin strategizing about how to create it. Many different things go into creating the career and life you desire, but such usually begins with a career vision. Perhaps then the operative question becomes, what vision do you have for your career and personal life? Consider the following reflective questions and answer on a separate sheet of paper or on your computer. Feel free to discuss this matter before completing this exercise and certainly after completing it. Remember, your vision is subject to revision due to shifting interests, life realities, and new opportunities. So, a career or life vision is a *living* document as opposed to an air-tight, unchanging plan.

1. My vision for my career is

2. My vision for my personal life looks like

3. What I most want in my career life is

4. What I want most in my personal life is

96　*Emotional Intelligence*

5. When I think of the future, I

_____.

6. I am very optimistic/pessimistic about my career and personal future. (circle optimistic or pessimistic). I am very optimistic because

_____

_____

If I am very pessimistic, I could begin to change towards becoming more optimistic by _____

_____

7. If I could look 7–10 years down the road, and my personal and career life were very fulfilling, how would my life and career look?

_____

_____

Remember, as Goleman (1995) and Frankl (1969) theorize, so much of being successful revolves around the attitude we choose to take. On a continuum of 1–10, with 10 being high on optimism, where would you score yourself? Why? How might you improve your optimism score just one point? My own work as a counselor suggests that most people make incremental gains over time as opposed to huge, sudden improvements. What I learn from my experiences is that we must be invested in our lives for the long term. That being said, ongoing self-reflection and evaluation is important for assessing positive change. Here is a suggestion: take a month and grade yourself on a weekly basis for four weeks. Evaluate your attitude on a 1–10 scale with 1 representing a *less adaptive attitude* and 10 a *very adaptive attitude*. Track yourself each day of the week and average out your scores with a weekly mean score (say 7 for week 1). Then, at the end of the month, sum and average your scores. If your score is lower than you would like (say 5 or less), do not berate yourself, as this is the compassion aspect of EQ and mindfulness. Instead, ask yourself, how can I improve my attitudinal average by one point the next month? Make sure you revise your self-talk to be encouraging, as that is both healthier and also more likely ensures you will improve. Likely, your behavior will change to match your revised self-talk (Ellis, 1999).

Authentic Feedback

So often in our lives do we provide and receive feedback, make comments, or statements that are culturally accepted and understood, yet convey little in actuality. Most of the time such feedback does not pose a significant impediment in either our lives or others. For example, in society it is common to ask, "How are you?" when greeting someone we know. In US society, we understand this simply means "Hello." We all have likely made regular use of this expression—and I had given little thought to the matter. Many years ago, however, when running an international residence hall during the end of my doctoral program, I was given opportunity to consider this expression. It was early fall term, and while walking across campus one day, I crossed paths with one of the students living in my hall, a young man from an Asian country. I offered the usual, "How are you?" Whereupon, he proceeded to explain that he felt stressed, was homesick, hated the food, and so forth. Pausing to listen, I realized he took me seriously when I offered the question-cum-hello greeting, as he was as yet unfamiliar with our idioms of speech. I mentioned that I hoped he would feel better soon when he made friends and became integrated in his studies. He thanked me and we continued on our separate ways.

Later I reflected upon the encounter. Clearly, as someone new to US culture, he was unaware of the cultural nuance regarding this common greeting and took me at my word that I was curious as to how he was doing (and feeling). The more I considered the encounter, it occurred to me that I either needed to be more mindful as to whom I was speaking, or that I needed to be more authentic in my conversation. Probably in most instances, a typical, "How are you doing?" as a greeting is not a problem. Sometimes, however, it may well be an issue. The point is not to become overly cautious on greetings, but instead to live, and speak, with more authenticity. So, as an experiment, I decided to habituate myself on simply using the common term "hello," as that seemed authentic, and ceased the "How are you?" I had no problems nor misunderstandings with this change. Furthermore, when I inquired, "How are you doing?" I actually wanted to know that person's emotional state.

Some period of time late, during a time of intense stress related to frustrations around completing my dissertation and doctoral degree, I found myself feeling isolated. Even other doctoral peers appeared uninterested in my plight as after all, they had their own challenges (doesn't everyone in completing a doctoral degree?). During this arduous process, I began to notice how ubiquitous this "How are you?" expression was in society. The more I heard it, the more annoyed I became and more determined I was to expunge it from my vocabulary. There were moments when I wanted to scream back at the "How are you?" questioner with something profane, though naturally I refrained, albeit with occasional difficulty. Still, this frustrating process took me back to Carl Rogers' writings regarding the authentic self (1951). In reviewing Rogers' work, I became aware of just how inauthentic I had become. So, from that point forward I decided my energy would be directed towards more honesty in my discourse, though certainly using a slice of kindness. The following is an exercise in authenticity for consideration.

Authenticity Exercise

For this exercise, you will select three people whom you respect and trust. These people are ones you believe will be honest with you while at the same time will not use their honesty as a weapon for injury. Naturally, this trio should know you well enough to answer in-depth questions. They must also be willing to provide such answers of course. When they provide the answers, your role is simply to acknowledge their service with an honest "Thank you." You will refrain from a defensive reaction should one of these people provide answers you find difficult to hear.

98   *Emotional Intelligence*

So, monitor your self-talk accordingly. Perhaps using mindful meditation prior to meeting with the persons evaluating you.

> **Question 1.** You are to ask the people you selected to tell you: "What do you see is my greatest asset or strength?"
>
> **Question 2.** Ask, "What is something (e.g., attitude, behavior, skill, etc.) you would like to see me target for improvement?"
>
> **Question 3.** Ask, "If you had a problem and needed to talk the matter over with someone you trust, would I be the type of person you would select? Why or why not? If not, what would I need to change in order to become a listener?"

Now, these types of questions, most particularly number three, have much to suggest regarding the types of listener and counselor we may become. Going back to Rogers' idea of therapeutic presence, are you fully present (or present as much as possible) when counseling, listening to a friend or family member in need? If you were to ask a given client, "On a scale of 1 to 10, with 10 high, how understood did you feel in session today?", how might that client answer. I realize some clients are chronically negative, others desperately seeking approval. But, I have found many to be quite honest. How might one of the more honest ones answer? How might close friends rate you as a listener? Or rate your strengths? Discuss frankly your needed growth areas (i.e., weakness)?

Now, part of your task is also to answer frankly when others seek your input. Using compassion so as not to try and wound another, can you provide honest feedback? Are you willing to tell another person who seems a poor fit, "No I cannot recommend you for a _____ position." Will you be ready to explain why you have to dispense what is likely to be disappointing news to a client, student, colleague, friend, or co-worker? I have little sage advice other than the ethical what is in this person's best interest (and someone else's best interest), and the suggestion that you spend time practicing dispensing honest feedback. As one colleague told me 30 years ago, "No is sometimes the most therapeutic response." After all these years, I am inclined to agree. I would add that few people hearing "no" are going to appreciate it.

Building and Maintaining Healthy Collegial Relationships

Building and maintaining healthy relationships with co-workers is one of the most important functions of emotional intelligence (Goldman, 1995). In point of fact, conflict with co-workers and supervisors and toxic workplace environments are typically among the primary reasons for changing jobs. When I reflect on my own 30-plus years in the field, my experiences reinforce the importance healthy relationships play in the workplace. Sadly, some of the most toxic environments I have had the misfortune to have worked in were mental health treatment centers. One actually was a residential psychiatric facility where, although the rank and file staff (e.g., counselors, child-care workers and social workers) were committed professionals, the administration's influence permeating the center was noxious. The director of the facility had a smooth, avuncular façade, whereas in reality he was a master manipulator and pedophile. I was unaware of the latter sinister aspect of his persona, yet fully cognizant of his insincere, pernicious manner. A couple of years after I had left the center, he was arrested and convicted of multiple counts of sexual abuse of minors. As of this writing, he remains in prison.

The ability of such a monster (well, that's what he *was* to the children and adolescents) to exist in a treatment system and even to flourish, illustrated a systemic failure. That systemic failure, however, was aided and abetted by individual professionals within, all of whom lived by an ethic to conduct themselves in a manner that did no harm to those they treated. In the aftermath, numerous stories emerged of staff observing questionable behavior by the director but were told to mind their own business (in so many words). One day, thankfully, this fragile house came crashing down upon this evil man, the center, and enabling staff. Sadly, there were many innocent staff injured in the aftermath of the fallout around the former director. My takeaway lesson is that someone, preferably some persons, need to step up and confront the person or persons in authority. No doubt, such is scary, professionally risky, and too often dissent is muzzled, until the carnage cannot be ignored. (Note: witness the Catholic Church's sex abuse crisis. FYI: I am a Catholic.)

Mercifully, the above, representing perhaps the worst case example of a dysfunctional workplace, is rare in number. Yet, the failure of anyone to come forward and confront the many questionable activities witnessed had much to do with the low level of trust among the staff. All administrations must be accountable to boards of responsible professionals, to say nothing of the staff they supervise. In the example I have described, there was significant failure on all parties, more on upper-level administration and the supervising board. Yet, as a former staff member, I too share a responsibility, as I had witnessed a couple of questionable incidents. I did speak with a superior, but was advised, "Oh, the director's just chummy with the kids." Despite my inner voice telling me otherwise, I acquiesced due to a more experienced colleague and because I needed the job and paycheck. Yes, I was young, in a vulnerable position myself, and unwilling to risk my career. With great shame, I spent a couple of years ruminating over what I, insignificant as I was, might have done differently.

Therefore, with no further self-flagellation, this section is devoted to collegial relations. First off, there may be points in your career when you face a career-changing (or life-changing) moment as in the previously described agency scandal. During such times, you will need to consider many issues such as your career and, more importantly, the vulnerable people served by your profession. You will need to strategize on how to address concerns while at the same time doing so in a constructive manner. It is to be hoped that you will not face such a traumatic system's failure as my former colleagues and most egregiously the children endured. Still, you may need to take risks for the sake of ethical and legal issues. In many cases, of course, workplace conflicts are just that and not something sinister. Regardless of the issue or issues, you need a strategy for how to resolve the types of issues and challenges that come your way. Here are some considerations:

100 *Emotional Intelligence*

Conflict Resolution 101

1. First off, how big is the conflict you are facing? Does it represent a major ethical or legal concern? Or, is the conflict simply a matter of disagreement between you and another party? This is an important distinction to consider.
2. The best advice herein, is also the most difficult. You need to approach the colleague with whom you have the conflict. My experience is most of us fear a potential confrontation. (I do!) Nevertheless, seek out that colleague anyway.
3. Prior to speaking with the colleague, prepare yourself. This involves revising your self-talk to be more optimistic. Now, you cannot control the other person, but you can tell yourself, "I will be non-confrontational in my approach and will not react even if the other party lashes out." You might even role-play the future meeting with a friend or co-worker, or use an empty chair exercise playing both yourself and your colleague. Most often, addressing the conflict is less stressful than dreading the meeting.
4. Seek first to understand. Be willing to hear the other party, and make compromises if you can. Sometimes of course you cannot (e.g., ethical issue).
5. Review the conflict resolution process. What went well? What went less well? How might you improve the next time a conflict arises?
6. Finally, get support for yourself, especially if the resolution process did not go well. Support means perhaps speaking with a trusted, more experienced colleague. Be careful not to make this a triangulating relationship whereby the absent party gets scapegoated.

In addition to the suggested conflict resolution above, it would be prudent to consider operational procedures for developing good workplace relationships. One would imagine, for example, that a collection of mental health professionals would be the ideal setting for harmonious workplace relationships. This is precisely what I thought at the onset of my career and was to discover how horribly naive that belief was! The reality is counselors and related mental health professionals come in all variations on the insecure-to-secure continuum (or should I say *spectrum*?). Then, stir in all the stress involved in treating children, adolescents, and adults, many of whom have severe and persistent mental illnesses, legal issues, and so forth and you have the potential for severe stress and burnout.

Counting full-time, part-time, volunteerism, practica, and internships, I have experience is some 20 agencies in the USA and abroad. In addition, I frequently ask colleagues about the health of their workplace, using the 1–10 scale with 10 being high. While such is scarcely a scientifically validated study, the results do suggest something. For the most part, I would say a mean of 6 (rounding off) would be a good estimate. I do find very healthy, functional agencies, schools, and suchlike as well as those where the tension is thick as the Ozark humidity of my childhood. Now, the operative question becomes, "How can I create and maintain healthy collegial relationships?" The following are suggestions from myself and others.

Developing and Maintaining Healthy Collegial Relationships

1. *Be appreciative.* Colleagues and superiors hear a lot of complaining and less of the word "thanks!" Furthermore, be specific in your appreciation as it sounds more genuine.
2. *Treat your colleagues and superiors with respect.* Respect is a gestalt composed of many components such as kindness, good listening, honesty, emotional regulation, and so forth. A thought worth considering is: "When I feel respected the other person is doing _____." Fill in the blank.
3. *Conflict resolution.* As in the previous set of recommendations, seek first to understand the other party. Remain emotionally regulated even if the other party is not. Moderating your behavior usually helps during conflict.
4. *Be on time.* This is a basic but you might be surprised how many people struggle with this. Anyone will be late on occasion but some make a habit of it. Be one of those who is punctual coming and going to and from work.
5. *Develop a sense of presence.* I always go back to Carl Rogers regarding presence as he focused so much on it (Rogers, 1951). Presence is associated with good attention, being focused, and if you have a role in a meeting, being prepared. When asked by students, colleagues, and others about how to develop healthy relationships I suggest they work to become a good, active listener. Good listening does not seem to come natural to most people as too many are focused on moving the conversation topic to their interest. Learn to listen very well to colleagues and allow silence to permeate at critical points.
6. *Be the best counselor and colleague you can be.* Respect usually is earned over time and competence—fueled by work ethic and attitude—is critical.

To make the case further, here are some poor workplace habits that create toxic environments:

1. *Gossip.* Almost all of us do this sometimes. Now, the issue is how hearsay enhances or harms workplace relationships. My experience is the latter as opposed to the former.
2. *Bullying.* Sadly, far too much workplace bullying goes on. Counselors and related professionals are not immune from this regressive practice. You will need to speak out against bullying and stand up to is should someone try and bully you. There is always your supervisor, Human Resources, and hopefully allies to support you. Know your workplace rights!
3. *Unethical practice.* If you wish to have the opportunity for a respectable career, you must know and follow your professional ethical code. Without question, a percentage of counselors and related mental health professionals choose to veer from ethical practice. In doing so, they harm vulnerable people (clients, students, colleagues, etc.), and do a great disservice to the helping profession.
4. *Being an unsupportive colleague.* Given the demands of the profession in schools, agencies, hospitals, and rehabilitation centers, everyone needs healthy support

102   *Emotional Intelligence*

systems. Unsupportive, uncaring colleagues are ones to avoid. Ask yourself, "Would I find someone like me a support co-worker?" Well, would you?

5. *Poor self-care.* You might wonder why I have selected this as a characteristic creating workplace dissatisfaction. My own experience is poor counselor self-care is the most violated tenet in the ethical code. Poor self-care means you are likely to be feel compromised physically and emotionally and this is likely to affect your mood and behavior at work. If you do not have a self-care plan, you will need to develop one.

In addition to the previous lists, I have created one that provides emotional intelligence strategies for consideration. As with the lists, these are more for consideration and "food for practice" than hard and fast rules. They all are practices I have found helpful in my daily life and self-care practice. As a long-time counselor, counselor educator, international trainer and consultant, and meditation teacher, I have found the following list helpful. Many people I have worked with, supervised, and trained have also found these helpful. Now, if you have a practice that works for you, perhaps you will not need additional strategies. Regarding myself, I typically find it helpful to consider additional strategies regarding self-care. Furthermore, there are few practices more relevant to good EQ than regular, ongoing, daily self-care. For a counselor, such will be imperative for long-term practice and good health.

Emotional Intelligence Strategies

This is a list of self-reflection exercises and reminders for the days when you are doubting yourself. The reminders are simple and easy to perform. The difficulty lies in doing them on a regular, in some cases, daily basis.

1. Begin each day with acknowledging three "gratitudes" (or any time before falling asleep at night).
2. Each day, practice the Three Cs on your self-talk. Set a goal of 3–5 times per day.
3. Regarding the previous suggestion, remind yourself you are more than your cognitions or emotions. My advice: Do not believe everything you think.
4. When your fail at something, or are disappointed, ask yourself, "What is this failure/disappointment trying to teach me?"
5. Surround yourself with people who may challenge you but accept you for who you are. While you may not be able to choose your family or co-workers, you can select your friends.
6. Learn to breathe slower and with intention. Meditation is encouraged even if only for 5 minutes a day.
7. Visualize yourself succeeding. Remember also that "successful failures" bring you one step closer to success.
8. Set measurable goals for your career and personal life. Remember to evaluate them regularly to measure success. Once again, failure is not a problem provided you are having successful failures.

Emotional Intelligence   103

9. Seek to become a better listener. Focus far more on being present to what the other person is saying and less on your response.
10. Learn a valuable lesson from people you encounter, whether the experience was pleasant or unpleasant.

Lessons Learned

Like everyone else, my life has been composed of numerous chapters. Some have been more enjoyable, others quite challenging, and none have been easy. There is, of course, nothing unusual in these statements. Everyone has joys and heartbreaks in their life regardless of culture, geography, socioeconomic standing, and all other ways of commonality and difference. At one time in my life, I was seriously contemplating life as a Trappist monk. In making this disclosure, I wish to make it clear I have much respect for any spiritual path that includes a meaningful life, with universal love and respect for others, most especially those of different ways and means.

While working to complete my doctorate, I traveled the hour-plus to the monastery the first Saturday of each month. One of the monks, a former psychologist, held all-day meditations attended by many, including myself. Typically anywhere from ten to 15 people from various walks of life—doctors, lawyers, small business owners, and teachers among others—would sit silently in a semicircle on small Zen-style benches. Our leader Fr Brendan (pseudonym) would help us to center ourselves with minimal guidance, and then regulate our day with 30-minute meditation sessions, followed by 5 minutes of walking in a circle, and then back to 30 minutes of sitting. The first two or three times I attended, the flotsam and jetsam of my thoughts almost made those Saturdays unbearable. This struggle illustrated to me just how badly I needed to learn to sit in silence and harmony. It was a metaphor for the carnage going on in my personal life, which included the death of my grandmother, who had raised me together with my four siblings, a painful divorce, and an academic career on the fast-track to a *cul-de-sac*. I was very unhappy, aimless, and frankly a mess.

"I have no idea whether our way of life is right for you," Fr Brendan had counseled me. "The more important thing for you is to life in harmony with yourself and the world around you." He went on to say that his one certainty was that the discipline of meditation would be good for me. In addition, he encouraged me to continue reading mystic Trappist Thomas Merton, as well as Thich Nat Hahn, a famous Vietnamese Buddhist teacher, monk, and pen-pal friend of previously mentioned Thomas Merton. I devoured several books of both these different, yet similar monks to the shameful neglect of my doctoral studies, infuriating my mentors! I rationalized my new priorities by telling myself that I was trying to reclaim my life and that it likely took precedent over even a PhD. That rationalization went over far less well with professors and my doctoral committee.

So, while the catechism aspect of Catholic readings didn't exactly "take" for me as I have always been more a spiritual free spirit, the meditation was pure freedom, at least once the practice became more habituated in my life. Daily, I meditated prior to work or class, and sat in silence for ten minutes prior to bedtime. My Saturdays

104 *Emotional Intelligence*

of all-day meditation at the monastery became days circled on the calendar to look forward to, as opposed to that of Browning's Child Roland approaching the Dark Tower. In summary, meditation had transformed me, at least to the extent of me finding a more peaceful inner life. Outwardly, I continued to struggle with my studies and with a sense of "What do I do next?" My old problem of living in the future continued to plague me.

One Friday, as I was driving back from a workshop I decided to stop in at the monastery. Fr. Brendan was available and we met for coffee on the back porch of one of the out-buildings. We sipped coffee and talked while observing the sunlight playing against the woods. He listened patiently, and never offered the standard "pat" answers I have always found so unsatisfying in organized religion. At some point during our roughly two-hour talk, before he was called to his monastic duties, he offered a suggestion. "Look, I cannot pretend to have the answers for you. You need to find those yourself. But, here's something that I believe will help. Each day, maybe on rising from bed or before you fall asleep at night, I want you to acknowledge three gratitudes." He paused to let that sink in. "That's all?" I replied. "That's the easy part. The hard part is I want you to acknowledge three gratitude's every day for the rest of your life. *That's* the hard part."

During the drive back home, I considered his suggestion. In general, I liked the idea of acknowledging the positives, as it certainly seemed that might just help me pull out of my personal doldrums. From that day forward, I began to acknowledge three daily "gratitudes." In the early days, I would often forget the practice until I was nearly asleep. Thereupon, I would roll onto my back and cite three in a low, soft, often sleepy, voice. With no pun intended, three gratitudes became the habit I would take from the monastery. More than any other practice, including meditation and my distance running, three simple gratitudes have helped me develop a more meaningful, optimistic outlook than anything else. Truthfully, I did not always feel this way, and in fact it took me a full decade of daily practice before I realized the full benefit of daily gratitudes.

The lesson I have learned is that while monastic life was not for me, Fr Brendan's simply suggestion has helped me change my personal outlook for the better. He was also correct in that the difficult part—and the far more important aspect—was acknowledging gratitudes every day. Instead of canonical hours in chapel, I have three gratitudes, along with daily meditation. When I train and consult overseas and with my own students at Niagara University, I emphasize meditative silence and three gratitudes. I cannot say what such means for my students and training participants. What I do know, however, is what these simple practices have meant for my life. No, I am not a monk and never will be such. But I have developed a meaningful outlook on life and my simply daily practice of sitting in silence and three gratitudes have been the lynchpin to greater understanding and happiness, even on my down days.

9 Technology and Distance Delivery
Twenty-First Century Realities for Counselors

The counseling profession has definitely entered uncharted waters with regard to the use of technology. Without question, advanced technology, as exemplified by the internet and high-technology devices such as smart phones along with social media outlets, have revolutionized the way commerce, education, and even counseling are delivered (Ziv, 2014). The counseling profession has firmly established a presence on social media and the internet as well. All major counseling organizations likely have an active Facebook page and daily I witness counseling programs and professional counselors posting on LinkedIn. University libraries are now virtual, providing counselors, counselor educators, and students the opportunity to access a wide range of professional journals that previously would have been inaccessible. I am in contact with colleagues all across the globe and frequently counselors conduct video sessions via the internet. An Australian friend of mine living in New York City has monthly counseling sessions with his psychiatrist who practices back in Sydney. Recently, I have been consulting on a mindfulness education project with a psychologist colleague working in a remote indigenous area in Australia's Northern Territory. Without question, our professional world now runs through technology, and technology will evolve and shape the counseling profession in ways we likely could not have imagined in past eras.

For the most part, technology has been used to enhance or provide education, health, and mental health services to remote communities that previously would have received very little in the way of such important services. Naturally, any such advance in technology also opens the pathway for unintended consequences. Internet bullying has become a serious problem for P-12 schools just as online harassing, mobbing, and stalking have become serious concerns for private citizens (StopBullying.gov, n.d.). Then, there have been numerous incidents of talented hackers corrupting health and other sensitive personal records. Most notably, the 2016 presidential election was arguably decided by the intrepid, or sinister, Julian Assange (along with the Russian government). Network security has become a multi-billion dollar business as hackers attempt to breach firewalls on a daily basis in governmental systems, hospitals, universities, and private businesses.

So, while the internet and communication technology have provided the counseling profession with an amazing tool to expand into the far reaches of the globe, it also has provided a means of personal and professional destruction. The good

106 *Technology and Distance Delivery*

news is that it is likely that the average counselor, professor, student, or client faces a small degree of risk. The bad news is that anyone can be targeted by a malevolent hacker. While remaining abreast of the latest technological advances is a high reach for anyone of my generation—those of us who are immigrants to technology as opposed to the natives, meaning the millennials—all counselors must make the effort to remain relevant. We must furthermore educate ourselves in ways that client privacy might be impacted by nefarious trolls lurking under hidden virtual spots. The *ACA Code of Ethics* (ACA, 2014) devoted an entirely new section to address technology issues in counseling (Standard H: Distance Counseling, Technology, and Social Media). The 2014 edition of the ethical code was one of the first such codes to address technology in counseling and requires that counselors actively attempt to understand emerging technological advances impacting the profession and to develop knowledge and skills in relevant technology. You can rest assured, however, that future editions of the ethical code will have a greatly expanded section on technology!

Distance-based Counseling and Virtual Technology

Counselors are using a variety of technologies to counsel clients in novel ways. Distance counseling is actually not a nouveau concept, as for decades telephone crisis lines have been operating. In fact, I provided over a decade of evening crisis work myself as a graduate student and counseling professional. Currently, however, the ways and means of technology make the old phone system look as obsolete as the slide rule to the computer (another anachronistic device I was trained on!). While some counselors use email for counseling clients, most likely are using a visual and audio system to provide distance counseling. Some of the concerns revolving around distance counseling are related to privacy, security, crisis intervention, "phantom" clients (those using an alias), quality of transmission, and payment (Reeves, 2011). The NBCC (2014), through the Center for Credentialing and Education (CCE), established the first certificate in internet counseling named the Distance Certified Counselor (DCC) for counselors wishing to demonstrate their facility in the distance area (see www.cce-global.org). While certification as a distance counselor is voluntary, counselors would be wise to seek advanced training in using distance technology. Furthermore, all counselors will need to become more facile in the use of technology to serve clients in the future. Counseling agencies will need highly trained Information Technology staff to address issues of security and privacy.

The Case of Paul

Paul is a recent graduate from a counseling program and has landed a job in a remote part of the US mountain west region. He works in a remote town in a small county clinic with two counselors, a nurse practitioner, and two support staff. While Paul's city and county have a tiny population, the county is larger than the state of Vermont, with one town more than 100 miles from another settlement. Paul, who also is a paramedic, has a certification in trauma counseling and much of his work involves treating PTSD. The lone physician in another remote town 100 miles away hears of Paul and contacts him. He informs Paul that many of his clients are suffering from PTSD and requests Paul begin counseling clients via Skype. Paul is very interested to use distance technology to expand his reach and provide mental healthcare to people in remote county areas. Paul's intentions are certainly admirable but what are some of the ethical and legal considerations he should address prior to offering distance counseling services for traumatized clients?

> **Discussion:** First, will Paul be operating under the auspices of the clinic or as a private practitioner? What does the state law require for distance counseling services? Does his professional liability insurance cover distance counseling? He should further review the 2014 ACA Code of Ethics to ensure he is practicing in an ethical manner. Does he, or the clinic, have encrypted software to protect client privacy? Skype, for example, is not considered a secure delivery pathway. Finally, what are the risks and liability involved in counseling traumatized clients via long distance?
>
> **Question:** If you were Paul's clinical director, how might you advise him on this matter?

Ethical and Legal Considerations

The Code of Ethics (ACA, 2014) includes a number of standards pertaining to distance counseling. Counselors must ensure that clients understand they have the option of in-person counseling if they so choose (Standard H2.a). This standard also requires the counselors to be facile in addressing risks and limitations of technology. For example, what happened in the event of technology failure when counseling a client at a critical point (e.g., crisis intervention)? Does the client have access to a private space for the counseling sessions? I can recall counselors complaining that their clients would sit at the dining room table while their children played in the next room. Some clients would connect while sitting in coffee shops during online sessions. In the latter, the counselor would need to refrain from providing a service until the client relocated to a private space. There are many additional questions to consider with regard to distance counseling: what about different laws if counseling across state and even national borders, and the contingency plan in the event the client voices a suicide plan (or harm towards a third party), previously mentioned concerns regarding confidentiality, and finally, whether distance counseling is even appropriate for a particular client's issue. In short, providing distance is not as simple as connecting through Skype or another such program.

I can recall one case when working overseas several years ago. The clinician was provided counseling initially by phone and later by an interactive, more secure Skype-like program. The reason for the distance counseling was that the client had been diagnosed with agoraphobia and did not feel comfortable in leaving his cramped apartment. The counselor came to consult with me on the client. After discoursing with the counselor, who had seen this client for over a year, we decided the treatment plan would be amended to include the client would eventually venture to the agency for in-person counseling (after an extended systematic desensitization period of treatment). Admittedly, this plan turned out to be overly optimistic as the client did not like the "artificial" process through the internet. The clinician providing internet services came to believe distance counseling was not helping the client address his shut-in life. This necessitated in the counselor physically going to the client's apartment and providing in-home counseling. (In-home counseling has its own particular risks of course.)

As previously discussed, a counselor providing distance counseling must be knowledgeable with legal as well as ethical issues. Licensure requirements for professional counselors (ACA, 2016b) provide helpful information and links to State and Territorial websites for more complete information of distance therapy requirements. Wheeler and Bertram's excellent resource, *The Counselor and the Law*, eighth edition (2019) is a highly recommended resource as well. For example, 19 states currently regulate electronic communication involving counselors but only within their respective state (Alaska, Arizona, Arkansas, California, Colorado, Iowa, Louisiana, Massachusetts, Minnesota, Nebraska, Nevada, New York, North Carolina, Oregon, South Carolina, Ohio, Texas, Utah, and West Virginia). Nineteen state counseling boards and the District of Columbia report an absence of any law or regulation addressing the use of the Internet with clients (Alabama, Connecticut, Delaware, Florida, Georgia, Hawaii, Kentucky, Maine, Michigan, Missouri, New Hampshire, North Dakota, Oklahoma, Pennsylvania, Rhode Island, South Dakota, Vermont, Washington, and Wyoming). Only one state, Arkansas, has an addendum to its licensure law specifically addressing technology-assisted therapy, requiring additional training and supervision. Six states specifically state that they do not support electronic communication under the scope of practice for professional counselors (Maryland, New Mexico, South Dakota, Tennessee, Virginia, and Indiana). One state, Mississippi, will only grant licensure to state residents and/or those who pay state income tax.

Now, the above variation between state and territorial laws could potentially pose major challenges for counselors providing therapy across state lines, and rest assured such practice is widespread. A counselor in New York may experience little complication is providing services to a client in, say, Pennsylvania, which has no regulators law regarding distance counseling (as of this writing). However, that same New York-based counselor could be in troubled professional waters should they offer services to a client living in the states of Arkansas or Mississippi where distance counseling is regulated. Furthermore, we are unsure of the standing if the New York counselor provides services to clients in one of the six states that specifically do not support electronic communication for counselors. Again the confusing question becomes "Which state's laws take precedence?" A best practices type of approach, as a well as ethical one, is that the counselor should be in compliance with her state of residence and that of the clients she serves (Wheeler & Bertram, 2019). In some cases, this means the counselor cannot provide counseling through the internet.

Counseling across state lines also carries with it a long list of questions for consideration. For example, must a counselor be licensed in the states where clients reside? Or only the counselor's state of residence? Should the income generated

Technology and Distance Delivery 109

by the New York-based counselor be subject to tax in states such as Pennsylvania, where her clients reside? Which state will regulate the therapeutic services offered? Then again, what about outlier laws in select states? I am specifically referring to two court cases, Boynton *v.* Burglass (1991) and Thapar *v.* Zezulka (1999). The former is a Florida court decision stating that psychotherapists have no Tarasoff-like duty, though they may warm with immunity if done in good faith. The latter Thapar case is more problematic. Thapar *v.* Zezulka was where a Texas State Court judge ruled that counselors have no Tarasoff-like duty in Texas. Furthermore, and of more concern, counselors who do breech confidentiality to warn have violated the client's privacy and may be subject to litigation (Wheeler & Bertram, 2019). To further complicate matters, some states such as Tennessee, have passed *matters of conscience* legislation providing for values-based referrals, usually on the basis of LGBTQ issues. Finally, six states (Oregon, Washington, California, Hawaii, Montana, and Colorado and the District of Columbia) provide for legal physician-assisted suicide. Would the New York counselor be in legal jeopardy for providing counseling services to a terminally ill Oregon client seeking PAS services in his state? Would a counselor in Tennessee making a values-based referral on the grounds of religious beliefs be subjected to disciplinary from the American Counseling Association or another similar professional organization? Would such action by the Tennessee counselor be grounds for an ethics investigation in another state lacking conscience legislation? I can find no case law to offer any informed opinion, but would strongly advise counselors involved in such distance work to speak with their attorney.

So, where are we left regarding the confusing morass of nonexistent or conflicting case law between states and territories for counselor offering distance counseling across legal boundaries? Moreover, what about counselors and related mental health professionals offering their services across state, territorial, and international boundaries? I can imagine some serious concerns if, for example, our New York counselor were counseling a client living in Saudi Arabia who desired to discuss his same-sex attraction in a country where homosexuality is punishable by death. Thus, the only reasonable conclusion I can draw from this murky state of affairs concerning counseling across borders is that one needs to proceed deliberately and with great caution! This caution light will require prudent legal advice from a counselor adept at negotiating this ethical and legal minefield. Thus far, counselors and related therapists providing such services have essentially flown beneath the radar of magistrates and litigation professionals, but given the evident proliferation of the internet and online services (e.g., ordering computers, groceries, furniture, etc.), such stealth is unlikely to continue much longer. So, counselors be warned!

By sounding the warning sirens, I by no means mean to imply the counselor profession should not be involved in distance counseling through virtual means. In point of fact, counselors can no more ignore virtual service delivery than, say, the medical profession. Again, the virtual world opens up the remote, far reaches of the globe to health, education, and mental health professionals that in past times were previously not considered. In a way, the current virtual era takes me back ironically to my childhood in the rural Ozarks. As a grade school student, I recall reading an article in the *National Geographic*. The article was on Australia and the challenges

110   *Technology and Distance Delivery*

that the remote continent and country faced, particularly for those living in the Outback. The vast distances on a continent roughly the dimensions of the continental USA are staggering with regard to education and healthcare needs. The tyranny of distance helped fuel the creation of two iconic remote Australian services: The Royal Flying Doctors Service (RFDS) and The School of the Air (SOA). Given my years in Australia, most especially summers volunteering in Outback schools and communities, I have been witness to both services in action. One of my friends, a retired remote teacher and principal, was a valuable resource for the School of the Air, as he had begun his teaching career with SOA on a remote cattle station in the uber-remote Northern Territory.

The SOA was originally broadcast through radio and TV, and currently is delivered through the internet (www.assoa.nt.edu.au/visitors-centre/the-centre). Children on remote cattle stations and aboriginal settlements throughout Queensland, the Northern Territory, and Western Australia would tune in to a remote teacher based in Alice Springs, Katherine, Cairns, or another central location for attendance and lessons. Parents would often provide tutoring and help with lessons. Then, during high school years, Australian children would go off to a boarding school, often far from their families and communities. During formative years, however, the SOA provided an educational life link to remote children across the sparsely populated landmass.

This Australian practice of education and healthcare delivery helped to spawn what must be one of the first distance counselling (double l's in Australia) services. Remote Australian public and sectarian schools began to realize the need for "guidance" services in remote schools. This led to training and hiring remote school counsellors, many of whom likely had similar training to our 1950s and 1960s school guidance counselors in the USA. During my first summer in 2013, I travelled throughout much of Australia's very remote, sparsely populated Northern Territory with a remote school counsellor. Along with my colleague Cheryl, we would sometimes drive four-to-six hours to a remote school and spend anywhere from a day to a school week. As some schools were so remote, we sometimes had to be flown. Cheryl's eight schools covered a distance roughly the size of Arizona! She would offer play therapy for younger children and individual and groups for older ones. I would assist her in groups and with some individuals, and we both provided training on behavioral issues, trauma, crisis intervention, teacher self-care, and the like. In between visits, she would call and speak with parents and teachers regarding how a particular child or adolescent was progressing. As the Northern Territory education budget was Lilliputian, she was one of only two counselors for the entire top-end of the Northern Territory—north of Alice Springs in the dead center—meaning roughly the size of Texas, though with a population of around 250,000. No doubt more counsellors were needed, as sometimes she would get to a very remote school only once or twice a term.

Cheryl had created a website with information remote teachers could access for mental health information and download sample forms and information sheets. Much posted was on mindfulness-based stress reduction, healthy activities, and ways to resist peer pressure, bullying (called *teasing* in the Northern Territory) and what to do if a student was feeling suicidal. In fact, suicide rates among indigenous Australians are among the highest in the world (Higgins, 2019). The overwhelming social and emotional needs of remote, indigenous Australia are overwhelming to the point of absurdity. The Royal Flying Doctors Service (RFDS) staff are now trained in basic mental health first aid. Despite the Brobdingnag mental health challenges, my experience was entirely worthwhile as many teachers, principals, families, and children were very appreciative of counseling and consultative services. Cheryl also gave me a good education in the origins of serving socio-emotional needs in the remote indigenous schools. During my initial two months in the Outback, I took several calls and messages from remote teachers and principals regarding suggestions for addressing severe social-emotional needs of indigenous youth. Much of my training and consultation involve suicide prevention.

There are naturally Australian counsellors and psychologists providing distance counseling services through the continent, although few seem to be doing so in remote communities. This deficit likely is due to challenges in technology, culture, and the difficulties in establishing rapport with populations understandably mistrustful of "whitefellas." Nevertheless, the opportunity remains, especially as technological improvements have been coming to places as remote as, say, the very remote community of Maningrida, Australia, way up on the north coast of Arnhem Land, where during the wet season of heavy rains, the region becomes an island that requires flying in and out. With crocodile-infested waters, no one will be swimming should they drive into the swelled rivers! The lessons learned in the Outback have been very instructive regarding the delivery of educational and counseling services and has spurred my thinking regarding how ever increasing technology will impact the profession.

To say a little more regarding distance counseling, I am reminded of Thomas Freedman's influential book, *The World Is Flat* (2004). What Freedman meant by "flat" is that commerce, education, health care, and so forth were now being driven by the digital revolution. Driving this revolution, arguably, are giants such as Amazon as well as intrepid individuals with slick *YouTube* channels. For the counseling profession, all you need to do is go on *YouTube* and keyword search for counselors and you will be inundated by private practitioners marketing their wares. The professional website *LinkedIn* also has become the high-technology approach to marketing, networking, and promoting oneself, graduate counseling programs, and individual counselors. As of this point, I am connected to just above 400 professionals, which I am finding is a small number with regard to many other professionals. One colleague has over 5,000 connections! On a related note, consider the ubiquity of online counseling programs and while several have shuttered, others such as the University of Phoenix remain. Furthermore, traditional colleges and universities nor offer online classes as well as degree programs.

A Glimpse into Counseling's Virtual Future

It requires no stretch of the imagination to state that the virtual world will drive the counseling profession just as it has done with commerce, education, and all other

112 Technology and Distance Delivery

industries. What specifically this means is yet to be determined though I will make some cautious predictions. First of all, evening crisis calls will be very impacted by sophisticated operating systems. At some undermined point in the future, a person in crisis will call the helpline where a virtual "counselor" will field the call. Using sensitive devises to monitor voice tone, as well as the specifics of what the caller articulates, the operating system will use a triage process through a series of questions to determine whether to send the call to a *live* counselor, or make a follow-up plan to a local mental health provider. After a recent call to a major retailer, where I spoke with a facile operating system for some ten minutes before finishing with a live person, that future may not be very far away. In addition, I can see avatars used in counselor education programs where student counselors can begin practicing their counseling skills with virtual human-like creations through cyberspace. These avatars will present with symptoms of PTSD, depression, major psychosis, and other *DSM*-type diagnoses. Student counselors will be able to hone and refine their skills regarding trauma treatment and crisis intervention under very realistic conditions. In a sense, our graduate counselor education training programs will resemble the high-technology type of training airline pilots undergo in flight simulators. These aspects of advanced technology likely represent the positive impacts of technology on our profession. I have previously referred to more sinister operative slipping through the portals, hacking into confidential counseling and psychiatric records, outing people who receive treatment for a variety of sensitive issues, traumatizing many and leaving other unsure of seeking services even when sorely needed. No doubt, advanced technology is neither inherently good nor evil, but the use of such is the determining factor therein. Thus again the need for hospitals and treatment agencies to have well-trained Information Technology teams. This latter point will be very challenging for small treatment centers and private practitioners, as they may lack the resources to pay for this.

So the operative question, it seems to me, is "How can the counseling profession remain relevant in such a fast-paced, virtual, 'flat world,' environment?" This highly advanced era will require professional organizations such as the ACA, all similar organizations, counselor education programs, and counseling professionals to invest very heavily in information technology—even more so than at present. Counseling organizations virtual presence will be very interactive providing an array of services that can only be speculated about at present. Without question, professional conferences will garner as many if not more attendees through cyberspace than at the actual event. Related organizations such as the NBCC and the CCE already offer trainings online, but future educational services will offer more advanced, interactive trainings than are presently available. At some point, the very term *distance counseling* likely will become an anachronism. In fact, do not be surprised if, at some point in, say, 20 years' time, virtual counseling does not exceed face-to-face counseling. Given the convenience, improving technology, and that most client-age populations will have grown up and lived through virtual means, I expect this to happen in my lifetime. That change will require counselor education programs, licensure boards, and codes of ethics to be upgraded as well. To be succinct, counseling's future is a virtual certainty.

Lessons Learned

It had been a very long, arduous week in the remote Northern Territory School system. I had just completed another trauma training to remote teachers at an aboriginal school some 90 miles from the remote school headquarters office in Katherine. The principal and I were having coffee to end the day and week. Suddenly, the phone gave off a shrill ring, shattering my brief respite. "It's the principal up at Morningstar* (pseudonym) community and he seems upset," the receptionist called out to me from her desk just outside the principal's office. I had just delivered a 90-minute training after traveling several hours the previous day where I had delivered trainings, provided co-therapy, and spent much of the day consulting with teachers regarding student behavioral issues. I sat down my coffee mug and picked up the phone. The principal on the other end of the line was in near panic mode. Evidently, there had been some conflict in the community encompassing his very remote indigenous school and that problem had traveled into his school as well. There had been fights, screaming, and *en masse* acting-out behavior, threats of violence, and even suicide threats. To complicate matters further, Cheryl, the traveling remote school counsellor, was working at another remote school far away and not available. "I'm desperate for help mate!" he pleaded.

I was nearing the end of a very "full-on" two months of volunteering with the Remote Indigenous Schools in Australia's remote and sparsely populated Northern Territory. I had delivered numerous trainings on trauma care, student behavioral issues, self-care, preventing burnout, suicide prevention, providing the occasional co-therapy with Cheryl, one-to-one coaching with teachers, and numerous other duties as assigned. I was assigned to the central office in the big town of Katherine, population around 8,000 or so, though usually I spent the week in some remote indigenous community. On weekends, I would travel back to Katherine to stay with friends. Bone weary from a very draining week of trainings and dealing with acting-out students and frustrated teachers, the last thing I wanted was to field a crisis call late on a Friday, particularly from a principal on record for "not believing in touchy-feely stuffy like counselling." Yet, here was that therapeutic agnostic on the other end of the line pleading for such assistance. Stifling my initial schadenfreude towards him, I focused my tired brain on his concern.

Evidently, there had been allegations of child sexual abuse towards a community member, leaving two extended families at odds with one another. This allegation and conflict had stirred up a lot of turmoil at school, including one child who was now threatening suicide. The community was one of the most remote in the Northern Territory, which was quite a statement when considering the area's remoteness. There also was no hospital, but merely a small outpatient clinic. In other words, no easy, available psychiatric hospitalization. During the wet season (November to April), the community was accessible only by plane. Therefore, it came down to me, a weary individual who was nearly ten thousand miles from home, counseling from a distance to an adolescent from a very different culture.

The first Australians, often called the traditional land owners as a way of showing respect and refuting Australia's former racist "Terra Nullius" (no owner) policy of former times. Although Australia is a very successful western country with a diverse population, indigenous Australians live in developing-world conditions on their remote lands. The average aboriginal school child speaks at least two languages, and in some cases as many as four. School absenteeism runs very high and some schools will go through years with no graduates. Addiction, trauma, and suicide rates in indigenous communities are among the highest in the western world (Creative Spirits, n.d.). Against this backdrop, school staff and community leaders struggle to craft strategies to address complex issues. Sadly, both territorial and commonwealth officials have been remiss on providing adequate mental health resources to remote schools and communities, complicating and exacerbating this unfortunate situation.

"What's the situation with the student?" I inquired. He explained she was a 13-year-old who had made a previous suicide attempt about a year ago. She had been living with her aunt and uncle as her parents were "on the drink in Darwin" (alcohol addicted and homeless) and unable to care for her. She had evidently been a victim of sexual abuse herself, and the community allegation had triggered her. From a decade-plus of phone crisis experience, I checked for safely (her aunt and uncle were reliable), suicide plan (which she had, according to the principal), and means (she would hang herself, a common method of indigenous suicide in the Northern Territory). The principal then handed the phone to her aunt, who claimed to have met me on my previous visit to the community. I listened as the indigenous woman outlined her niece's behavior. My most pressing concern was location, and as I was several down rough, dirt roads from their community. After some talk back and forth, her aunt finally asked, "Can you speak with her? She's here with me?" Such great distances continue to bring their challenges even in the twenty-first century. Phone service could drop regularly in the Northern Territory, and internet service was "dodgy" at best. Just as she came on the line with a meek "hello", we lost phone contact.

Our receptionist was a British woman and trained nurse, who assisted as tech person, bus driver, and cafeteria hand, and she frantically worked the phone to get them back online. After some minutes, she shook her head. Then, "Hey, I can reach them through the computer." In a previous era, the short-wave radio was how Outback towns communicated with each other prior to the 1980s, when phone service became more common. Most communities, however, maintained a short-wave radio for the very reasons we were just then experiencing, yet the internet was more reliable and easier to work. After a tense few minutes, she raised them through the internet, as they evidently had the same idea. I oriented myself with the system and began communicating with the student. Fortunately, she had remembered me speaking in one of her classes. "You the one who speaks in a funny language," she said over the fuzzy system. She meant my American accent, with perhaps my Ozark twang, with which many of the indigenous children (and adults) seemed to be intrigued. This seemed to have piqued her interest and that aided in my building rapport with her. She seemed a little more at ease.

I asked her many questions related to her anxiety and depression. "Yes, I have a sad face," she said in reference to the emotions chart the traveling remote school counsellor had taught her. I asked as to the origins of her sadness and she replied "family business," meaning her home. She did admit to trusting her aunt and uncle,

Technology and Distance Delivery 115

and did not wish to hurt them. Feeling more confident, I asked what she needed to get back to a happy face. Not surprisingly, she did not know. My response was that together she, her aunt and uncle and myself, would need to find out. "Would I get to talk with you?" she inquired. I replied if she would like or that Cheryl could call her. The additional complication was the traveling remote counsellor would not be able to get to her school for a couple of weeks as there were crises at two other schools she was assigned to work with (she covered eight remote schools). She liked and trusted the school counsellor but realizing the immediacy of the situation, I suggested she and I speak the following day. I then made a safety plan of her checking with her aunt if she felt unsafe. We also covered assets (which she called "positives"), which included her aunt and uncle, her religious faith, and her best friend. After speaking with her aunt, we hung up.

Fortunately regular phone service had been restored the following day (Saturday) and I checked in with the student, who was feeling better and safer, and her aunt who seemed most relieved. I reviewed our safety plan with her and her aunt and explained Cheryl would be in touch soon and likely would get to her school sooner than scheduled. The principal, formerly an adversary, was very praiseworthy of my help as was Cheryl, who would be following up with her very soon. The following week after debriefing with the regional coordinator of remote schools based in Katherine, we reviewed the impossibility of providing adequate mental health services to remote communities with only two counsellors to cover 15 remote schools spanning an area the size of California. She was sympathetic but explained the Northern Territory's conservative ethos was a "harden-up" mentality (i.e., "get over it!") that flew in the face of current reality of indigenous Australians depressingly high suicide rate. One wonders naturally what the response would be were the children white.

During my initial two-month experience in remote Australia, I learned many lessons! One was the importance of effective technology, to say nothing of the need for governments to provide more access to mental health services in remote regions, especially to indigenous people. Given Australia's wealth, it was concerning and embarrassing to see how little investment it had made in their remote schools' mental health services. But having spent extended time at eight remote indigenous schools, I would have to say that a sense of cultural humility was my primary lesson learned. The social and cultural issues are so complex in remote aboriginal communities most outsiders would have no understanding of them. I dealt with "poisoned cousins," that is, relatives who are not permitted to interact with one another due to cultural taboos. There were issues of black magic between feuding families, children who spoke three or four languages although they could barely read a sentence, schools with no graduates for years on end, and an addiction and trauma rate that was perhaps the world's highest. But I also witnessed the great athleticism evidenced in Australian League Football (AFL), the amazing aboriginal artists' paintings, and cultural celebrations of song, dance, and artistry to which I had never previously been exposed. At first glance, their world seemed primitive, yet indigenous Australians are arguably the world's oldest culture at 30,000–60,000 years (cultural anthropologists debate this).

Thus, Australia's indigenous people are both ever-present and, paradoxically, invisible to most Australians, save for negative media stereotypes. Despite the ever-present and overwhelming developing-world poverty, addiction, abuse, and trauma, I was constantly amazed at the resilience and spirit of so many indigenous people. It seemed to me the media and politicians never focused on the successes of the traditional people, although daily these were evident. I met an amazing indigenous artist and, although I am no critic, her paintings of the remote region were among the most vibrant I have seen. I was so touched that she wanted me to move to the area. "I'll take you around and introduce you to my people. Then they will trust you." She on to express that governmental leaders either flew in and out of drove in and out in a day. Thus, they showed no respect nor learned why the conditions were present. Granted, the issues are complex, but a more serious time investment would likely help. Working more collegially with indigenous leaders would be wise and, although this happens to some extent in remote Australia, I saw little evidence of it in the lands I visited.

During my final week, this cultural disrespect was in full view. I was asked by the community elders in one remote area to attend a meeting with governmental officials. During this meeting, the patriarchs, using me as an example, asked for the government to fund a full-time counsellor to address addiction issues, suicide, and community violence. The government duo promised to do so quickly. I was believing these men until I took note of the indigenous leader's body language. All the indigenous men had their arms crossed rigidly, with skeptical looks on their faces. After the governmental duo and gone to the airstrip for their return flight to Darwin, I asked the chief elder about the promise. He explained they had heard *many* promises from governmental officials, few of which were delivered on. Just days later, the Northern Territory Government announced cuts to health and mental health services throughout the territory. Thus, there would be no counsellor, despite the demonstrated need and low cost. So it goes for the Australian Traditional Landowners.

I conclude there is much we need to learn about indigenous cultures in order to begin to provide effective services. We can provide remote counselors (more are needed) and better technology. Providing counselors truly interested in cultural relevance and respect, however, is the much more difficult part of the equation. Perhaps the most important lesson any counselor can learn is a sense of cultural humility. During this recounted experience, my first of several international forays in Australia and South Africa, I learned a lot from my colleagues and most especially the indigenous teachers, community leaders, and certainly the children. I am a wiser, if not more effective, helper due to my experiences in remote Australia and other distant lands. The irony to me is that I seem to know less with each passing year and yet believe this actually is a good sign. I look forward to returning to the remote Northern Territory and have found both the faraway, distant land, with its traditional people, culture, and wildlife, and the otherworld-like landscape, very much like home.

10 Nurturing and Managing Your Career

This chapter is devoted to preparing for your job search and managing your career. In this chapter, the focus will be devoted to preparing for the job search, including preparing a résumé or curriculum vitae (CV), letters of reference, cover letters, interviewing, and issues of licensure and credentialing. There also are self-reflective questions for continued growth, visioning, professional activity, and additional matters related to your career. While the focus of the text is broad, that is, for beginning and veteran counselors, some information may speak more directly to those new in their career. Other exercises may be equally pertinent to those both in beginning and late stage careers. One of the critical skills for counselors to learn is that of self-reflection. In essence, reviewing what has gone well, what went less well, and what one learned from both. Then, we can apply the lessons learned and likely be more successful in the future.

Self-Reflection Exercise for the Conclusion of the Internship

Through your practicum and internship experience, or in your counseling career, you have gained a broader understanding of how to identify and address the educational, career, emotional, and mental health needs of the students and clients you have counseled. Another aspect of your experience is how what you have learned fits into the needs of your chosen career. Examine and respond to the following questions.

1. What specific skills and interests have you gained through your career/ practicum and internship experiences? How have these experienced helped you grow as a counselor?
2. The process of providing counseling services is a challenging one. During this helping process, what have you learned about yourself? As a counselor? As a person?
3. What lessons have you learned from working with people who differ from you (e.g., culturally, sexually, politically, socially, spiritually, etc.)? How have these experiences helped you grow as a counselor?

118 *Nurturing and Managing Your Career*

4. Specifically, how have your experiences providing counselling helped you grow as a person?
5. What specific skills, talents, and interests do you currently possess? What are your three strongest counselling skills or attributes?
6. What type (or types) of counseling setting are you considering for your first job after graduate school? Or, if an experienced counselor: What type of counseling setting or settings would you like to transition into?
7. Regarding item number 6, what specifically interests you about working with the setting(s) you have listed?
8. What advice would you give to a counselor just beginning her or his career?
9. Considering your experiences on practicum/internship and in your graduate counseling program in general, what changes would you like to see? Or: What changes would you like to see the profession make?
10. Regarding cultural considerations, how well did your practicum or internship prepare you? What recommendations would you make to the faculty in your program? What recommendations would you make to the leadership in the counseling profession?
11. Regarding professional ethics, how would you rate the staff at your placement or in your career? Did they seem ethical in their professional work (e.g., counseling, clinical discussions, supervision, etc.)? How would you rate your own ethical practice? What needs improving in your practice (if anything)?
12. What was the most important thing you learned on your practicum or internship? Why? Or: What has been the most important thing you have learned in your career? Why?

Preparing for the Job Search

Because the practicum/internship is all about preparing to become a professional counselor, this book would not be complete without some basic orientation to prepare for the job search. Although this section of the text is a brief overview (there are many more comprehensive job search books and websites available), it will provide some basic information and point the way for further information that may be helpful in assisting you in landing that initial job. If you are an experienced counselor, then the expectations will be much greater given your years of experience. Regardless of what stage you are in your career, a job search involves many facets: planning, résumé writing, mock interviewing, applying, interviewing, following up, dealing with rejection, entertaining an offer, accepting a job, negotiating salary, and relocating to name a few. The remainder of the chapter focuses on the basics of this process.

The Visioning Process: Creating Your Dream Career

Career professionals will tell you the first step to success is the ability to visualize a desired goal. Interestingly, many clients I have counseled and students I have taught do not have a clear vision for their careers. The lack of such is likely to set one up for some degree of struggle. Baseball great Yogi Berra supposedly made the following statement: "If you don't know where you're going, you'll likely end up somewhere else." Thus, the need for vision works regarding vocational life and personal life as well. The second, and more important task, is to strategize on how to realize that vision. One of the most popular methods for strategizing is creative visualization, or *visioning* for short (Capacchione, 2000). Successful people in every occupation tend to use some type of visioning process. Some notable visionaries are Nelson Mandela, Mohandas Gandhi, Martin Luther King, Jr., and Mother Teresa. Vision includes optimistic thinking, which is strongly correlated with success (Seligman, 1998). Visioning is a simple process requiring just a few basic pieces of information:

- **Personal history**. How did you arrive at your current personal and occupational station in life? What experiences led you to becoming a professional counselor or counselor educator? What valuable lessons have you learned along the way? What advice might you give to someone considering counseling or counselor education as a career?
- **Values.** What values are important to you? Psychologist Milton Rokeach (1979) conducted extensive research in the study of values. His findings suggest that the most successful people find work that is congruent with their personal values. For example, if your religion or spirituality is important to you, then perhaps you should find a spiritually affiliated school or agency. If working with inner-city youth is where your passion lies, a job in a wealthy suburban school may not be a good fit for you. So, what are your top five values? How might these values guide your job search and counseling career? Prediction: Should a potential job hold significant values conflicts, that job likely is not a good fit for you regardless of salary. Consider your values carefully when thinking of accepting as new job.
- **Professional identity.** Sure, you know you want to be a professional school/ rehabilitation/career/mental health/addictions counselor. However, profes- sional labels such as "counselor" do not tell the entire story. For example, some mental health counselors may decide to retrain to become school counselors or vice versa. In addition, many experienced counselors may move into admin- istrative roles, such as clinical director, and do more administrative work and less actual counseling. A few readers may even wish to earn a doctorate in Counselor Education and become a counselor educator. Would your long-term goals include moving into administration? Would those changes be healthy for you? Why or why not?
- **Goals.** What are your immediate, short-term, and long-term career goals? Are you interested in running a school counseling center? Being director of a college counseling center? Becoming dean of students at a large university? Moving overseas for work? Becoming president of the American Counseling Association (ACA), American School Counselor Association (ASCA), American Rehabilitation Counseling Association (ARCA), and the like? Goals are fluid and subject to personal changes over time, but it is still a good idea to set goals and to revise them periodically as your interests and values change

120 *Nurturing and Managing Your Career*

over time and through experience. Career goals, like those in a treatment plan, provide targets to measure success against. Furthermore, it is acceptable to not meet target goals. Sometimes we discover that we may have been aiming at the wrong target and failure is what saves us from much woe! Nevertheless, set goals and assess goal achievement. Then, reevaluate what further action you may wish to take. That could be revising goals, dropping some, or creating new ones.

- **Action plan.** Everyone with a vision needs an action plan to achieve it. An action plan is a rough road map to success and should consist of concrete steps leading up to the vision. The visioning process should also involve estimated time frames to provide a sense of how you are proceeding towards your goal. Action plans also are flexible as circumstances will intervene. Life will happen of course, bringing unexpected exciting and disappointing news. Nevertheless, plan ahead anyway, as that is your best option.

Sample Action Plan

If your ultimate goal is to become president of the ACA, your action plan might look something like this:

1. Become active in the state affiliate of ACA (1–3 years).
2. Transition into a state leadership role through the following steps (1–2 years):
   a. Serving on the planning board for the state conference
   b. Serving on the editorial board of the state journal
   c. Running for president, vice president, or another office of the state organization
   d. Submitting manuscripts to the state journal and national ACA-affiliated journals
3. Attend the annual ACA conference for networking opportunities with established ACA leaders.
4. Volunteer, make presentations, and host receptions at ACA conferences to boost your profile with the organization (3–6 years).
5. Get published in academic journals, national newsletters, and in venues such as *Counseling Today*. Sit on ACA committees and task forces to further boost your profile and understand the organization (3–4 years).
6. Run for secretary or vice president of ACA (2 years).
7. Finally, you run for president, using everything you have learned previously regarding visibility, a coherent platform, networking, and so forth. You win!

Even if you are not presently interested in becoming ACA president, this example illustrates that setting a clear goal helps you strategize how to work to

Nurturing and Managing Your Career   121

reach that goal. You should also be flexible with timelines and remember that you will have some failures along the way. Do not let failures get you down too much, as they offer the opportunity for self-reflection and reassessment. In fact, failures can provide the incentive and the wisdom for future success. Perhaps the inventor Thomas Edison is the best example of this ethic. Edison's experiment failures far outnumbered his successes. Yet, he needed the failures to help pave the road to his success, and his numerous failures are overshadowed by his successes. So, be of the mindset of allowing your failures to teach you healthy lessons.

Thus, when creating a visioning plan:

1. **Be conscious of the present.** Think long term as in the previous example. However, do not let long-term planning trip you up in the present. Doing well in the here and now is the first step to achieving your long-term goals.
2. **Set a time frame.** Remember, long-term goals will take time and you will need to revise them when setbacks and life circumstances change (e.g., marriage, divorce, children, moves, promotions, job loss). Disappointments will happen. I can recall having numerous job rejections and feeling quite discouraged. Then, I received some prudent counsel. I was encouraged to reframe each rejection as "One rejection closer to landing that first job." This simple act of reframing provided a greater sense of purpose and lessened my sense of failure. So, when you are not having the success you desire, reframe your thoughts accordingly. Positive, rational self-talk is a must for resilience and future success.
3. **Be flexible.** Your goals will change over time and that may be good. For example, you may start out with the long-term goal of running a university counseling center, but decide over time you are more interested in being a training director at a college counseling center. This would be an example of clarification, or simply learning that the original goal was not as congruent with your values and interests as previously thought. Remember, life is dynamic and all about change.
4. **Review your action plan periodically.** You need to check on your progress regularly. If you are not being successful, why not? In addition, what does success actually mean to you? Have your interests and values changed?
5. **Be mindful.** Mindfulness means being grounded in the present moment, nonjudgmentally, while connected to others. Make sure the goals you have set actually fit with your values. This may be the most difficult process you encounter in your career journey. You may need years of struggle, professional counseling, and some type of meaningful self-reflecting practice to a mindful career.
6. **Failure is okay.** As previously referenced, failure can be very transformative. That is, learn from your failures and tell yourself something like, "That's one failure closer to success." Personally, without the lessons my failure taught me, I would not be writing this book you are reading as I had many rejections from publishers.

122 *Nurturing and Managing Your Career*

Some techniques for career visioning are as follows:

- **Open-ended questions.** "What do I want in my career?" and "Now that I know what I want career-wise, how can I create it?"
- **Meditation.** Many people have a meditation practice that calms and centers them. Some people use meditation as part of the creative process. Numerous books and articles proliferate in society. Some download applications to their smart phone for daily use.
- **Visualization.** When you picture yourself 5, 7, or 10 years down the line, what does that picture look like? What does your career involve? Where are you living? Who else is in the picture?
- **Focusing.** This assists in clarifying how to plan and prioritize the preceding visualization process. For example, what needs to happen before you can open your own private practice?
- **Career journaling.** For many people, journaling allows them the opportunity to document how their career is proceeding, and what challenges, satisfactions, struggles, changes, failures, successes, and so on they are facing. Not everyone finds journaling helpful, but for those who enjoy it, journaling can be a type of self-discovery regarding career and personal insights.
- **Collage making.** Do not denigrate this potentially creative exercise. Collage making can be fun as well as helping you create a picture of your career dreams. Create a collage to explore your future dreams and goals. This provides a concrete example of what your desired future may resemble. You might be surprised at what it resembles!
- **Informational interviewing.** Choose two or three people whom you respect and who know you well. Ask them to address the following questions about you:
    1. What qualities do you possess that will help make you successful in your career?
    2. What steps do you need to take to realize your career goal(s)?
    3. What is your strongest quality?
    4. What is your chief weakness?

                                              (Hodges & Connelly, 2010, p. 14)

The Career Center

The career center on your campus can offer numerous services for the soon-to-be-graduated intern. One of the most valuable services is the letters of reference bank. With this, your field supervisor(s) and advisor can write letters of reference that can be stored at the center. Reference letters can be open or closed. Open references mean that the student has the right to inspect the letter. Closed letters cannot be read by students. Students frequently ask me, "Should I have an open or closed file?" I always feel somewhat torn, because I believe when we agree to serve as a reference it should be an open process. However, I also know that some hiring committees view closed files as more authentic. So, make the best decision you can. You may feel more confident in closed files if you are confident about the people who are writing the letters. I have written reference letters both for open and for closed files and my letter would be the same for both. Once again, it also comes down to how much trust you have in the person writing the reference letter. Ideally, people would not write reference letters for students unless they honestly had faith in the students' counseling ability. As a realist, however, I know such is not always the practice.

Career center counselors can also critique your résumé and cover letter (you might show them to your supervisor or a colleague as well). It never hurts to have fresh eyes examine your materials for errors, accuracy, and to make sure you present yourself in the strongest possible light to a potential employer. Remember, initial screenings of résumés and cover letters often are to screen out applicants. You want to be "screened in," so spelling errors, wrong dates, or simply misleading information will get your application relegated to the recycle bin.

Professional Networking Sites

You should also consider using appropriate social networking sites such as LinkedIn. LinkedIn provides a method of building vocational connections. Refrain from using social sites such as Facebook as a professional networking vehicle. Facebook works fine for transmitting social and familial information, but many people post compromising photographs and information on such sites and that can derail a promising career before it begins. Professional sites such as LinkedIn are typically understood to be more appropriate sites for networking with other counseling professionals. LinkedIn offers an easy, quick method of linking with fellow counselors and even soliciting recommendations. It is likely that in this rapidly accelerating electronic world, sites such as LinkedIn represent future "career centers" or at least as an ancillary career center (though certainly not as good as an actual career counselor). Naturally, the American Counseling Association (ACA), American Mental Health Counselors Association (AMHCA), American School Counselor Association (ASCA), and organizations such as the National Board for Certified Counselors (NBCC) have their own networking capabilities (another perk of membership). Regarding networking, the following section provides some guidance.

A Networking Questionnaire

Networking at social and professional events can be very helpful to your career. Developing relationships is important as people in the profession of counseling are more likely to recommend you when they have a positive impression. The following informal assessment may serve as a general guide for your networking practice.

124 *Nurturing and Managing Your Career*

Instructions: Answer each question by circling the number that best represents how your behavior. Higher scores suggest more comfort engaging in networking.

1=Strongly Disagree   2=Disagree   3=Neutral   4=Agree   5=Strongly Agree

1.	I enjoy attending professional social functions.	1	2	3	4	5
2.	I tend to take the initiative in introducing myself to people I don't know.	1	2	3	4	5
3.	On a scale of 1 to 10, with 1 being low and 10 high, my comfort in social situations is between 7 and 10.	1	2	3	4	5
4.	I listen attentively, providing others the opportunity to speak without interruption.	1	2	3	4	5
5.	I ask questions related to topics of interest others have mentioned to me	1	2	3	4	5
6.	I carry business cards and offer them to colleagues and from whom I collect cards.	1	2	3	4	5
7.	I make an effort to remember people's names and use them in future conversations.	1	2	3	4	5
8.	If someone I meet suggests I call to discuss their school/agency/treatment center, I follow up on their suggestion in a timely fashion.	1	2	3	4	5
9.	If someone is not interested in talking with me, I move onto someone else without feeling rejected or resentful.	1	2	3	4	5
10.	I am active on LinkedIn or a similar website	1	2	3	4	5

Average score = _____

If your average score is below 3, you may need to focus on addressing issues of social engagement and comfort. Some additional questions for consideration:

On the 1–5 scale, with 1 low and 5 high, how satisfied am I with my networking score?   1 2 3 4 5 (circle your score)

If you are not satisfied with your networking score, you could improve your score by _____. (Answer verbally/write out)

Now, review your answers to the previous questions. Then, consider the following questions:

1. What do my answers suggest to me regarding my people skills?
2. How could I begin to improve my people skills?
3. If I feel uncomfortable in social situations, how could I begin to feel more comfortable?
4. When you see yourself in the mirror, ask "Am I the type of person I would want to be friends with?" Why or why not? If no, what might you change? Remember, effective people skills are not necessarily about being popular. The issue is integrity and conveying a sense of interest and presence to those around you.

Requesting References

As you complete your final internship and prepare for the job search, you should be soliciting letters of recommendation from professors and field supervisors. Your letters of reference ideally should be written by counseling professionals, such as professors in your counselor education program, your faculty advisor, major professor, field site supervisors, and possibly supervisors or professionals in related fields who may be able to address pertinent areas related to counseling work. These references may be required to either write a formal letter on your behalf, or merely be accessible for a verbal discussion about you with a potential employer. Although most counseling applications typically require three references, some may ask for five. So be prepared for the possibility of needing additional references. Again, you would be wise to seek references from those with whom you have a good relationship as they likely will write you the strongest reference. Your candidacy will be sunk by tepid praise, so be prudent!

Prior to sending off your résumé or cover letter, you must *ask* each person on your list if he or she would be willing to serve as a reference. This may seem elementary, but you might be surprised how many times I have received a phone call from an employer asking about an applicant who never asked if I would serve as a reference. Such unexpected calls are always embarrassing and usually sink the counselor's candidacy. Failure to ask if a former supervisor or professor will serve as a reference sends the message you potentially don't respect your references well or that you were sloppy in your approach. So remember to ask!

Consider the strength of the referral before asking anyone to serve as a reference. As one who has written scores of reference letters for the past two decades, my guideline is I must be able to write a strong letter of reference or I will refuse to serve as a reference. Be aware that weak or nebulous references are worse than none at all. So, as soon as possible during your final semester, line up your references. As you do so, consider the following:

1. Provide your referral sources with a résumé or CV. This helps them fill in the gaps about your vocational life. No matter how well I know a student, I always learn something additional from his or her résumé or CV.
2. Do not ask your references to write a letter at the last moment. This shows poor planning on your part and your reference may not be able to write the letter with short notice, or might be annoyed at such a last-minute request. Ideally, give your references two weeks to write letters of reference.
3. Make sure you keep your references informed as to how your job search is proceeding. I personally appreciate hearing how my students are progressing on the job search. When you land a job, let your references know—they will be happy to know their supervision and hard work has paid off.
4. Although most applications now suggest emailing letters of reference and may not require a mailed letter of reference, be ready just in the event a school or agency does the business in the twentieth-century way. Likely, all will be managed through electronic means.

Developing a Résumé or Curriculum Vitae

A résumé or CV provides a description of your educational and occupational life. The résumé or CV provides a sketch of you for a potential employer's perusal. This is no time to be overly modest; your résumé is your calling card and summary of your professional life. Be your best self. But be honest in whatever you write on your CV or résumé! Overly embellishing on a résumé or CV (e.g., lying) can cost you a job and maybe even a career.

The recommended reading list at the end of the chapter offers many comprehensive references to help you craft a résumé and conduct other aspects of your job search. I highly recommend you consult one or more of them. Here are some basic tips to get you started (Hodges & Connelly, 2010, p. 34):

- Your education and transferrable skills are of critical importance. Your experience, training, education, and skills serve as a bridge to desired employment. Make sure you design your résumé or CV in a manner that clearly highlights your training and skills areas. List all degrees, degrees in progress, certifications, work history, awards, and so forth.
- Make sure your résumé makes chronological sense. Begin with the most recent position and work your way back. In addition, I recommend that you list your graduate assistantship just as you would list a job—because in essence, it is *job-like*.
- Claim the highest skills ethically possible. For example, if you have co-facilitated counseling groups for two years, certainly list that. Do not, however, list that you developed and oversaw the group treatment model at your school or agency if this is untrue.
- Be able to elaborate on anything you list. For example, if you list that you are proficient in Dialectical Behavioral Therapy (DBT) for example, you must be prepared to demonstrate you have mastered the basic concepts of this theoretical approach to trauma treatment. Ability to document certification would also be very helpful.
- Include membership in relevant professional organizations. Membership demonstrates a stronger commitment to the profession. It also suggests you are more likely to keep informed of research and emerging trends in the counseling field. My personal opinion: all counseling graduates and professional counselors should hold membership in the ACA, their particular counseling specialty area (e.g., ASCA, AMHCA, American Rehabilitation Counseling Association [ARCA]), and their state counseling organization.
- Make your résumé or CV reader friendly. When a search committee member first looks at your résumé or CV, he or she will give it a 30-to 45-second speed read (Bolles, 2015). Make sure it is clearly organized. Use a common 12-point font (such as Times New Roman).
- Do a spelling and grammar check. Have a career counselor or someone else you trust read it for content and mechanics. Misspellings and poor grammar are likely to get your application eliminated from consideration.

Nurturing and Managing Your Career 127

- There is no one "right" résumé or CV format. Make sure your résumé makes sense, flows logically, is factually accurate, and fits with the counseling position for which you have applied. For example, if you are applying for an inner-city high school counselor position, make sure your application letter reflects the particular demographics of that school, as opposed to an elite private school.
- Cover your most recent years of work experience in the greatest detail, depending on your age and years in the field. Do not be discouraged if you are a recent graduate of a counseling program. At your age and experience level, you are not expected to have many years of professional experience. After all, everyone starts somewhere.
- Having held multiple jobs is no longer the problem as it was in previous generations. In this era, people are expected to have held three, four, or even more jobs (Bolles, 2015). In higher education, the general understanding is that you must "move out to move up," and that is likely to be reflected in your résumé or CV. However, when you enter into a professional counseling position, you will be expected to stay at that job for four-to-five years. Job hopping—leaving or trying to leave a job every one-to-two years—will hurt you in future job searches.
- Be factually correct. You are responsible for anything you list in your résumé or CV. If you are caught lying or embellishing, the least you will lose is a job. In some cases, you may forfeit your career. Be warned: potential employers have little tolerance for the ethically challenged!
- Provide all contact information. List landline and cell phone numbers, email, and so forth.

In developing your résumé and cover letter, I encourage you to use language that describes your experience, skills, and interests in a concise, descriptive, and eloquent voice. The best way to illustrate your work in the cover letter and résumé is with action words that present your case in a lively manner. Here is a sampling of action words for consideration:

1. Accomplished
2. Chaired
3. Controlled
4. Coordinated
5. Executed
6. Headed
7. Orchestrated
8. Organized
9. Oversaw
10. Planned
11. Produced
12. Programmed
13. Administered
14. Built
15. Charted
16. Created

17. Designed
18. Developed
19. Devised
20. Founded
21. Engineered
22. Established
23. Formalized
24. Formed
25. Formulated
26. Implemented
27. Incorporated
28. Initiated
29. Instituted
30. Introduced
31. Launched

32. Pioneered
33. Spearheaded
34. Conserved
35. Consolidated
36. Decreased
37. Deducted
38. Diagnosed
39. Lessened
40. Reconciled
41. Reduced
42. Yielded
43. Accelerated
44. Achieved
45. Advanced
46. Amplified

128 *Nurturing and Managing Your Career*

47. Boosted
48. Capitalized
49. Delivered
50. Enhanced
51. Expanded
52. Expedited
53. Furthered
54. Gained
55. Generated
56. Improved
57. Lifted
58. Maximized
59. Outpaced
60. Stimulated
61. Sustained

62. Centralized
63. Clarified
64. Converted
65. Customized
66. Influenced
67. Integrated
68. Merged
69. Modified
70. Overhauled
71. Redesigned
72. Refined
73. Refocused
74. Rehabilitated
75. Remodeled
76. Reorganized

77. Replaced
78. Restructured
79. Revamped
80. Revitalized
81. Simplified
82. Standardized
83. Streamlined
84. Strengthened
85. Upgraded
86. Upgraded
87. Transformed
88. Aligned
89. Cultivated
90. Directed
91. Enabled

Below is a sample résumé. Remember, there is no one right résumé format. The books listed at the end of this chapter give plenty of additional styles to choose from.

Sample Résumé

Reggie Martinez, Master's Candidate, BA, AA
327 Springdale Ave.
Palouse Hills, WA 96332
(817) 555-0234 (c)
rmartinez@hotmail.com

Profile
Master's degree candidate seeking a challenging counseling position at a community mental health clinic.

Summary of Qualifications
- Five years' experience supervising college students in collegiate living groups, providing peer advising, crisis intervention, and educational programming.
- Nearing completion of 700-hour practicum/internship in community counseling agency.
- Trained in grief counseling during practicum/internship.
- Developed an outreach program for Latino youth.
- Selected as the Graduate Student of the Year at Washington State University.

Education
Master's Degree Candidate (will graduate in June 2021) in Clinical Mental Health Counseling, Washington State University, Pullman, WA (CACREP-accredited program)

Bachelors of Arts (2016) in Cultural Anthropology at Western Washington University, Bellingham, WA (Minor: Psychology)

Associates of Arts (2015) in Psychology at Seattle Area Community College

Related Work Experience
Mental Health Counseling Practicum and Internship (2019–2021), The Rainbow Center, Moscow, ID.

- Provided individual and group counseling to clients in Spanish and English.
- Co-facilitated support groups for parents of gay and lesbian children.
- Developed a grief support group for parents who have had children die.
- Presented psychoeducational workshops to schools, service organizations, and law enforcement officers.
- Served as crisis counselor for evening crisis call center.
- Assisted in rewriting the *Rainbow Staff Employee's Manual*.
Resident Director, Department of Housing and Residence Life, Washington State University, Pullman, WA (2019–2021)
- Director of International Student residence hall, with students from 33 countries.
- Oversight of 150 undergraduate and graduate students and scholars-in-residence.
- Supervisor for five residence advisors.
- Responsible for coordinating educational programming in residence hall.
- Mediated conflicts between residents in the residence hall.
- Provided crisis intervention and referred students to the university counseling center.
- Participated in Safe Haven training for gay, lesbian, and transgender students.
Resident Advisor, Department of Residential Life, Western Washington University, Bellingham, WA (2014–2016)
- Floor supervisor in coeducational collegiate residence hall (30 students).
- Responsible for educational programming.
- Served as peer counselor for students.
- Referred students to the counseling center, health services, and the career center.
- Mediated disputes between students on the floor.
President, Student Government Association, Seattle Area Community College, Seattle, WA (2012–2014)
- President of student organization representing 25,000 community college students.
- Responsible for oversight of student fee budgeting, programming approval, and selecting committee chairs.
- Voting member of Seattle Community College's Board of Trustees.
- Charged with lobbying for student needs, such as a new student union, recreation center, and campus residence halls.

Awards

2020–2021, Graduate Student of the Year. Presented by the Association for Gay, Lesbian, and Transgender Student Association, Washington State University, Pullman, WA

2012, 2013 Seattle Area Community College's Presidential scholarship

Publications

Martinez, R. (2020). Barriers to providing counseling services to Latino clients: Some reflections from the trenches. *Journal of the Washington Counseling Association, 12*, 22–34.

Martinez, R. (2019). Experiences as a first generation Latino graduate student. *The Advocate, 10*, 3–5.

Martinez, R. (2016, October 15). Racism and homophobia: One Latino's struggle for acceptance. *Seattle Post, 57*, pp. A.1, 22.

Additional Training

Trained in Dialectical Behavioral Therapy (Rainbow Center, 2019–2020)
Washington State Certified Mediator
Solution-Focused Counseling, Pullman, WA, June 22–25, 2019

Professional Memberships

Chi Sigma Iota (Counseling Honorary)
American Counseling Association (ACA)
American Mental Health Counselors Association (AMHCA)
Washington State Mental Health Counselors Association (WSMHCA)

Hobbies

Running, cycling, traveling, and writing poetry

References

Sam Cogan, PhD, Associate Professor of Counseling, Counselor Education program, College of Education, Washington State University, Pullman, WA, (509) 633-0134, e-mail: scogan@wsu.edu.

Angela Hermes, MS, LMHC, The Rainbow Center, Moscow, ID, (509) 714–1027, e-mail: hermesa@yahoo.com.

Harriet Wilson, Ed.D, Assistant Dean of Students/Coordinator of International Students, Washington State University, Pullman, WA, (509) 618–9090, e-mail: hwilson@wsu.edu.

Writing a Cover Letter

In writing the cover letter, you want to keep several elements in mind:

1. Open the letter with a respectful business-like address such as "Dear Director," "Dear Search Committee," or another title that conveys respect. Do not use informal titles even if you know the persons to whom you are writing. Remember, the cover letter indicates you understand professional protocol.
2. As with your résumé, type using a standard 12-point font (such as Times New Roman or another more traditional style). If you are delivering hard copies— less common in this electronic era—have your résumé and cover letter printed on quality, heavy stock paper.
3. In the opening paragraph, explain why you are interested in the job and show that you understand the population the organization serves. For example, if you are applying for a position as a school counselor in an inner-city school or alternative school, briefly illustrate your knowledge of and experience with that student population.
4. Keep it brief: one to one and one-half pages. Employers are busy people and tend to cease reading if the cover letter is too lengthy. A too-lengthy cover letter may also read like an "I love me letter," and potential narcissism is a turn off. Smart employers want team players who can forge good collegial relationships.
5. Hit the highlights of your qualifications for the position: cite your counseling experience (practicum/internship) and theoretical approach. (If the school or agency uses a particular approach, indicate your knowledge and experience with it if appropriate.) In addition, if you have special training in a particular approach (e.g., DBT, EMDR, ACT, Mindfulness Based CBT, etc.), indicate that as well.
6. If you have experience related to the counseling field, you certainly want to mention that. Related experience (such as working as a case manager, teaching assistant, resident advisor, bachelor's-level addiction counselor, etc.) should also be mentioned. Such suggests you understand what is involved in professional work and are thus better prepared for the job.
7. If you have experience doing something interesting such as teaching overseas, a Peace Corps or AmeriCorps volunteer, or anything that is outside the typical experience (whatever you deem that to be), list it. Such experience could make a difference.
8. In the final paragraph, wrap up by stating that you look forward to meeting to discuss your interest and fit for the job. Provide your phone number and email address.

132 *Nurturing and Managing Your Career*

Here is a sample cover letter:

Sample Cover Letter

March 13, 2021
1339 Easy Street
Vista View, AR 72301

Personnel Department
Hickory Ridge School District
5555 Cardinal Lane
Hickory Ridge, AR 72709

Dear Personnel Officer:

Please consider me an applicant for the school counseling position at Hickory Ridge High School. I noticed the advertisement in a recent online edition of the *Northwest Arkansas Times*. Currently, I am a graduate student completing my studies and will graduate with my master's degree in school counseling this May at the University of Arkansas. In addition to coursework, I have completed 700 hours of practicum and internship at a local high school. I have also served as a teacher's aide in a public school for 5 years and have a good understanding of both academic and personal issues that impact a student's learning environment.

My practicum and internship were spent at Fayetteville Technical High School, where I assisted the school counseling staff with academic, career, and personal counseling. This past semester, I co-facilitated two counseling groups for students at risk for dropping out of school. I also led an after-school group targeted at gang prevention.

During my counselor education studies at the University of Arkansas, I was selected for the counseling honorary Chi Sigma Iota, and have even served as president. During this past year, I also worked part time at the Beacon Light Center, where I provided personal, career, and academic counseling to at-risk adolescents.

My résumé and three letters of reference requested in the advertisement are being forwarded from the Career Center at the University of Arkansas. I would welcome the opportunity to discuss my interest in the school counseling position with you in the near future. If you have additional questions, please feel free to contact me at (123) 456–7890 or through e-mail at noone@hotmail.com.

Respectfully yours,
Althea Jefferson

The Job Interview

Some questions you will face in an interview will be generic, whereas others will be specific to a school, agency, or college counseling center. The sample questions in this section are not comprehensive, but it is to be hoped that it will give you a sense of the types of questions you should be prepared to answer. It may also be helpful to have a career counselor, classmate, spouse, or friend play the role of interviewer. As previously stated, practicing before the interview is *highly* recommended.

There are a couple of important points to consider before interviewing. If you do not know the answer to a question, please say, "I don't know." This displays both honesty and a lack of pretension. As a veteran interviewed, I can usually spot someone trying to "manufacture" answers when they have no idea what they are speaking about. After all, you have just completed a master's program and are not expected to know everything. So, do not act as if you do know it all.

Second, you do not want to be too lengthy with your answers, as those interviewing you will lose interest. Bolles (2015) suggests the 50/50, two-minute rule. The two-minute maximum suggests that you keep your answers thorough, but brief. The longer you talk, the less interested the interviewer (or search committee) will be in your answers. After all, if you are too wordy at the interview, you may be too talkative as a counselor. In addition, the longer you speak during an interview, the greater the likelihood you will disclose something you would rather not disclose (Hodges & Connelly, 2010). Be brief, thorough, and use discretion in your answers.

Here are some sample interview questions:

1. **Why do you want this job?** This is a critical question and you want the search committee to believe this school, agency, or college counseling center is your primary interest and focus. Be able to tie your answer to the mission of the organization. Something like, "I enjoy the challenge of working in an addictions treatment agency and wish to make my career in this counseling field. Your agency treats addicts in recovery utilizing CBT and DBT for trauma and offers an extensive training program and continuing education for employees." Don't say, "I think your school is a good stepping stone for my career." This latter response suggests "You're just a short step on my career path and I'm not committed to you."

2. **Tell me about yourself.** This is your opportunity to take initiative in the interview. What interviewers want to hear is how you can tie your brief biography into why you are a good fit for the job. I would suggest that you weave your personal experience and strengths into a 60-second answer that sums up your "fit" for the position. For example, "I grew up in a family of teachers, with my mother a principal, my father a school counsellor, and have maintained a high value on education. I volunteer with disadvantaged children every year in the Big Sister/Big Brother program. I believe my personal background and training as a school counselor have provided me valuable experience for working

134   *Nurturing and Managing Your Career*

alongside teachers, counselors, and administrators such as those here at Levett Middle School."

3. **What special training or skills do you offer?** This is where additional training or related skills and experience come in handy. For example, if you are a trained or certified mediator, mention that. Perhaps you have several years supervising collegiate residential living communities, or advanced training in art therapy or adventure-based therapy; mention this and tie the experience into how much it has enhanced your counseling ability. Remember, administrators are always interested in getting multitalented employees.

4. **What is your experience with this particular clinical population?** This is where your practicum/internship comes in handy, as does any related experience. Again, use your professional and related experiences to address the question. Weave in your practicum and internship experience, training, related experience volunteering with special populations, and so forth.

5. **Could you describe your strengths and weaknesses?** Everyone has weaknesses, and you are no exception. An overused line I have heard *way* too many times in job interviews goes something like: "I'm a perfectionist and very hard on myself." To me, this sounds contrived and scarcely original. My interviewer response to that question was: "You know everyone tells me that. What's another challenge you have grappled with?" So try to relate a weakness that can be turned around into a strength. For example, "Well, I am young and have just completed my graduate degree. But, I'm a quick learner and in a couple of years I will be older and more experienced. I'm also very willing to take coaching and feedback." The strength aspect of this question is much more honest and original. Cite your experience on practicum and internship, related work, and so forth.

6. **If offered this position, how long could you see yourself working here?** In most cases, it is best not to give a specific time. Instead, you might answer something like, "I would like to work here as long as I have fresh challenges and opportunities. And, I hope to be challenged and have opportunities here for several years to come." If they pin you down with demands for a year answer, something suggesting long-term is best. For example: "I would foresee myself working at this agency/school/hospital for 5–7 years." Of course, one never really knows!

7. **What theoretical counseling approach do you work from?** This is often a tough question for recent graduates of master's degree counseling programs, as the program may not have provided one single approach. So, cite the approaches you have primarily used on practicum and internship and under what situations you used them. Also, let the committee know you are open to learning new skills, techniques, and approaches. As trauma treatment is an issue, developing competence with efficacious approaches such as Acceptance and Commitment Therapy (ACT), DBT, EMDR, Mindfulness-Based CBT, etc.

8. **What are your professional goals?** Wise interviewees will tie their answer to the job at hand. For example, if you are interviewing for a school counseling position, you might express that you would like to direct a high school

counseling office. You might also mention a few marking points along the way (such as attaining licensure, national certification, additional training, etc.). The dreaded "I have no goals" or "I don't believe in setting goals" is guaranteed to end your candidacy for the job. You might be surprised at the number of interviewees who profess to a dearth of professional goals! Believe me, hiring committees and supervisors do not like such answers! So, set goals and measure your progress regularly.

9. **How do you handle conflict?** Be judicious with your answer, but be authentic. Inability to get along with co-workers is a huge reason people are fired or quit their jobs. A possible answer to this question might be something like this: "I work to calm myself, reviewing the main points of the disagreement. Then, I try to seek out the other party from the standpoint of trying to understand his or her point of view. If we then cannot come to agreement, perhaps asking a colleague or supervisor to mediate might be a good idea."

10. **What if a parent, teacher, coach, and so forth, demand to know what you and a student or client is working on in counseling?** For school counseling applicants, this is a question to see how well you remember your professional ethics (and legal issues as well!). You might want to briefly allude to the relevant legal issues in your answer. Remember, laws vary from state to state. So, know the relevant laws for the state you plan to work in. Further, be aware of your school or agency's policy on how relevant information is released.

11. **Regarding research, what is your specialty area?** If you are completing a doctorate in Counselor Education and Supervision and applying for an academic position or a research position, you need to be able to articulate your research interests, experience, and publications. In addition, check out the department's website to see how your research interests match those of the current faculty. It is also worthwhile to scope out whether the opening is a replacement position ("Why did the last person leave?") or a newly created position.

12. **Have you ever been fired from a job?** If you were terminated for a cause, explain what that was. Emphasize how you have learned and grown from this experience. Remember, the world is full of successful people who were fired from previous jobs. Self-disclosure time, I was fired and although certainly a disappointing and painful experience it was the genesis for in-depth soul-searching and professional growth. Ironically, I believe I am succeeding now only because I failed earlier.

13. **What did you like about our agency/school/treatment center that interested you enough to apply for the job?** This is a critical question. The interviewer(s) want(s) to hear your in-depth knowledge of the agency or school and its programs, missions, goals, client population, talented staff or faculty, and so forth. Be brief but thorough. Illustrate that you are knowledgeable about what they do. For sure, check out the website to learn as much as you can. If you know someone who works at the school/agency, ask him or her relevant questions.

14. **What do you see as the pressing issues in the field for the next decade?** This question is designed to see how well you understand the profession and

136 *Nurturing and Managing Your Career*

potential changes. Good answers also illustrate that you have kept up on professional reading of journals. The "pressing issues" are subjective, so be prepared to support any answers you give. For example, a potential answer might be, "I believe multiculturalism is the most important issue because of the large influx of immigrant and multicultural populations and the fact we live in a globally interconnected era."

15. **How have you or how would you support multiculturalism?** Be prepared to address how you support multiculturalism and include specific examples. Concrete examples might include having served on the school district's diversity task force, having counseled multicultural populations, having studied and/or worked abroad, and so forth. Remember, everyone has some part in multiculturalism as multiculturalism includes race, culture, socioeconomics, gender, sexual orientation, geography, and so on.

16. **What professional counseling organizations do you hold membership in?** If you are preparing for a job search and are not a member of a professional counseling organization, I'd strongly suggest you join the pertinent one: e.g., ACA, ASCA, ARCA, etc. The lack of a professional membership suggests you may not be committed to your profession and that you may not be up to date on current research, laws, ethics, and other important related professional issues. When directing programs I would not hire any candidate who was not a member of ACA and/or ASCA, AMHCA, etc.

17. **What salary would you expect to receive?** Never quote a specific figure. Answer with something like, "Somewhere in the advertised range," or "Something reflecting my training or experience." Never state a dollar amount until you receive a job offer! This is a mistake too many inexperienced job seekers—and even some experienced ones—make.

18. **What do you know about the mission of this university, school, or agency?** This is a question that is becoming more commonly asked in interviews. Make sure you have read and understood the mission, which should be posted on the university/school/agency's website. In addition, be prepared to explain why your experience and background fits the mission of the organization. If you do not know the mission, search committees will interpret that to mean you were not prepared for the interview, and do not understand the school or agency.

19. **Why should we hire you?** All interviews are an attempt to address this overarching question. This question usually comes at the end of the interview and is the candidate's opportunity to state his or her special qualifications and fit for the job. You need to be brief and sound confident, but not cocky. Here is one possible answer, "I believe myself to be the best candidate for this addiction counseling position because I have spent the past 2 years counseling in a residential addiction treatment center. I also have experience counseling trauma survivors and have completed DBT training. My plan is to make a career as an addictions counselor and one day to run a clinic such as this one. Hire me as a counselor and I'll make you very happy you did." Suggestion: practice your answer with a friend or colleagues. Then ask if they would hire you based on your answer.

20. **Do you have any questions for us?** Of course you do! This is your opportunity to take control of the interview and it comes at the tipping point. I cringe when

Nurturing and Managing Your Career   137

I hear job candidate's state, "No, I have no questions." Such an answer implies the candidate did not do her or his homework. You must always have questions to ask, even if you already know the answers to them.

(Hodges & Connelly, 2010, pp. 68–70)

Inappropriate Questions

Unfortunately, some interviewers will ask inappropriate questions during interviews. This may be unintentional (although ignorance is no excuse) or deliberate. Most public and private institutions sign an Equal Opportunity Employment Commission (EEOC) statement that pledges they will not discriminate based on race, age, creed, national origin, disability status, sexual orientation, veteran status, gender, and so on. Thus, questions concerning any of these issues should generally not be raised in an interview.

Examples of inappropriate questions might include the following:

- "Are you married?" or "Do you have children?"
- "What church do you attend?"
- "Mind if I ask you some personal questions?" (*Of course you would mind*— everyone minds! I was once asked this very question at an interview for a counseling position! Yes, I did mind! No, I did not accept the job when offered.)
- "What political party do you belong to?"
- "Do you have a *normal* sexual orientation?"
- "How many times a day do you pray?"
- "I don't see a ring on your finger. Are you dating anyone?"
- "Are you related to anyone who could help us politically?"

The professional way to respond to illegal or inappropriate questions is to be tactful and ask clarification-type questions. While it might be very understandable if you were to get angry and respond in a likewise manner, you are a professional and professionals conduct themselves professionally even when the interview team or an administrator does not.

> **Example of illegal/inappropriate question:** "Are you married?"
> **Potential answer:** "How does that question relate to the job?" or "Why is this important information to know?" You might use humor to defuse the situation: "Hmmm … I don't think the interview police allow that question." A more low-key and humorous approach does not suggest that illegal or inappropriate questions are any laughing matter, but rather they provide the interviewee an opportunity to set a message in a manner that does inflame the situation.

Inappropriate or illegal questions should rightfully lead you to wonder about the day-to-day ethics of the workplace. Should you be asked illegal or inappropriate questions on an interview, you may wish to consider whether you want to work at a school or agency with such lax ethics and callous disregard for federal

138   *Nurturing and Managing Your Career*

law. Once the interview is over, you may consider contacting the appropriate person (usually in human resources) and informing him or her of your experience. You also have the right to contact your state's department of labor and file a complaint. Naturally, as a vulnerable person on a job search, it is wise to consider the ramifications of reporting versus not reporting. Consider the potential risks versus the rewards. Just as important for you, ask yourself what type of school, agency, or academic department you want to work in. If the potential job site does not seem a good fit for your personal values, you will likely be unhappy working there. As a counselor who spent more than 20 years providing mental health and career counseling and advising, I have heard many sad stories from employees whose values are not a good fit for their place of work. Accepting a job is a bit like a marriage; you can get out of it (thankfully!) but the getting out is emotionally draining and very expensive.

Dealing with Rejection

On the path to career success, you will experience some rejection. This section of the chapter offers concrete suggestions to manage your disappointment if you do not get a position that you wanted. Fortunately, such rejection is not personal (except in rare cases), will pass, and does not have to keep you from landing another viable job. Rejection is also universally experienced as everyone has been rejected for something he or she desired. Feeling bad and perhaps angry that you were passed over for another candidate is also natural and I have found the best antidote is to remind myself that I learned from the experience. Further, that is one rejection closer to a job offer. I suppose this is the upbeat, CBT part of my psyche.

So, you have just suffered a setback in your job search. That dream job—the one you seemed perfect for—was given to someone else. Perhaps you had a great interview where the search committee seemed to hang on your every word (or so you thought). You left the interview convinced you would soon be getting a call with a job offer. Then, with a brief and stilted phone call, your dreams burst into flames of disappointment. You hang up the phone stunned and numb from the shock of rejection. You try to make sense of it, but your mind cannot seem to accommodate the unexpected setback. "How could they have selected someone else?"

This scenario has been experienced by just about every job seeker in history. The critical factor is to acknowledge that you will have failures. For each job advertised, typically only one person will be selected. This means, of course, that if 30 applicants apply for a mental health counseling opening, 29 will be disappointed. Thus, job rejection is not only a common shared experience, there is almost no way around some degree of occupational rejection.

There are several reasonable reasons for job rejection:

1. A more qualified candidate was selected. Or, the interviewer or search committee *thought* the successful candidate was more qualified. Remember, the job search and hiring process is an inexact science at best- for both parties.

Nurturing and Managing Your Career 139

2. The successful candidate seemed a better fit for the position. A candidate with less experience might be hired because he or she has a counseling specialty area other candidates lack (e.g., trauma counseling experience, play therapy experience, mediation training) or simply seemed to connect better with the search committee.

3. Fit has cultural and gender implications. For example, if all the current counseling staff at a school are female, a male candidate may have a better chance at the job. No interviewing committee will admit to making such considerations, but believe me, they do consider such.

4. The successful candidate was simply better prepared than the other finalists. Bolles (2015) makes the point that the most prepared applicant will likely be hired over a more qualified one. Preparation includes a well-crafted résumé or CV, succinct and error-free cover letters, and good interviews. A more qualified candidate could torpedo his or her candidacy by lack of preparation in these critical areas.

5. A candidate's behavior was inappropriate during the interview. Inappropriate behavior could be having more than one drink at dinner with search committee members, making racist or sexist jokes, rudeness to committee members or others, or raising inappropriate topics during the interview. Remember, you are always "on the clock," even during breaks.

6. A candidate displayed a lack of confidence at the interview. You might be the most qualified candidate, but if you do not present as such, someone else will get the job offer. Self-critical comments such as "It's nothing," or "Anyone could have done it," or, "My colleagues actually did most of the work," send the wrong message. Be confident, not cocky or self-absorbed, but confident. One of the most qualified faculty candidates I helped interview was so self-critical that although he was the best candidate with regard to experience teaching, counselling, and scholarship, we selected another candidate with less stellar credentials though a quiet confidence.

7. A candidate was dishonest. Were you caught in a lie on your résumé or CV? Did you overly embellish your credentials during the interview phase? Be honest, it will save you a lot of angst. Honesty will also relieve you of the need to "keep your story straight" in addition to being ethical behavior.

8. A candidate's appearance was unprofessional. Granted, the counseling profession is not as formal as that of say, banking or finance. Nevertheless, play it conservative: women should wear dress slacks, skirt, or dress. Men should wear a tie or sport coat. Do not go overboard with cologne, perfume, or jewellery.

9. The search was a failed one. Sometimes a committee will not hire because of a shallow applicant pool or a general dissatisfaction with the finalists. This happens, so work to not take it personally. As the saying goes, a person (or persons) failure to see your value is not necessarily an accurate statement of your value.

10. There was behind-the-scenes politicking. My experience is you can never really know what goes on behind closed doors. Politics certainly comes into play at times and a surprise candidate can emerge with the job offer even if the

140 *Nurturing and Managing Your Career*

interviewing committee suggested another candidate. I was once on interview committee that ranked the candidates 1 to 5 and the pertinent administrator selected the fifth-ranked candidate! I have seen this happen more than once.

11. A candidate posted inappropriate content on the internet. Social networking sites have created a medium for sharing information and meeting new people. They also contain and chronicle much outlandish behavior. Make sure your online persona matches what you wish to convey in your job search.

(Hodges & Connelly, 2010, pp. 88–91)

Transforming Your Disappointment

Fortunately, most applicants are resilient and understand there will be other job opportunities. The important point is to learn from disappointment and adapt that knowledge to new opportunities. When you get the disappointing phone call, email, or in past eras, the thin envelope, here are some suggestions for dealing with job rejection:

1. Allow yourself some time to adjust to the situation. Do not push yourself to feel "okay." Talk the situation over with a trusted friend or colleague. Be honest with yourself about the disappointment and pain. Remember, there will be other job opportunities.
2. Stay physically active. Activity routines are a staple of health, especially during a job search. Physical activity works off anxiety and depression and promotes relaxation.
3. When you have a little distance from the disappointment, reflect back on the experience. What went wrong? What seemed to go well? How could you improve for the next application or interview? This aspect of self-reflection is a critical task in the job search process.
4. Get feedback from someone in the professional field. If you are seeking a school counseling position, ask a professional school counselor to look over your résumé or CV and for tips. Practice interviewing with a career counselor or a professional counselor and have him or her grade you.
5. Identify two or three close friends/colleagues you can get support and a reality check from.
6. If needed, go in for personal counseling to address your frustration and the stress generated by the lack of getting hired.
7. Monitor and reframe your self-talk. Notice if you are telling yourself negative messages, such as "I'll never get hired" and "Nobody wants me." Reframe to more positive and realistic self-talk, such as "I'm having difficulty but I'll keep applying and improving and someone will hire me," or "Someone will eventually give me an opportunity and I'll be ready."

Professional Self-reflection

1. How would you describe your current job search?
2. Ideally, where would you like to be in your professional life? Describe the job, geographic location, salary, and anything else that seems pertinent.
3. How can you begin to create the professional life you described in the previous question? Cite anything that could help you accomplish your professional goals.
4. If you were recently rejected for a job (or jobs) you wanted, what did you learn that could help you in future job searches?
5. What supports do you have for this transitional time? Examples of support can be family members, friends, a spiritual community, fellow graduate students, support groups, and the like.
6. What personal strengths do you have that will assist you in coping with this transition time? Examples of personal strengths are a positive outlook, good work ethic, fitness routine, and the like.
7. Think of when you were faced with previous challenges. How have you coped with previous disappointments? How can previous experience assist you now?
8. Think of someone who has been successfully transitioned through job rejection and then found success. Ask them for tips on how you can do the same.
9. Ask yourself, "What else can I do to become the strongest candidate possible?"
10. When you are hired into a professional counseling position, how will your life be diffe rent? What joys and challenges might the new professional role present?
11. What would potential employers find attractive about you? What criticisms might they have? What is your ratio of strength to criticisms?
12. Networking is an essential component of a successful job search. What can you do to create an effective supportive network?
13. When writing cover letters, résumés or CVs, interviewing, and so forth, what message would you like to convey? How can you create that desired message?
14. If you were looking to hire a counselor or counselor educator, what qualities would you be looking for? Now, how well do you match up to those qualities? If you do not match up to the desired qualities, what do you need to do to meet them?
15. If a potential employer were to say, "Tell me five reasons why I should hire you," how would you answer?

(Hodges & Connelly, 2010, pp. 94–96)

142 *Nurturing and Managing Your Career*

Evaluating a Job Offer

Congratulations, you have a job offer! This is a big deal even if you are not interested in the job. When you receive an offer, it may be tempting to accept on the spot, especially during tough economic times. Be aware that if you accept the job unconditionally, you may be losing any leverage you might have in the negotiation process. Certainly, you want to express excitement and gratitude on receiving the offer and you may even feel the salary and benefits are very good. Still, as this is a big step, ask for a few days to think it over. Most employers, reasonable ones anyway, will respect this request.

Be thorough in your decision-making process, because you do not want to hastily accept a job only to find there is something you missed in the process (e.g., moving expense reimbursement, annual raises). There are many issues to consider:

- What life changes would accepting this job entail?
- What expenses would I incur by accepting the job (e.g., moving expenses, selling or buying a home, uprooting children from school and friends, moving away from family)?
- What would I be gaining by accepting this offer (other than a paycheck)?
- What would I be giving up by accepting this job?
- Does the salary range seem equitable compared to other jobs of this type? Will it be enough to live on? In addition, what will my counter offer be?
- How excited am I about this offer? Would I want to work with the staff? Does this position offer good potential for professional growth?

If you are still unsure about accepting the job, a simple and common technique to try is a pro–con exercise. Using a pen, split a sheet of paper down the center. Label the left side "pro" and the right side "con." Then, list all the pros and cons you can think of. Naturally, you want the pro list to be longer than the con list. If the con list is longer or the lists are of about equal length, this should give you pause before accepting the offer. Let us examine such a list:

Pro	Con
1. It is a job.	1. It is an expensive area.
2. It includes good salary and benefits.	2. It requires an expensive move.
3. It is in a desirable area of the country.	3. It is far from friends and family.
4. It has good potential for promotion.	4. I might get other offers.
5. I would have likable colleagues.	
6. The area has job potential for my partner.	
7. I am excited about the job!	

In this case, the pros outnumber the cons, although there are significant cons in the list. Thus, this candidate has a difficult decision to make. There are some

Nurturing and Managing Your Career 143

significant pros as well, and the most significant one may be item number 7— excitement about the job. Some readers may be in the enviable position of entertaining several offers at once, and the pro–con lists would be longer than a list for one offer. Regardless, the ultimate decision to accept or reject the offer can be a difficult one. Talking the matter over with friends, family, spouse, or partner and if need be, a counselor all can be helpful.

Here is another example of a counselor weighing an offer:

Pro	Con
1. It is a very good job.	1. It is a 500-mile move.
2. We love the location!	2. I will be leaving friends.
3. They will help my partner search for a job.	3. My partner will need to find a new job.
4. Excellent potential for promotion.	
5. I like the staff/faculty.	
6. The salary and benefits are very good.	
7. They will pay $3,000 for the move.	
8. We are close to family.	
9. I am very excited about the job!	

In this example, the pros seem to far outnumber the cons. It is likely that this counselor would have an easier time making a decision of whether to accept the position than the previous scenario. Another method of assessing whether or not to accept a job involves a decision tree. In the following example, continue down the list until you arrive at a "no" answer. A "no" answer would suggest that you seriously consider whether accepting this job is a wise decision.

Step 1: Do I want really this job? Yes or no?

Step 2: Does this job fit my needs or my family's needs regarding professional challenge, financial security, benefits, stability, and lifestyle? Yes or no?

Step 3: If taking this job necessitates a move, would I or my family be willing to relocate? Yes or no?

Step 4: Would the relocation be worth the disruption in our lives (distance from family, friends, school change, spouse's or partner's job change, etc.)? Yes or no?

Step 5: Are the administration and staff (or faculty) at this position actually supportive of diversity? Yes or no?

Step 6: Do I feel committed to this job for three-to-five years? Yes or no?

Step 7: Does the job environment seem healthy (e.g., healthy collegial relations, small annual turnover rate, and supportive supervisor)? Yes or no?

Step 8: Can I say, "This is the type of job I'm excited about?" Yes or no?

Step 9: Do the pros of accepting this job outweigh the cons? Yes or no?

144 *Nurturing and Managing Your Career*

If you answered "yes" to the question, "Do the pros significantly outweigh the cons? Yes or no?" this should provide you some insight. If you answered "no," that answer has the same guiding principle as "yes." Another critical question to consider is: "Am I excited about the prospect of this job?" Well, *are you*? (Hodges & Connelly, 2010, p. 81).

If You Reject the Offer

Be professional. Thank whoever has offered you the position. If the person asks why you are turning down the offer, be as honest as you feel comfortable. For example, if the staff seemed rude, you might want to consider whether you would actually disclose that. If you are rejecting the offer because of salary, because you found a job that offers a better fit with your goals, or because you have found one in a preferred geographic location, that likely will not be as difficult to mention. Remember, the counseling profession can be very small, so do not burn any bridges.

If You Accept the Offer

This is the place all job seekers want to be; they have an offer and have decided to accept it. Now, your work is still not done. Anyone extending a job offer understands that a savvy candidate will attempt to negotiate the best possible terms. Many people, and this may especially be true of counselors fresh out of graduate school, may be uncomfortable with negotiation, especially during tough economic times. Determine what salary you and your family need, then practice negotiating with a career counselor or friend. Here are some things to keep in mind regarding negotiation:

- You may have been given a specific salary figure (likely). Your ability to move that figure upward will depend on what you have to offer (e.g., special training, related experience, publications), your apparent skill level, and how much the employer wants you.
- Beyond salary, what are the other negotiables? Is a costly move involved? Are you a dual-income family and losing one income with the move? Can the employer assist your spouse or partner in finding a job?
- How competitive is the benefit package? What and *who* does the health plan include (e.g., domestic partners, stepchildren)? What about the retirement package? If you are young do not discount this issue because it will become increasingly important over time. In fact, in my experience many Americans have inadequate pensions.
- How many vacation days do you receive per year? How many sick days?
- What type of annual salary increase or merit increase is offered? Will you have a probationary period? Does the job involve tenure, and, if so, what is the length of time before you can apply for tenure?
- What opportunity is there for advancement in this clinic/school/agency?

Nurturing and Managing Your Career   145

- Will the employer pay for you to receive additional training (e.g., attending conferences, workshops)?
- Regardless of what transpires, be courteous during the negotiation phase. Do not become rigid and make statements such as "This is my final offer!" Be flexible when necessary without giving in on everything. For example, you might be more flexible on salary, but hold the line on moving expenses.
- When you agree to a package, get the agreement in writing.

Your new employer will expect you to be enthusiastic when you begin. Be realistic and give yourself time to adjust to a new place, new colleagues, and new challenges. Remember that most people struggle in their jobs not because they lack the skill, but because of conflicts with co-workers (Bolles, 2015). Therefore, extend yourself to your new colleagues by asking for their input, ideas, and critique. Be respectful when you disagree in staff meetings, and learn to listen to people you find difficult.

Final Thoughts on Completing Your Internship and Beginning Your Professional Career

- Remember, your career as a professional counselor is just beginning. The first job you begin your career with is unlikely to be the one where you finish your career.
- Because you are new in the profession (e.g., recent graduate) and lack licensure (or certification for many school counselors), your initial job out of graduate school may not be one you stay with for the long term. However, remember that, although the initial job after graduation may not be ideal, it provides you the opportunity for professional growth and to receive supervision for licensure. State licensure and 3–5 years' experience give you professional mobility.
- Although graduate school experiences vary, many graduate students experience their counseling programs as nurturing environments. Do not expect your first professional job to be like your graduate program. In fact, it may seem fast paced and, at times, callous.
- Make sure to keep your résumé or CV current so that when more desirable positions become available, you are ready to apply. Advice: Try and stay in your first job a minimum of three-to-five years. This provides time to grow as a professional, become licensed/fully credentialed and suggests you are not just in and out the job door. Of course, life sometimes happens and one has to make adjustments.
- Take advantage of all trainings your school, agency, college, and so forth, has to offer. As a professional counselor, you should be a lifelong learner. Certificate trainings in specific clinical, legal, or professional issues are great ways to upgrade and expand your skills. Take advantage of these.
- If the agency, school, or college counseling center has a preferred treatment approach (e.g., DBT, cognitive behavioral therapy [CBT], solution-focused therapy [SFT]) keep an open mind about it, even if you prefer a different

146   *Nurturing and Managing Your Career*

theoretical approach. Working from a new theoretical modality also broadens your experience and enhances your clinical skills.

- Set some professional goals for yourself, such as to develop expertise in the treatment model you are learning (e.g., CBT, DBT), to develop harmonious relationships with the staff, to stay in the job for two years, to receive training in a new skill area, and so forth.
- Keep a folder of the applications you make for employment. Many students, especially doctoral students looking for an academic job, may make 20 to 30 applications. You want to keep the positions you apply for from merging together in your mind and a file of all applications filed can assist with organization. In addition, some search committees work slower than others do. I once applied for a job and did not hear from the search committee until six months later.
- Anytime you apply for a counseling position, be sure to examine the website of the organization.
- Use appropriate social medial sites for career networking. LinkedIn is one of the preferred networking sites career professionals use. LinkedIn is relatively easy and simple to use and provides an efficient way to link with colleagues in your area, state, country, and abroad.

Conclusion

Congratulations! You are nearing the end of your graduate counseling program and preparing for the job search. The good news is the demand for counselors is high and that translates into very good job prospects. Having said this, make sure you prepare thoroughly for all interviews. Even if you are unsure you want the job, treat it as if you do as such is valuable practice, and also you never really know what you will end up liking or disliking job-wise. I have experienced such a sea-change in my own career and many former students have informed me, "I thought I would hate this job and discovered the opposite." (The converse of this statement can be true as well.) So, be prepared for all interview and follow suggestions in this chapter and other valuable recommended resources.

Recommended Reading

Here are a number of texts I have used and found helpful in counseling students regarding résumé and cover letter writing, self-exploration, visioning career goals, and the job search process in general:

Bolles, R. N. (2015). *What color is your parachute? A practical manual for job-hunters and career-changers.* Berkeley, CA: Ten Speed Press (updated annually).

Capacchione, L. (2000). *Visioning: Ten steps to designing the life of your dreams.* New York: Tarcher/Putnam.

Enelow, W. S., & Kursmark, L. M. (2007). *Cover letters: Trade secrets of professional resume writers.* Indianapolis, IN: JIST Works.

Hodges, S., & Connelly, A. R. (2010). *A job search manual for counselors and counselor educators: How to navigate and promote your counseling career.* Alexandria, VA: American Counseling Association.

Parker, Y. (2002). *The damn good resume guide: A crash course in resume writing*. Berkeley, CA: Ten Speed Press.

Yate, M. (2007). *Knock 'em dead 2007: The ultimate job seekers guide*. Avon, MA: Adams Media.

Lessons Learned

I had recently completed my master's degree in Community Counseling and was well into my job search. Unfortunately, I was having no luck as I had yet to land a job offer despite scores of applications and several interviews. Granted, living in western Oregon, it seemed that every third person I met was either a counselor or social worker, so there was a lot of competition. What concerned me far more was that although I was getting the odd interview, I was not landing the job. My faculty advisor suggested I seek the services of the campus career center. A career center staff reviewed my résumé and cover letter format and, finding little of concern, made some peripheral suggestions before putting me through a mock interview. We developed the types of questions I had been asked in previous interviews and she role-played being the director of a mental health clinic. After a very realistic mock interview, she sat back and shrugged.

After commenting that she could not see any obvious problem with my interviewing approach, she then inquired about my follow-up, and the types of agencies I had applied to. Once again, she just shook her head. Unsure of what else to do, she suggested I just keep applying. "It's like getting a date," she began, "you might have a few rejections prior to someone saying yes." I nodded, stifling the urge to say I did not find her analogy very encouraging. Regardless, she had the right idea. I would keep applying; after all, what choice did I have?

I continue making application for entry-level counseling positions, expanding my search to the broader four state region instead of the immediate area. I was able to land several phone interviews, most of which seemed to go quite well, though all ended with me receiving a brief letter thanking me for my interest but stating they had hired someone else. Feeling even more discouraged, I returned to the career center and was assigned a different staff member—one who was actually trained in counseling. She suggested a few career counseling sessions focused on my "story" and also my self-care plan. I was unsure about her strategy but, having nothing better in mind, agreed.

I soon became more impressed with my career counselor. She had been in human resources for several companies before moving into higher education and completing a master's degree in counseling. She was well-versed in the hiring and firing of employees and knew hiring trends very well. Yet, despite the fact we developed a strong alliance, there were no *ah-ha* moments in our sessions. Then, on our third and final session, she gave what came to be the best advice that anyone had given. She suggested reading Richard Nelson Bolles' iconic book on careers. Now, upon her suggestion, I was unenthusiastic. I had leafed through the text previously and was unimpressed with it. While it was creative in an off-beat way, the text did not resonate with me. In fact, the drawings and format seemed chaotic at times. However, with absolutely nothing to lose, I checked out a copy from the university library.

148   *Nurturing and Managing Your Career*

Reading through the text I continued to be only mildly impressed at best. In truth, there seemed little helpful information for my discouraging situation. I was simply a job search loser whom no one seemed to want to hire. To make matters even worse, I was receiving all sorts of unsolicited, well-intentioned advice from friends and acquaintances. Some advice, such as informational interviewing, was sound, though I had already done much of that and still had no offers. One person, a corporate executive, opined I should just show up at various agencies, résumés in hand and demand to see the "man in charge!" No doubt I disavowed his advice without explaining the "man in change" usually was a woman.

I was going to return Bolles' book to the library but for unexplained reasons continued reading. Finally, a single page caught my attention. The author was explaining how job seekers needed to reframe each rejection as one more step closer to success. To illustrate this, he had a page with lines of the word No! printed on the page until at the lower right hand corner, in cardinal red was the word Yes! Suddenly, something moved in my very discouraged, learned helpless mind. I realized my attitude had to change, else I would continue to become more and more discouraged and eventually lapse into a depression. So, I immediately bought into the author's advice on reframing my sense of rejection. Then, I decided, each rejection is one step bringing me closed to an offer. I also began to ask myself what went well on this application or interview, what went less well, and how I could be more successful next time. Now, with a mere application and even an interview, it can be difficult to know how to improve. Still, a type of learned optimism, manifest in my improved self-talk, became my modus operandi.

If nothing else, I immediately felt much better. Everyone in my circle noticed my improvement. When I explained, I was met with furrowed brows as clearly no one saw this as anything significant. All were pleased I seemed more upbeat, however. I was finding my inner resilience and that made a huge difference. As the rejection letters continued, I stayed with my reframing of rejection. Then, out of the blue, a local treatment center called me for an interview. I had applied for the position so long ago I had forgotten about making the application. I went for the interview well prepared and, like most, it went rather well. The three staff members who interviewed me—a counselor, social worker and a lone administrator—all seemed pleased. In fact, at the conclusion of the interview, I was offered the job! Shocked at this sudden turn of fortune I immediately accepted it. I had been so focused on getting an offer, I had neglected the part on negotiating. Nonetheless, I was happy.

More than 30 years later, long after having moved on from my initial professional hire, I have retained my optimistic outlook. I can say that maintaining optimism in the face of discouragement can be very difficult. Daily, I practice reframing my negative self-talk in order to keep my mood upbeat. This is not to imply that grief, sadness, and discouragement are not part of my existence, as I am as subject to the whims of life as anyone else. The difference is that I know these challenging times will pass. That very knowledge has made a huge difference in the quality of my life. As I reflect back over three decades of my life, no one single strategy has ever worked as well for me as the simple reframing of my self-talk. The story I am telling myself has moved from one line to an entire autobiography. The lesson I learned is that success often comes through the crucible of defeat and discouragement. The best way through this personal and occupational brief patch likely lies in changing one's attitude.

You know, the easy part is changing my self-talk from negative to positive. The hard part lies in doing it every day for the rest of my life. Even when I do not feel positive, I force myself to change my inner story as I have discovered over and over that such an approach is worthwhile.

11 The Counselor as Leader and Activist

This chapter is an outlier from what most of you may have encountered in traditional counseling textbooks and journal articles. Having made that statement, this very text also is unusual in that I have primarily authored it as a narrative using the personal pronoun "I" as opposed to a traditional, impersonal APA style of writing. Traditional dispassionate, technical style is very important so as to be clear in research journals. However, there must of necessity be room at the counseling publication table for a more personal, essay-type style. The monthly periodical *Counseling Today*, as well as APA's *Monitor* are prime examples of essay-type writing. Likely, these reach far more counseling professionals than professional journals such as the *Journal of Counseling and Development* and the *Journal of Professional Psychology*, to cite a couple of notable examples. My point is not to denigrate research publications as they are critical to the success of the counseling profession. Moreover, I wish to emphasize ways individual counselors can take personal responsibility in the field. Furthermore, there are far more professional counselors in agencies, hospitals, schools, and chemical dependence treatment settings than counselor education faculty teaching in universities. In this vein, this chapter addresses the counselor as activist and leader in the community, school, agency, and university.

Back to the Past

During my master's degree program, the program had a required course titled something like, *Organization and Administration of Human Services*. The course was taught by one of my favorite professors and was very different from the corpus of the curriculum. In addition to a text, we also read from popular books such as *In search of excellence: Lessons from America's best run companies* (Peters & Waterman, 1982). A significant portion of the classroom discussion revolved around developing our own management style. This puzzled me as I had absolutely no intention of becoming a manager. Other than clinical supervision, I had no interest in running a clinic or other agency. But, for sake of the grade, my fellow students and I were forced to write a paper on developing a management style as part of the grade. Furthermore, classroom presentations were part of the schedule. As this was my last term in my master's program and was more than 30 years ago, I recall few specifics. What I have

The Counselor as Leader and Activist   151

never forgotten, however, is struggling to articulate a management philosophy and the realization that I have never previously considered myself a leader. I was a good supporter and adviser to leaders, but no leader myself.

Fast-forwarding to the present, my professional life has involved almost as much management and leadership roles as clinical and educational ones. My further experience is that all counselors in training must understand they will of necessity need to become facile in developing a management style in addition to a clinical supervision approach. Clearly, these two supervisory roles must of necessity be linked in a meaningful way and cannot be totally distinct. To my astonishment, I was hired to run a community mental health clinic after completing my doctorate degree! This opportunity could best be described as accidental, as I had gone on a job interview for a line counselor position in a rural eastern Oregon community. Once the interview began, the executive director informed me they had elevated the job to director of Clinical Programs, and the successful candidate would oversee all clinical functions: mental health, addictions, intellectual disabilities, the day treatment program, and evening crisis service.

Having prepared for an interview as a simple counselor, I was completely caught off guard and fumbled and stumbled my way through the interview. After the interview was completed and I commenced the eight-hour drive back to western Oregon, I found myself relieved. After all, having only run college residential living groups, and been completely unprepared to interview for a position I had not applied for, much less actually *run*, a clinic, surely they would select a more appropriate candidate. After all, *almost anyone* would have been a better candidate than myself at that point. At least, so I thought.

The following Monday while back at work, I received a call during my lunch hour. I was working for an agency where I provided career counseling and assessment and also assisted providing testing, counseling, and advising in the agency's alternative school. The call was from the executive director who had interviewed me for the clinical director position the previous Friday. Assuming he was making a courtesy call to inform me that he had decided on another candidate, I was only half-listening. Then, most shockingly, he offered me the job! So surprised, I asked him to repeat what he had said. He chuckled and did so. Recovering, I asked for a day to mull over the offer. In truth, the job was well out of my comfort zone as I had never supervised professional counselors in the work place, only master's degree students on clinical placements. I was planning to turn the offer down but realized this was indeed an opportunity. After talking over the offer with a close friend (who also was a counselor), I decided to accept the offer. Fortunately, the executive director was a good mentor, and I learned a lot about management during my time at the clinic. There were many challenging times and frequently I felt over my head with responsibility, but I stayed on. Thereafter, I ran a university counseling center and further honed my clinical supervisory and management skills. Later, as a department chair and coordinator of a counseling program, admittedly very different management roles, I continued to develop my management and supervision style. I actually refer to my supervision and management approach as Solution-Focused Supervision and Management. Essentially, I focus on the positive and build from there. Naturally,

152　*The Counselor as Leader and Activist*

I do have to address deficits and provide occasional discipline, but have found this style seems my best fit.

So, the rest of this chapter is devoted to making sure anyone reading this text does not get as blindsided by workplace realities as I was. Furthermore, I tell all students in our Clinical Mental Health Counseling and School Counseling programs to remember than one day they will be some kind of supervisor. They must select a supervision style that best fits them and develop a management style that assist them in addressing workplace conflicts, coaching employees, evaluating employees, and in hiring and, unfortunately, firing staff. Get ready!

Political Realities: What They Do Not Teach You in Graduate School

Several years ago during an internship class, the topic of politics emerged. It was late fall term and a presidential election was looming large. Coming from a politically active family where my grandfather and uncle had held state and county offices, I was dismayed to learn several of the students were not planning to vote. While I supported their right to choose not to participate, they needed a basic civics lesson. As they were on placement in mental health agencies, I inquired how many of their clients used Medicaid for reimbursement. (Note: A few of the students were Canadians, courtesy of our location on the US-Canadian border.) Several hands went up. Then I asked, where Medicaid originated from and none of these twenty-something students knew. After my brief history on Medicaid's origins, I asked them, "Okay, given that Medicaid's creation was a political process, what is our responsibility as counselors?" Some voiced the need to be up to date on current events while others pointed out Medicaid had been around longer than their parents. I admitted as much, then reminded them the Affordable Care Act provided mental health coverage many would not have had. This expansion of services also meant more clients for the agencies and thus more jobs for counselors. So, I reiterated the point regarding the political process and the counseling profession while careful to respect their political points of view.

At this point a couple were confused, as their parents opposed Medicaid expansion and the Affordable Care Act, aka "Obama Care." Several students however, admitted they had not considered the impact of politics on eligibility for counseling services, noting working poor likely could not pay out of pocket for counseling services. Then, I brought up the issue of Medicare reimbursement, which licensed counselors still lack. I asked if they know how the profession could get the right to bill Medicare. Sadly, only one knew, even after the talk on Medicaid. I explained the arduous political process of lobby the U.S. Congress, and how a Medicare reimbursement bill would need to pass both legislative chambers and be signed into law by the president. At this point, the light began to brighten in their youthful eyes. "Alright, so what can we do?" asked one. I turned the question back to the class and a healthy discussion ensued. The result of the discussion was that counselors need to study the health and mental health care positions of political candidates and that of political parties. By the end of the class, all agreed the intersection of politics and the counseling profession was very important. Now, not all agreed on particular politics, of course, as such is to be expected.

The Counselor as Leader and Activist   153

Politics has always had a profound impact on health, education, and welfare services (Hodges, 2015; Remley & Herlihy, 2016). Medicare, Medicaid, the Affordable Care Act, American with Disabilities Act, and most recently, Gay marriage (Obergfell *v.* Hodges, 2015, Supreme Court decision) are all examples of how the broader political landscape has impacted the counseling profession. More specifically, the Ward *v.* Wilbanks (2010) decision represents perhaps the best example of the legal-political impact on the profession. Julia Ward, a graduate student in Eastern Michigan University's School Counseling program, was dismissed from the program after she refused to counsel a student who was gay. Ward had refused the EMU counseling faculty's requirement she undergo a remediation process. The faculty agreed Ward, an evangelical Christian, had the right to her personal opinion. However, as the American Counseling Association Code of Ethics (2014) mandated clients not be discriminated due to sexual orientation and further that a values-based referral was also unethical. Now, an evangelical Christian counselor could retain his own personal opinion, but cannot impose that belief on the client or the counseling process. He would thus need to bracket off his views and focus on assisting the client.

The Ward case was decision in favor of EMU. However, upon appeal, the case was thrown out. Both parties eventually agreed to an out-of-court settlement. The ending of the Ward case, however, has left a murky legal picture. Counseling programs, especially those holding CACREP accreditation, hold forth with ACA ethics (or those of ASCA, AMCHA, etc.) and maintain the ethics of the EMU faculty. In the meantime, however, several states have passed "conscience" legislation providing values based referrals and barring counseling and related graduate programs from dismissing students on the basis of such (Wheeler & Bertram, 2019). state legislation of this type illustrates the impact of the political process on the counseling profession and that of psychology, social work, and related fields. Counselors will need to be informed of political candidate's agendas with regard to delivery of counseling and additional mental health services. The Ward case has spurred a stream of laws that fly in the face of the counseling profession's pluralistic nature, to say counter to the code of ethics. This legal versus ethical conflict has put counselors and many clients in a difficult position.

As I write this text, the current political situation in the country is quite volatile, with political and sectarian divisions running as deeper than any time since my childhood, when the Vietnam War and the Civil Rights Movement shook the country like a massive ongoing earthquake. As I was writing this chapter, the current US president made the statement that four female, Democratic members of the House of Representatives should "go back where they came from" (Dwyer & Limbong, 2019). The irony is that three of these Congress women were born in the USA and that the president is himself married to an immigrant and had immigrant parents seems to have slipped past many citizens, the media, and the president himself. Regardless of who makes such a statement, what political party that person fronts, and whatever office or position they hold, such an ignorant, hate-filled, discriminatory, fear-mongering statement poses great challenges for a large percentage of the population and a grave threat to a pluralistic nation. As conservative columnist George Will put it, you cannot simply undo hate-filled rhetoric with mere statements to the contrary (Cillizza, 2019). My point here is not that conservatives or Republicans cannot be good counselors. Rather, the emphasis here is understanding that a free and open democratic society is a wager that all persons are welcome, regardless of ethnicity, national origin, religion or lack thereof, sexual orientation, and so forth. This particular ethic is echoed in the profession's code of ethics (2014) and in all related mental health professions (e.g., AMHCA, ASCA, APA, NASW, etc.). So, the critical message herein is, how will you as a professional counselor advocate for the rights of the downtrodden? More to the point, how will you do so with those clients of a different political orientation, religion, or sexual orientation? If you have not been confronted by someone of great difference in a counseling session, then be prepared because at some point that will occur. Can you bracket off your values to provide counseling to a neo-Nazi mandated for therapy? How about that client who believes you are heading to hell based on your beliefs or unbelief? Pick the challenging type of client and consider how you will bracket off your values to address this person's needs.

Finally, what has moved the counseling profession forward is not merely the research studies validating the efficacy of counseling, but sustained political activism by counseling organizations such as the ACA, AMHCA, and others, and, of course, by individuals. Research evidence certainly is crucial, but political action for licensure, insurance reimbursement, civil service eligibility, Medicare reimbursement, and so forth. involves ongoing activism and lobbying efforts. Licensure in all states and three territories, for example, did not simply happen due to the good hearts and minds of elected officials (least anyone be so naive), but through step-by-step, ongoing, efforts by state and national counseling organizations (e.g., ACA, AMHCA, and state counseling affiliates, etc.) as well as individual counselors. So, be prepared to work through your local, state, and national organizations to effect change. Just recently, the counseling profession won the rights to maintain diagnosis in Licensed Professional Counselors' (LPC) scope of practice (Gray, 2019).

The ACA, AMHCA and numerous state affiliate organizations (e.g., New York Mental Health Counselors Association or NYMHCA in my state) are organizations that have strong track records of successful advocacy on the part of the profession. Your membership and active support of their legislative efforts is of the utmost importance to both the future of the profession and yours as well. The stronger the counseling profession, the better positioned you will be for an active and successful career. I strongly encourage you to maintain a lifetime membership in professional organizations (e.g., ACA, ASCA, AMHCA, and state affiliates) and to actively participate in legislative efforts to the extent feasible. If nothing else, utilize websites such as the ACA's Governmental Affairs. You can locate this important resource through the following link: (www.counseling.org/government-affairs/actioncenter) Remember, rights usually are won through a political process and while the counseling profession has been very successful in most right to practice endeavors (e.g., licensure, diagnosis, testing, etc.), many professional battles lie ahead. Most particularly, Medicare Reimbursement, and improving the diagnosis issue in several states.

So, for a viable and successful counseling career, be engaged in professional organizations and become politically active. We need thoughtful Republicans, Democrats, and Independents for a successful future.

So, You Are the Director or Clinical Director: Now What?

I wrote earlier about being an accidental director at a community mental health clinic. Once I accepted the position and commenced, I fully realized the magnitude of the responsibility. I was overseeing all clinical programs involving over 30 staff, grappling with the State regional psychiatric center, trying vainly to build a working relationship with the county Sheriff's department, plugging holes in our overly ambitious contract with the local State prison, and trying to build relationships with the local school district. In the midst of all this, I was also trying to carry a case load of ten clients per week as I wanted to continue practicing.

The first week, one of the counselors inquired about my management style. With no better answer, I replied that I planned to develop one. That same first week, three important independent contractors working in our prison outreach providing sex offender and addiction treatment abruptly quit over disagreements with another contractor. To make matters even worse, several counselors and social workers brought me a letter of complaint against one of the part-time psychiatrists, demanding he be fired. Had I not needed the job and had it not been for the guilt I would have for what this would do to the executive director, I just might have walked! Using the one day at a time 12-step philosophy, I survived.

I would like to say that my occupational life settled down and became much smoother, with few conflicts and that I felt that I was in the right place in the universe. Such a statement would be a total fallacy as some of the staff were in real conflict with each other. I held several mediation sessions which, although stressful, ultimately resulted in a lessening of tensions, though without resolving the underlying issues. Every day I wondered if I would last even six months in the job. How soon before a letter demanding I be fired was circulated? At roughly the six-month mark, the situation at the clinic smoothed out. The reason for this change occurred gradually. The staff began to see I wasn't about to just leave and due to putting in extended time building relationships, better relationships paid off. Some staff did leave, though most remained. Interestingly, when the youngest member of the treatment team put her stamp of approval on me, the remainder followed her lead. It was enlightening to observe that it wasn't the executive director's input, not the psychiatrist's, nor the longtime administrative assistant's influence, but rather the force behind a mid-twenty-something counselor. This forceful, bright, opinionated, and very talented woman was the linchpin to a more functional team.

You see it isn't always the person with the lofty title, the one with the MD after their name, nor even that of the most intellectual member of the team. My own experience as a director of two clinics, line counselor, and volunteer in many agencies and remote schools overseas, is that it is the people who best know how to create and nurture friendships. The persons with the titles may reap the credit (or blame), but the catalyst sometimes are like the young woman above. They are the ones who actually move the agenda forward or stop it in its tracks. So, my advice to those reading this chapter is job number one likely will be to discover who the "doers" in your school, hospital, or agency are and cultivating a strong working alliance with them. Had I not developed such a positive relationship with the

156   *The Counselor as Leader and Activist*

youngest member in the clinic, my tenure as clinical director likely would have been a fast and abysmal failure. Fortunately I had just enough of what Daniel Goleman (1995) calls emotional intelligence or EQ to get past my nascent ego. You will need a strong sense of EQ and good emotional regulation so as not to over-react to potentially flash-point encounters with upset clients, staff, and outside persons. I also recommend a good, ongoing self-care plan that you make daily use of. So, be prepared!

Supervising Counselors and Related Professionals

If you have been newly promoted to a supervisory role, there are many considerations you will wish to entertain. First of all, if you were promoted as an internal candidate, as many in agencies are, your role is somewhat more complicated. The advantage to an *inside* promotion is that the said person knows and understands the agency, its staff, strengths and weaknesses. The disadvantage is that lingering conflicts can make the supervisory role muddied. More concerning perhaps, are the colleagues you may have had friendships with as equals. Suddenly, you are now the boss and along with the role change will come relationship changes. Staff members who may have been you friends become annoyed that you no longer socialize with them on weekends or hang out with them in the break room. On occasion, you must provide critical feedback to them regarding their performance, perhaps even discipline them for infractions, and god forbid, fire them for insubordination or unethical behavior. Many times in my academic and practice career I have witnessed a popular counselor or professor ascend to the level of supervisor only to suddenly find she is no longer popular and may even be viewed as the enemy! The outside hire will carry with her previous expectations and in this regard may feel freer to make changes without the same level stress. After all, she does not have the weight of previous friendships to cause stress. (There will be other kinds of stress of course!)

There are various supervisory methods to use with practicum/internship students. The type of supervision provided will mostly depend on the orientation of the on-site clinical supervisor. Although numerous studies have been conducted on the effectiveness of supervision on counselor development, no evidence supports one methodology being superior to another (Granello & Granello, 2007). Interestingly, only once in my entire counseling career has anyone ever asked me, "What is your theoretical supervision style?" This question was asked of me at an interview for a faculty position in counselor education, not in a treatment facility. But, when you become a supervisor, be prepared to articulate a particular theoretical supervision style. In fact, my belief is that most supervisors in the field would likely be stumped at such a question. I have actually discovered this by querying clinical supervisors and been met with furrowed brows or statements to the effect of, "well, I have my own style." Probably, your field supervisor *has* developed his or her own style after several years of experience both in being supervised and in providing supervision. Most supervisors are likely influenced most by the persons who supervised them during their graduate school training or an influential supervisor when they were a newly minted counselor or other therapist. The next section of the chapter briefly reviews some of the more common approaches to clinical supervision for readers' consideration.

Bernard's Discrimination Model: One of the most commonly employed and researched supervision models is the Discrimination Model, originally published by Bernard (Bernard & Goodyear, 2009). The discrimination model is composed of three separate foci for supervision (i.e., intervention, conceptualization, and consultant) and three possible supervision roles (i.e., teacher, counselor, and consultant). The supervisor could, in any given moment, respond from one of nine ways (three roles × three foci) (Bernard & Goodyear, 2009). For instance, the supervisor may take on the role of teacher while focusing on a specific intervention used by the supervisee in the client session, or the role of counselor while focusing on the supervisee's conceptualization of the work. Because the response is always specific to the supervisee's needs, it changes within and across sessions

The supervisor first evaluates the supervisee's ability within the focus area, and then selects the appropriate role from which to respond. Bernard and Goodyear (2009) caution supervisors not to respond from the same focus or role out of personal preference, comfort, or habit, but instead to ensure the focus and role meet the most salient needs of the supervisee in that moment. Supervisors utilizing the discrimination model must be very organized and mindful regarding the supervisory relationship and be clear as to what role they are "playing" out with the supervisee.

Psychodynamic Approach to Supervision: Psychodynamic supervision is based upon Freud's model of transference and countertransference (Frawley-O'Dea & Sarnat, 2001). Frawley-O'Dea and Sarnat (2001) further classify psychodynamic supervision into three categories: patient-centered, supervisee-centered, and supervisory-matrix-centered.

Patient-centered, based on Freud's model, focuses the supervision session on the patient's issues and behaviors. The supervisor assumes a didactic role with the goal of assisting the supervisee to understand and treat the patient. The supervisor is viewed as a dispassionate expert and thus an authority figure. As long as the supervisee agrees with the supervisor, less conflict is inherent (Smith, 2009). Given that the psychodynamic supervisor is posited as an authority figure, some supervisees may have difficulty voicing disagreement, particularly if they are struggling with confidence—something not unusual with beginning counselors. Likely, most counseling students are not under supervision from a psychodynamic supervisor (although some practicum and internship students may well be supervised by such, especially in large urban areas).

Supervisee-centered supervision, which focused on the content and process of the supervisee's experience, became popular in the 1950s (Falender & Shfranske, 2004). The supervisor's uninvolved, authority role remains the same, but as attention is transferred to the supervisee's experience as a counselor, the approach becomes more experiential than didactic (Falander & Shfranske, 2014). Still, as the supervisor remains the distant authority figure, the supervisee remains in the position of the "inferior." Now, proponents of the psychodynamic-based supervisor would point out that all supervisors would be the authority figure regardless of the supervision model

158 The Counselor as Leader and Activist

utilized. While this point is true (or should be), the model may lend itself more to a scrutiny than a process-oriented conversation.

The supervisory-matrix-centered approach differs in that, in addition to focusing on the client, it also addresses the supervisor–supervisee relationship. No longer is the supervisor and austere, uninvolved expert. The relationship is very relational with the supervisor expected to actively participate in establishing a two-way conversation with the supervisee (Frawley-O'Dea & Sarnat, 2001). The relationship also involves an examination of parallel process, defines as the supervisee's interaction with the supervisor that parallels the client's behavior with the supervisee as the therapist.

Feminist Model of Supervision: Feminist theory asserts that an individual's experiences are reflective of society's dominant values, attitudes, and opinions (Brown & Brodsky, 1992). Feminist counselors view the client's experience with context of society. Thus, anxiety, depression, BPD, and so forth. may be viewed as a consequence of an oppressive society (Brown & Brodsky, 1992). Many feminist counselors are ardently opposed to the *DSM* as a tool of a patriarchal society (Haynes, Corey, & Moulton, 2003).

Feminist supervisors then may counsel the supervisee to acknowledge power differentials in the client–counselor relationship and encourage the supervisee to understand the role of privilege. Given the supervisor holds a position of power over the supervisee, the relationship may form grounds for more collaborative discussions, at least to the extent possible. Feminist supervisors may also focus on empowerment of the supervisee and in turn facilitate the counselor's working to empower clients, many of whom may live along the margins of society as disempowered individuals, couples, and families. Feminist models of supervision have become more popular in recent years.

Integrated Developmental Model: The Integrative Developmental (IDM) Model of supervision developed by Stoltenberg, McNeill, and Delworth (1998) is a popular and well-researched supervision model (Smith, 2009). The IDM describes three levels of counselor development:

> Level 1: supervisees are generally entry-level students who are high in motivation, but also high in anxiety and fearful of evaluation;
> Level 2: supervisees are at mid-level and experience fluctuating confidence and motivation, often linking their own mood to success with clients; and
> Level 3: supervisees are essentially secure, stable in motivation, have accurate empathy tempered by objectivity, and use therapeutic self in intervention.
> (Falander & Shfranske, 2004)

The IDM emphasizes the need for the supervisor to select skills and interventions appropriate to the level of the supervisee. When supervising a level-1 supervisee, the supervisor would want to balance the supervisee's anxiety and dependence by a display of support and direction. If supervising a level-3 supervisee, the supervisor would emphasize autonomy and engage in a more constructivist discussion. The critical factor in IDM is in matching feedback with the supervisee's appropriate

The Counselor as Leader and Activist   159

level, otherwise the supervisee may feel either overwhelmed or restricted. A supervisor who refuses to engage in more parallel conversation with a level-3 supervisee is likely to encounter a high degree of frustration and resistance. Likewise, a supervisor who expects autonomous behavior from a level-1 supervisee likely will increase the supervisee's anxiety.

The IDM has become a popular supervision model and offers many advantages, especially in breaking down supervisees into working stages of development as such may make sense to supervisees. IDM however does have weaknesses as it focuses predominantly on the development of graduate students in training and pays little attention to post-degree supervision (Smith, 2009). Furthermore, IDM present few suggestions for specific supervision models that are applicable at each specific supervisee level. An alternative development model developed by Ronnestad and Skovholt (2003) addresses IDM initial weaknesses by providing a framework to describe counselor development.

Ronnestad and Skovolt's Supervision Model: The Ronnestad and Skovholdt model is based upon a longitudinal qualitative study conducted by interviewing 100 counselors/therapists, ranging in experience from graduate students to professional counselors/therapists with a mean of 25 years counseling experience (Ronnestad & Skovholt, 1993). Ronnestad and Skovholdt analyzed data and developed a stage model, a theme model, and a professional model of development and stagnation (2003). The first three phases (The Lay Helper, The Beginning Student Phase, and The Advanced Student Phase) essentially correspond with the levels of the IDM (Smith, 2009). The remaining phases (The Novice Professional Phrase, The Experienced Professional Phase, and the Senior Professional Phase) are self-explanatory in terms of the relative occurrence of the phase in relation to the counselor's career.

In addition to the phase model, Ronnestad and Skovholt's (2003) research enumerated 14 themes of counselor development. They are as follows:

1. Professional development involves an increasing higher-order integration of the professional self and the personal self.
2. The focus of functioning shifts dramatically over time from internal to external to internal.
3. Continuous reflection is a prerequisite for optimal learning and development at all levels of experience.
4. An intense commitment to learn propels the developmental process.
5. The cognitive map changes: Beginning practitioners rely on external expertise, seasoned practitioners rely on internal expertise.
6. Professional development is a long, slow, continuous process that can also be erratic.
7. Professional development is a life-long process.
8. Many beginning practitioners experience much anxiety in their professional work. Over time, anxiety is mastered by most.
9. Clients serve as a major source of influence and serve as primary teachers.
10. Personal life influences professional functioning and development throughout the professional life span.

160   *The Counselor as Leader and Activist*

11. Interpersonal sources of influence propel professional development more than "impersonal" sources of influence.
12. New members of the field view professional elders and graduate training with strong affective reactions.
13. Extensive experience with suffering contributes to heightened recognition, acceptance and appreciation of human variability.
14. For the practitioner there is a realignment from self as hero to client as hero.

(Adapted from Ronnestad and Skovholt, 2003)

Ronnestad and Skovholt (2003) conclude that counselor development is a complex process requiring continuous self-reflection. They also conclude that much like the counselor–client therapeutic alignment robust influence on treatment outcomes, their results suggest a "close and reciprocal relationship between how counselors/therapists handle challenges and difficulties in the client relationship and experiences of professional growth or stagnation" (p. 40).

Cognitive-Behavioral Supervision: Just as CBT has become a very popular approach to counseling, cognitive-behavioral supervision is likewise common (Haynes, Corey, & Moulton, 2003).Cognitive-behavioral supervision makes use of tangible thoughts and behaviors, particularly that of the supervisee's professional identity and his or her reaction to the client (Haynes et al., 2003). Cognitive-behavioral techniques used in supervision include setting an agenda for supervision sessions, bridging from previous sessions, assigning homework to the supervisee, and capsule summaries by the supervisor (Haynes et al., 2003). The supervisor–supervisee relationship is akin to that of teacher–student and though is collaborative is directive with the supervisor leading.

Person-centered Supervision: Carl Rogers developed person-centered therapy with the belief that the client has the capacity to effectively resolve life problems without interpretation and direction from the counselor (Corey, 2017). Similarly, person-centered supervision assumes that the supervisee has the resources to develop effectively as a counselor. The supervisor then is not viewed as an "expert" in the person-centered model but rather as an experienced collaborator. The supervisor's role is to establish an environment whereby the supervisee can be open to the supervision experience in order to develop fully as a clinician (Lambers, 2000).

Solution-focused Supervision: Solution-focused brief therapy was developed as a therapeutic approach in the 1980s by de Shazer (1994). As the name suggests, the approach focuses on being brief and focusing on solutions as opposed to a focus on target problems. Therapeutic attention is devoted to building on the client's idea of a future goal and discovering the inner resources needed in order to achieve this goal (de Shazer, 1994).

To review, here are some common Solution-focused techniques:

The Miracle question: "If you woke up tomorrow and a miracle had happened and the issues of concern were no longer a concern, how would your life be different?"

Exceptions: "What's different when you are not drinking?"

Scaling Questions: "On a scale of 1–10, with one being low and ten high, how would you rate this counseling session?" Then the follow-up question of: "How could we raise the score one point next time?"

Acknowledging difficulty: "I can see that this issue has been very challenging for you."

Noticing improvement: "Okay, between now and next session, I want you to notice what's improved."

Graduating from therapy: "How will you know when you no longer need to come to counseling? What will be the evidence you are ready for graduation?"

(Kim-Berg & Szabo, 2005)

The Solution-focused approach lends itself well to clinical supervision as well as in counseling as the interventions are easily transferrable to clinical supervision encounters. The following constructivist questions might be utilized in supervision:

"So, how were you able to help the client improve their mood?"
- "How were you able to gain confidence this past semester?"
- "What have you learned about yourself during your practicum/internship/job?"
- "What would you cite as your clinical strengths?"

When addressing the supervisee's strengths, resources, and skills, the supervisor adopts the persona of the curious inquirer. For example, asking how the supervisee managed a particular situation, despite the challenges faced, enables the supervisor to acknowledge their ability to identify skills utilized in order to identify the particular solution.

One of the Solution-focused staples is the Miracle Question. Regarding a focus on specific goals, the supervisee may be asked, "If you went to sleep tonight and a miracle occurred related to your confidence as a counselor (or any issues of concern) where you were more confident, how would your work as a counselor be different? What would you notice? What would I notice?" The Miracle Question provides the format for the supervisee to drop anxiety and speculate on future success (Kim-Berg & Szabo, 2005).

Subsequent supervision sessions focus on solutions rather than problems. Soliciting, "What has improved?" at the onset of a supervision session, as opposed to "How are things?" encourages the supervisee to focus on their clinical growth. At the conclusion of the supervisory session, the supervisor summarizes the supervisee's strengths, skills, and improvement. The Solution-focused supervisor provides feedback based upon the supervisee's choice of language. Thus, the importance of active listening coupled with constructive type responses is highly emphasized. The following suggestions are offered regarding Solution-focused supervision:

- Utilization of active listening to what the supervisee is saying. (Example: "I hear you saying you are concerned about this client's ongoing depression.")

162　*The Counselor as Leader and Activist*

- Using constructivist-type responses to assist the supervisee identify, strengths, skills, and inner resources. (Example: "If you could bring that client into the supervision session right now, what might you say to them now?")
- Using encouragement by actively demonstrating interest and encouraging a more collegial supervisory relationship, though not an equal one. (Example: "You are making a good effort with this recovery group. Now, here's something to think of next session …")
- Citing and naming specific supervisee strengths, skills, and resources. (Example: "You have a made a lot of progress in confronting relapse.")
- Use of scaling questions to assist the supervisee in measuring clinical growth. (Example: "On a scale of 1–10, with 10 high, how would you rate your counseling skill at this point?")

The point of a Solution-focused supervisory approach into clinical supervision is to enhance the supervisee's experience and lessen their degree of anxiety thus enhancing the likelihood the supervisee will develop more confidence and competence. As the Solution-focused supervision approach is more collegial, supervisees may report feeling less anxiety during supervision sessions. It is also likely, however, that some supervisees may find an "over focus" on strengths limiting and may at times prefer explicit criticism. Research on the Solution-focused supervision model is not as extensive as more established models and more research in needed in this area of the clinical supervision literature.

Systems Approach to Supervision: In the systems approach to supervision, the crux of the supervision relationship targets mutual involvement of both parties (Holloway, 1995). Holloway describes seven dimensions of supervision: (1) central supervisory relationship; (2) the functions of supervision; (3) tasks of supervision; (4) the client; (5) trainee; (6) supervisor; and (7) the institution. The function and tasks of supervision are at the foreground of interaction, while the latter four dimensions represent unique contextual factors that according to Holloway are covert influences in the supervisory process. Supervision in any particular instance is viewed reflective of a unique combination of these seven dimensions (Smith, 2009). Thus, a systems approach to supervision covers multiple levels related to the various intersecting "systems" in which the supervisee and client exist. Examples of systems may be schools, businesses, correctional institutions, religious institutions, culture, families, and so forth.

Supervision Styles

You may discover that your field site supervisor may have a radically different style than one supervising your classmate. Some on-site supervisors are quite formal and require a student to tape an entire session. Others will listen to a brief segment of a tape, or none at all. Some supervisors will ask students to work on a particular skill, such as delivering confrontation or using a particular intervention. Supervisors vary greatly across the continuum of styles, opinions, theoretical approaches to counseling, and in how they deliver feedback (i.e., constructivist versus overtly negative in feedback).

The Counselor as Leader and Activist   163

It is clear that in the supervisor–student relationship, the power differential rests with the on-site supervisor. Thus, students must become facile in negotiating a delicate balance of appearing open to critique and at the same time developing appropriate assertiveness. Openness to critique would involve listening to feedback that may be critical. The assertiveness aspect of the student role would be to ask for clarification if he or she were unclear of the message. Consider this example:

Supervisor: I need you to work on the treatment plan more, ok?
Practicum student: I would like to do that. What specifically could I do to improve my performance in this area?

If you do not know what your supervisor is suggesting, or if he or she seems vague (such as in the given situation), seek clarity by asking questions. Good supervisors will appreciate your initiative. Granted, there are poor supervisors out there and some of you will have the misfortune of working under them. Having a poor supervisor, however, also provides you the opportunity to learn to deal effectively with such professionals, as you will encounter them in your career. When you do get a supervisor who seems to be a poor communicator, is overly critical, sloppy, or seems burned out, you need to find a "safe" area to debrief this. Safe areas could include other practicum or internship students and fellow graduate students in your counseling program.

If you believe your supervisor is incompetent or unethical (as opposed to merely ineffective), your first step would be to talk with your faculty advisor or the coordinator of practicum/internship placement (ethical issues are discussed in Chapter 3). Your advisor would then need to have a dialogue with your on-site supervisor or the director of the setting in which you have been placed. In many cases, a healthier relationship can be established, although, in some, you will likely be assigned a new supervisor. It is also possible that you may need a new placement, although that should be a last resort. It has also been my experience that in most cases (although not all), addressing conflicts with your supervisor paves the way for a more trusting and respectful relationship.

Theoretical Approaches to Supervision: Questions for Self-reflection

With regard to the previous reviewed clinical supervision approaches, consider the following questions:

1. Of the supervision styles profiled in this chapter, which style seems the closest "fit" for you? What makes that approach a good fit for you?
2. Beyond theoretical supervision approach, what additional attributes should a clinical supervisor possess?
3. For readers who have been through clinical supervision, what qualities did you appreciate in your supervisor? What areas could your supervisor have done a better job in? Finally, given what you have learned from your supervisor(s), how might the experience inform your own development as a clinical supervisor?

Professional Legal and Ethical Liability

Clinical supervisors in the universities (counseling service and Counselor Education faculty), agencies, schools, and hospitals are vulnerable to an array of legal and ethical challenges (Wheeler & Bertram, 2019). All clinical supervisors regardless of profession must be acutely aware of the additional liability they carry due to their advanced education, years of experience, and the professional role they have undertaken. Clinical supervisors must provide clear guidance to graduate interns and professional counselors and therapists in a clear, unambiguous manner. Bernard and Goodyear (2004) have provided a useful definition of supervision:

> Supervision is an intervention provided by a senior member of a profession to a more junior member or members ... This relationship is evaluative, extends over time, and has the simultaneous purpose of enhancing the professional functioning of the more junior person(s), monitoring the quality of professional services offered to the clients that she, he, or they see; and serving as a gatekeeper of those who are to enter the particular profession.
>
> (p. 8)

This definition underlines the special level of responsibility clinical supervisors provide not only to supervisees, but also in protecting the public. The ACA Code of Ethics (ACA, 2014), begins with an important statement regarding responsibility: "The primary responsibility of counselors is to promote the dignity and welfare of clients" (Section A.1.a). Standard F.1.a also states, "A primary obligation of counseling supervisors is to monitor the services provided by supervisees. Counseling supervisors monitor client welfare and supervisee performance and professional development." The ethical and legal ramifications are thus clear for anyone assuming the role of supervisor. Thus, supervisors must of necessity be well-educated, appropriately trained, and experience enough to assume such risks. As a supervisor or future supervisor, you will be held to a higher standard than supervisees. In fact, should a lawsuit be brought against a supervisee, it is most likely the supervisor will be named in the suit (Wheler & Bertram, 2019). This is known as vicarious liability and is based on the legal doctrine of *respondeat superior*, a Latin phrase which means the supervisor assumes responsibility for the supervisee actions. So, are you still interested in becoming a supervisor?

I can speak to the above Latin in a very personal manner. One day while at a clinical supervisors meeting two hours away, the counselor serving the daily on-call function neglected to interview a woman brought to the clinic on a civil commitment to the State Hospital as required by that state's law. Now, the supervisee had been trained in and state certified to initiate civil commitments but just made a grievous error in judgment! The woman's family sued and the case was settled out-of-court. Not only was the counselor in legal "hot water" but so was I as her supervisor. Fortunately, as all were operating as agencies of the clinic, we were covered. Further, as the clinic had far more resources than either the supervisee or supervisor (me), the clinic was named in the suit.

The Counselor as Leader and Activist   165

This was not to be the only unfortunate legal and ethical experience I was to have as a clinical director. In another case, I received the phone call no supervisor ever wants to get. In fact, fittingly, it was early on a Monday morning. As I was working on my second cup of coffee, an assistant warder from the local State prison called me. He informed me that he had good evidence one of our counselors providing counseling services to the prison had been having an affair with an inmate. I was shocked and unable to speak, as he filled me in on the details. Evidently, the inmate was a trustee and eligible for parole soon. The counselor allegedly had been driving the inmate to a seedy motel where they were having an affair. Just when matters couldn't get any worse, they got worse: the accused counselor had seemingly been a model contract employee (meaning she was not full time) and a very skilled clinician despite her young age. I cannot recall many specifics of the conversation thereafter as I was too shocked by the call. Fortunately, the counselor in question was scheduled to meet with me that very afternoon for a supervision session!

When she arrived, I appraised her of the accusation and that, upon the advice of the county attorney, she needed to obtain separate legal counsel. I also notified her she was suspended with pay until the investigation was complete and that I would need to notify the State License Board. Finally, after informing her she had a right to tell me nothing, I asked what had happened. Then, she broke into tears. Surprisingly, she denied the affair, though I certainly didn't believe her. She then left my office. Given eyewitness accounts of motel employees, her wallpaper-thin denial fell apart quickly. The least she lost was her license! Once again, as a supervisor, I was charged with addressing the fallout from a supervisee's poor ethical judgment. Incidentally, in some states, an affair with a client is a felony often resulting in prison time. Should the client be a minor, the prison time would be substantial and the counselor required to register as sex offender when released.

As a former director of two clinics, longtime professor who created and has taught professional ethics for 20 years, and served on the Ethics Revision Task Force (ERTF) that revised the current ACA ethical code, ethics have been central to my life. They are central to yours as a counselor and even more as a clinical supervisor. To drive this point home, I have my ethics class take a "no sex with clients" pledge. Most find it humorous, but the point is very serious. I further emphasize that should they violate ethical boundaries by having an affair, I will not write license boards nor magistrates asking leniency for them. The media is far too full of counselors and related mental health professionals, including professors of Counselor Education, who cross the ethical DMZ for their sexual gratification. You must make sure you follow professional ethics and do not become a member of this dubious fraternity.

Suggestions for Maintaining Healthy Boundaries for Supervisors and Counselors

1. Remember: The supervisor–supervisee relationship is a professional relationship and not a friendship. The relationship may be friendly, but is first about professional development of the supervisee and protecting the public. Maintain this professional and ethical boundary.

166　*The Counselor as Leader and Activist*

2. Similar to the previous, the counselor–client is a professional relationship governed by ethics and not a friendship. The relationship may be friendly at times, but is all about the client's personal development.
3. For supervisors, have at least a couple of colleagues to consult with should your objectivity as a supervisor be a concern. Choose colleagues your trust to be ethical and who will give sound, thoughtful counsel and not those who may simply tell you what you wish to hear.
4. Related to the previous, should you find you are becoming overly interested in a supervisee, seek consultation. You may even wish to seek counseling to address the issue. Finally, should your objectivity be compromised, you may need to refer the supervisee to another supervisor.
5. You must develop a healthy self-care plan to get your personal needs met. In addition to a healthy diet and exercise, and social support is critical. Likely, self-care is the most violated tenet of the ethical code. Develop friendships and cultivate personal relationships with appropriate people.
6. Find personal meaning through pursuits such as hobbies, journaling, spiritual communities, and any other healthy endeavor.
7. Read, understand, and live your professional life in congruence with your professional code of ethics. This practice will save you a lot of personal, professional, and legal grief.

Additional Considerations for Supervisors

A. Develop a supervision contract for the supervisee's learning objectives. Make sure these objectives are measurable for clearer assessment.
B. Provide your supervisees a clear understanding of your supervision style (e.g., Solution-focused Supervision, or another) and your theoretical approach to counseling.
C. Define the activities the supervisee is to be evaluated on. This list would certainly include counseling (individual, groups, couples, etc.), but might also include psychoeducational presentations, clinical intakes, or another professional activity.
D. Set the day, time, and location of each supervision session and main this schedule regularly.
E. Provide protocols for crisis intervention, legal or ethical concerns, and reasons for dismissal.
F. Keep clear and consistent records of each supervision session.

Hiring and Firing Staff

As the supervisor, you likely will be changed with helping to hire and sometimes fire staff members. Having been charged with both responsibilities, I can speak from experience in expressing the former is far preferable to the latter. You must, however, understand the relationship between hiring and firing. First of all, having interviewed scores of student applicants, professional counselors for hire, faculty

The Counselor as Leader and Activist   167

members, administrators, and certainly more than 20 years of interviewing clients, I have developed a reasonably fair (I believe so anyway!) method of assessing candidates. Having made the previous statement, however, interviewing is a very inexact science at best. In fact, my counsel on hiring and firing staff will be quite brief as this text is more about other issues. Hiring, evaluating and firing staff is a critical function, though likely written more completely in other texts. However, I will offer some basic considerations.

Each month for the past 25 years, potential employers call me for references for current and former students. I find these calls most enlightening for what I am asked and often what I am not asked. Some questions are expected such as, "Is this person dependable?" Virtually every potential employer asks me this question in some manner. Now, I tell all students that if I cannot provide a strong recommendation, I will not serve as a reference. This protects the agency or school, the applicant, and myself as well. Almost all callers ask how long I have known the applicant and how did I know that person? Most ask me about the applicant's work ethic, which is certainly predictable, though surprisingly not all ask this important question. Only a few, likely the more astute supervisors, ask me about the applicant's attitude towards accepting critical feedback. Frankly, this would be one of my highlighted questions were I hiring counselors. Another surprise, is that seldom am I asked about the applicant's ability to work across cultures. I would certainly ask this question as it is especially important in urban schools and clinics. Finally, I cannot recall ever once being asked about an applicant's grades! Funny, what with all the pomp and circumstance regarding grade point averages, graduating with honors, wearing honor chords at the graduation ceremony, employers do not ask about this area. One might then question, what grades actually mean with regard to working in the profession (outside of being Counseling Education faculty). So students, give your academics your best effort while in your program. Remember, however, that regarding landing the job, other attributes will take precedent. This usually includes, performance on practicum and internship, work ethic, attitude, cultural competence, and your ability to develop resilience.

Now, if I were hiring again, I would ask about attitude right off the bat. Nothing will be more important as a healthy frame of mind sets the tone for everything else. The same is true of an unhealthy frame of mind also. I would want to know about work ethic of course, but also how well they get along with others and how they manage conflict. I would ask about the applicant's ability to manage stress and maintain healthy self-care (I would ask each applicant about these as well of course). Finally, I would ask, "Would you hire this person and why?" To my memory, suspect as it is at my age, only one supervisor has ever pitched me this question. So, as I have said, what is not asked may be far more valuable than what is asked when it comes to references. Should be in a position of hiring counselors, do your due diligence and dig deeper by asking the types of questions that provide more background information on an applicant.

Firing will be a far more complicated and stressful experience than any hiring you will do. The reason is that you just never know when someone you fire will threaten or even initiate a lawsuit against you. Now, terminating employees should

168 *The Counselor as Leader and Activist*

not be too easy as then employer abuses would be more likely to occur. In fact, employer abuses are a real concern in the workplace, even in mental health settings. Regarding firing, there is no doubt that it is an unfortunate, unpleasant experience for all involved. Basically, it hurts the employee, often hurts the supervisor and may leave residual resentment among colleagues of the terminated employee. Firing should also be the last resort after a correction plan, coaching, additional training, and clear benchmarks for the employee to achieve. This means that unless the counselor or other employee has, say, had sex with a client, termination is a process not an immediate experience.

When you become a supervisor, you will need good supervision and consultation so that you can manage the challenges and stresses of supervising and terminating staff. I would definitely recommend you cultivate a supervisor or more experiences mentor/consultant who can guide you through the process. No doubt, school or agency legal counsel will be a significant part of your life as a supervisor as employee relations require thorough knowledge of the school or agency due process policy and strict adherence to that policy (Wheeler & Bertram, 2019). Ideally (and nothing is *ideal* in firing employees), the terminated employee would not be surprised to be fired. As we likely all know, fired employees often are shocked to lose their job, sometimes even when they have committed grievous offenses (read, sex with a client, stealing from the school/agency, abusive behavior, etc.).

Regarding termination, it is also fair to say that many people are wrongfully fired by abusive or capricious employers for sometimes the most frivolous or even false claims. Think also of women in the workplace who have been fired for refusing to have an affair with their supervisor. Think of those predatory supervisors who were able to get away with such egregious, abusive and illegal behavior. So, in such cases, one can sympathize with the occasionally intrepid former employee who hits back with a lawsuit. So, with all this information in mind, the following are some common sense steps you need to take prior to terminating a counselor or other employee.

1. Take time to talk: Moreover, make sure you actively listen to the employee you are having concern with. In addition, make sure that person understands your concerns.
2. Create an action plan: Create an action plan to correct the employee's behavior. The plan should have clear benchmarks the employee can aim for. This way, she/he understands what is required and provides the employer necessary information should termination be necessary.
3. Take corrective action: As previously noted, firing an employee should be the last option. Create a mentor for the employee—someone other than yourself—and have that mentor meet regularly (weekly or twice monthly) with the employee in question. The goal is for the mentor to help coach the errant employee to make the grade and retain her or his job.
4. Regroup: How well is the correction plan working? How is the employee doing meeting the bench marks? What does the employees mentor/coach say? Finally, how realistic is it the employee will be able to retain her/his job?

5. Reflection: Okay, has the employee made enough progress during the correction time to keep her or his job? If the answer is no or is not close enough to warrant more time, you likely will need to make the difficult decision to fire the employee. Naturally, second chances are important for most of us in this occupational life. However, if the employee cannot or will not change, do not be afraid to terminate that person. Furthermore, failure to fire an employee for cause may send an unhealthy message to co-workers and hurt agency or school morale.

6. Check with legal counsel: Naturally, you need to check with legal counsel prior to terminating an employee to make sure you have followed school or agency policy. Failure to follow due process could very well result in litigation against you and your employer.

(Adapted from Boykiv, n.d.)

Finally, I would encourage all readers to view their development as a supervisor and administrator as a process. That is, new responsibilities will require time for adaptation on the part of the employee. So, to use a mindfulness-based approach, give yourself time to adapt, use healthy self-talk, seek counsel from a mentor, and be nonjudgmental on yourself.

Lessons Learned

During my first year in the master's in counseling program, one of our classes was treated to a guest speaker. The man was a graduate of our counseling program and had been working in agencies for over a decade. I recall almost nothing about his presentation other than one particular part of counsel. At one point near the conclusion of his talk, he asked, "Okay, how many of you want to be counselors?" After glancing at one another in puzzlement, virtually all 30 (or so) hands went upward. "Alright," he continued, "in five to seven years, if you are doing well, most of you will be administrators." This latter statement was a shock to my ears. I recall thinking that I did not get into the counseling program to be a desk jockey! Afterwards, several of my class mated voiced similar sentiments. After all, most of us were young, idealistic, and anticipated careers working in direct line service in agencies and schools. The last thing I wanted at that point in my occupational life was to become a paper-juggling administrator.

I put the man's talk out of mind and went about getting through my master's, getting hired, then into the doctoral program three years later and working my way through the remainder of my education. I provided individual and group counseling in a variety of local agencies, was a graduate teaching assistant in Counselor Education and also the Psychology Department and generally put in my time until finally I completed my doctorate. I was hoping to land a position in a small college counseling center, but was not having much luck. Then, as I alluded in this chapter, went to an interview for a line counseling position in the rural mountain west. As previously mentioned, upon arriving to the interview, was informed the job had been upgraded to that of clinical director and was I still interested? In my mind, the

170 *The Counselor as Leader and Activist*

answer was "No!" The reality of my situation, however, was that my current counseling position was on a contract that was set to expire in another month. Thus, I explained my interest in hearing more regarding the position.

It was an odd experience to have prepared for an interview for an advertised job only to arrive at the interview and be informed the job description and classification had radically changed. One particular perplexing question was, "Why would you be interested in become a clinical supervisor?" In reality, the question had never entered my mind as I had applied and prepared for a different job! In fact, such was precisely my answer. Somehow—perhaps the abrupt change—the director and addictions manager seemed to view my response as both honest and appropriate. Still, one would expect such an answer would mean my candidacy would be torpedoed! Albeit, a candidacy I had neither imagined nor desired.

Making the eight-to-nine-hour drive home, I actually gave little thought to a job offer as it was clear I was scarcely management and supervisory ready. In fact, I had only supervised college and graduate students in academic programs and in residential living communities. My focus was on a continued job search. Much to my surprise, however, the executive director called me the following day when I was back at my job. Although I was expecting it was simply a courtesy call to inform me a rejection was imminent, the man then offered me the job! Shocked, I was momentarily hit with aphasia and unable to speak. Finally, I croaked out the excuse of needing to think about it overnight. He gave me three days to give him an answer.

I was totally uncertain of what to do and felt myself in a real quandary. I had no interest in becoming a clinical director as that involved supervising professional staff and taking on all sorts of scheduling, supervising, mediating, and other administrative responsibilities, and sounded like a real headache. All I wanted was to counsel people in need. The reality was, however, I needed a job. This was a challenging job with a decent salary and benefits and one that perhaps I could grow into. But, the responsibilities seemed so far outside my comfort zone. Thus, I sought out the counsel of a more experienced colleague. He was a seasoned professional and, in fact, a clinical social worker who had served in many roles throughout his career in the field. We had worked together at one agency, with his providing supervision and consultation to me. I had come to value his thoughtfulness and cool headedness.

He listened patiently to me as I outlined the job and my concerns regarding taking on the role. Finally, after a long monologue by me, he sat back in silence for a long moment before asking, "Why do you think they offered you the position?" I responded having wondered the same, but figured it was only because they were desperate. He chuckled, then offered the reframe of, "So perhaps they see you as the best candidate?" I shrugged and said something to the effect of, "I guess so." Both of us had a good laugh at my lack of confidence and enthusiasm. He continued his thought. "Look, this is an isolated rural location and likely you are the best they can get. So, if you turn it down, they may get someone even less qualified." He let that thought sink in. "This is your call, but it does represent a good opportunity for growth." He suggested I take the time provided and give the matter serious thought. "Make the best decision you can make. Remember, none of us were originally supervisors. We all began somewhere."

The Counselor as Leader and Activist 171

I talked the matter over with a couple of close friends and thought about it in my own mind. No doubt, the job was well beyond anything in my background and more than I had anticipated. Eventually, my thoughts returned to the presenter's prediction a decade earlier regarding my becoming an administrator. I wanted to counsel and grow in my clinical skills. If I were to bite the bullet and accept the job, my requirement would be that I also would carry a small case load of clients. After three intensive days of mulling it over, I called the executing director and accepted the job on the caveat I would also see clients. Surprised, he agreed to my stipulation.

As was mentioned in the chapter, I had *many* struggles in my role as clinical director. During the first six months, I considered quitting on a daily basis. There was a constant stream of crises: suicidal threats, staff conflicts, conflicts with outside agencies, challenges with the State Psychiatric Hospital in our rural region, hostility from our local hospital, and a litany of other issues. My main joy was in providing counseling to a variety of clients. Fortunately, I began to grow into my supervisory and administrative roles. The staff began to find me valuable—or at least valuable enough. After a year, I could honestly say that I enjoyed the role of clinical supervisor. No doubt, the responsibilities of the job wore me down, most especially evening crisis calls and addressing staff conflicts, and fencing with the State Hospital system. There were days when my management plan was no plan other than surviving the day and hoping direction would come the following morning. Fortunately, the ability to survive the day seemed to give me enough stamina to follow up the next day.

After a couple of years in the role, I was provided the opportunity to direct a university counseling center—something much closer to my heart and interest. But I was only offered the opportunity to return to higher education because I had been offered the position of running clinical programs. Having spent every week addressing crisis situations (e.g., suicide threats, dealing with violent clients, sex offenders, courtroom testimony, etc.), I was far more confident in my ability to manage difficult situations. There were *many* lessons learned during the arduous process of growing into my role as a clinical supervisor and administrator. My most significant take-away, however, is that we must at times take occupational risks that may be a stretch for us and perhaps leave us feeling somewhat uncomfortable, at least for a time. Had I gone with my initial inclination and turned down the job, my occupational and personal life would likely have turned out very differently. My belief is that things would have gone well, and I would have found an entry-level counseling position. It is unlikely, however, that my career would have taken the upward trajectory without this challenging and eventually rewarding job. So, here's my counsel for readers. When confronted with an opportunity such as I had, take time to think it through. Seek the counsel of someone who knows you well and has far more experience. Listen to that person's advice. If you need it, seek counseling for additional insight. Finally, you are the person who has to make the decision of whether or not to accept a supervisory role. Are you ready? I did not believe I was ready, but others thought differently and fortunately I was able to adapt, albeit with much difficulty. So, I will leave you with a few self-reflective questions for consideration.

172   *The Counselor as Leader and Activist*

1. What would be your motivation for accepting a position of director or assistant director in an agency, hospital, or school?
2. What excites you most about this offer? For example, would it be the salary, increased responsibilities, a bigger office, or something else?
3. If you were to solicit the advice of three people with more experience, would they recommend you take the position? Why or why not? (Naturally, you would be wise to seek out an opinion from such people.)
4. What would make you a good candidate to become a supervisor or administrator?
5. If a close friend of equal qualification to you were to seek out advice on whether they should or should not accept the offer as assistant director or director, how might you counsel them?

Let these and other related questions be your guide to scaling the occupational mountains and valleys of your career.

12 Healing the Divided Self

This text, and most especially this chapter, is intended for counselors serving on the front lines in schools, mental health clinics, hospitals, private practice, as well as the college and university settings of counselor educator professors, and in counseling services. This particular chapter is devoted to addressing both solitary reflection and collegial dialogue within and beyond the workplace. Essentially, it is to encourage counselors to open their hearts and minds so they will be better equipped to learn life's lessons when dealing with challenging clients, colleagues, and supervisors. In essence, our lives are full of rich learning experiences if only we can reframe difficulties as opportunities to learn and grow. Admittedly, this is far easier to speak and write about than to put into regular ongoing practice. This chapter is intended to serve as both a springboard and guide for counselors in training, professional counselors in the field, and those teaching in graduate counseling programs. It is hoped that this chapter will offer a variety of approaches to help readers explore the inner landscape of a counselor's life. As people can vary significantly with regard to what they find meaningful and fulfilling, this chapter is not a "decision tree" for a purpose-driven life, but rather offers examples for consideration.

The Inner Life of a Counselor

One might reasonably ask: why embark on such a journey in the first place? My rationale is that counseling is a profession that demands sometimes intense self-reflection regarding our personal motivations, ethical practice, and one's ability to work effectively with people who sometimes do not want our assistance. Counseling, perhaps like teaching, the ministry, and other notable service work, emerges from one's inward journeys, for better or worse. As I teach and counsel, I project the condition of my attitude onto my clients and students. The rewards and entanglements I experienced in counseling sessions in particular are part and parcel of the convolutions of my inner life. Viewed from this perspective, counseling holds up a mirror to the psyche. If I am willing to peer into that reflection, and not shrink from what I see, my opportunity for personal and professional self-growth is exponential. More simply stated, self-examination leads to self-understanding and is crucial to providing effective counseling work (Rogers, 1977).

174   *Healing the Divided Self*

Naturally, this focus on the counselor's inner life is not exactly a conventional approach to providing counseling assistance to clients. There is little doubt, however, that the more at peace we are with ourselves, the more effectively we are likely to be in addressing human needs in the clients we serve. As professional supervisors and educators, we often focus on the "hows" and "whats" of counselor training and supervision. For example: "What theoretical approach should I use?" "What particular technique should I employ with a client in grief?" Such questions are very relevant to the type of work we provide. But seldom, if ever, do we ask the following questions: Who is the self that provides counseling to needy persons? How does my selfhood form the way I relate to my clients, my supervisors, supervisees, and colleagues? Furthermore, how can this self-knowledge help counselors sustain and deepen the selfhood from which quality counseling emanates?

This chapter will contains self-exploration exercises to invite the reader to explore the inner landscape of their life along the distinct but related pathways of affect, cognition, and behavior, also known as the ABC of counseling. In addition to the building blocks of self-exploration and counseling, readers will explore the way we think about counseling and change. By affect, we mean the way we feel about ourselves and our clients. By cognition, how does our self-talk frame the lens in which we view clients and their distress? By behavior, how do we come to address issues in our own lives so that they do not impede progress between ourselves and our clients? As challenging cognitions, emotions and behaviors are part and parcel of the human experience, counselors certainly are not immune from these intrusive thoughts, emotions, and challenging behaviors. Our responsibility lies in becoming more mindful of how these ABCs impact our personal lives with loved ones and professional relationships with clients and colleagues.

Without question the journey to a deeper self-understanding of the self is lifelong and goes far beyond the pages of this chapter. Likely, this personal trek is life-long and involves much introspection, training, mentoring, education, and reflecting on and learning from joys and disappointments. As with any longitudinal journey, our lives have their difficult passages, sometimes leaving us to ponder if we have lost our way. Losing our inner direction, or perhaps our sense of purpose and meaning, may be where Frankl's Existential Vacuum (1969) enters our lives. My own experience suggests that the more familiar we become with our inner landscape, the more emotionally balanced, satisfying, and confident our lives and our counseling work likely will become. By embarking upon this inner journey, we can begin to practice responsible self-care and contribute to our own wellbeing and that of the clients we serve. Remember as well that by our actions we model healthy and unhealthy behaviors to our supervisees, colleagues, students, and clients. No counselor should need to feel pressure to strive for unrealistic and unhealthy perfection. Rather, be mindful as to whether your affect, cognitions, and behaviors are mostly congruent. Others certainly will notice.

The Authentic and the Divided Self

In his brief though useful book *Let Your Life Speak: Listening for the Voice of Vocation* (2000), Parker Palmer writes about the divided self and its impact on humans,

Healing the Divided Self 175

especially educators. Throughout his brief, though thought-provoking book, he often references himself as one having grappled with this division between one's true self and the ego-driven persona and its protective masks and self-serving facades. Palmer advocates that teaching is in itself a vocation, or calling as some would call it. He speaks of the Latin meaning of the word vocation, which is voice (2000):

> Vocation does not mean a goal that I pursue. It means a calling that I hear. Before I can tell my life what I want to do with it, I must listen to my life telling me who I am. I must listen for the truths and values at the heart of my own identity, not the standards by which I live- but the standards by which I cannot help but live if I am living my own life.
>
> (pp. 4–5)

Palmer's words hold much value for those of us in the counseling profession as well. While one might well debate the belief of counseling as a calling, a voice, if we follow his thinking, there can be little disagreement that understanding oneself though intensive self-reflection, through our own counseling work, and through a personal, even spiritual awakening, can be part of discerning one's vocation. In well over two decades of counseling clients from children to the elderly, in remote overseas communities as well as in the USA, I have had a front-row seat to the inner struggles of the human condition. That people chafe against how they see themselves, versus the person others desire them to be, seems to cut across all cultures I have encountered. Now, cultures vary with regard to rugged western individualism as opposed to a collectivist, eastern, and indigenous approach. Nevertheless, many persons of Asian, indigenous, and other cultures have disclosed to me their struggles with the divided self, whether of their own or another's construction. As one sixty-something indigenous woman from Australia's remote Arnhem Land said to me, "I felt torn between the life I wanted as a teacher and the role my family expected me to adopt." I recall a graduate school classmate saying that her biggest struggles had not been in her failed marriage nor her strained relationship with her family of origin, but that she had failed to become herself. For her, leaving a lucrative banking career to become a school counselor meant she was finally living her own life. Or, as a middle-aged male client in recovery expressed, his greatest failure lay not in his inability to maintain sobriety but in his failure to become himself. He went on to detail how the anesthetic of alcohol had been his coping mechanism, albeit a very destructive one that impacted and practically destroyed every area of his life.

The concept of an authentic self goes back thousands of years, of course, but I recall Carl Rogers writing some of the most cogent pages about it. In his seminal opus, *On Becoming a Person: A Therapist's View of Psychotherapy* (1961), Rogers recounts the fear many of his client's expressed in delving into an intense exploration of selfhood. He goes on to write that many fear discovering something unappealing, and perhaps frightening, through the uncovering of self during the process of counseling. However, Rogers tells us his clients came to appreciate their humanness, both in their personal strengths and their frailties. The operative question then becomes, what is this authentic self and how does one go about discovering it, and then living in harmony with it? Likely, there are numerous ways for self-exploration

176   *Healing the Divided Self*

and discerning our authentic live. Frequently, I have found open-ended questions helpful in the explorative phase. I have listed such sample questions below. These questions address the authentic self and also how that self is manifested in who we are as counselors.

The Authentic Self

1. Consider the question, *Who am I?* In a journal write whatever you believe this question means for you. That could be personally, occupationally, spiritually, financially, culturally, sexually, and so on.
2. Regarding terms such as the *authentic self*, what does such a term mean for you?
3. If you were to write a journal entry about your authentic self, what would you write? Another way to think about this is: *Who do you say you are?* Or, who are you as opposed to who others in your life want you to be?
4. How does (or might) understanding my authentic self-assist me as a counselor?
5. When did you first understand you wanted to be a counselor? What led up to that understanding of vocation or as Palmer calls that *voice?*
6. What do I stand for as a counselor? Beyond professional ethics, what do I value as a counselor?
7. What do I want my legacy as a counselor to be?
8. Consider an influential counselor. What do you recall most vividly about that counselor? What kind of impact has that counselor had on your own decision to become a counselor?
9. What do you consider the most important quality for a counselor to possess?
10. What is the most powerful experience you have had in your life? How has this experience helped shape who you are as a person?

To complete the thought regarding the authentic self, it must be admitted that there is no end point where a person ceases growing. Rogers once wrote that as beings we are always in a constant process of development and never quite a finished product (1961). In essence, we never quite reach self-actualization, even though we may be self-actualizing in our thoughts and behaviors. The same principle can certainly be applied to one's development as a counselor: namely, that we are always growing, improving, and becoming skilled at our clinical work. How much we develop and improve depends upon our work ethic, self-reflection, ability to take feedback, attitude, self-talk, and our willingness to lean from our clients among others. So, make periodic time to consider your authentic self. Consider keeping a journal on this question and seek counsel from persons who know and understand you well to discuss the matter.

Walking the Talk: A Must for Counselors

Regarding the previous section on the authentic self, certainly part of that self-involves living our values. Understanding and living out one's values in service to society goes well beyond any professional field or high salaried job. There can be

Healing the Divided Self 177

neurosurgeons who fail to live out their values and janitors who exemplify positive values in action, with the latter being more important to society than the former. In fact, at one university where I served as director of Counseling Services I saw this in action. There was a custodian at the university who was a very special person. She had been a military veteran, was an Emergency Medical Technician (EMT), and had a really calm disposition. She not only did her job very well, and college students and faculty can sometimes be very messy and careless regarding spills, dropping trash, failing to recycle properly, and so forth. Anyway, I will call this person "Jane." Jane always did her job without complaint and found a way to mentor students. She explained to me that she particularly kept her eye out for freshmen and transfers who were new at the university. As a middle-aged female, she became a natural resource for younger students and many students, female and male, sought her counsel. Not infrequently, students who presented at Counseling Services were referred by her.

One day while leaving the building she served, we spoke, as she was on a break from her broom closet turned office. I inquired as to whether she had ever considered becoming a counselor, given she was such a natural helper. She thanked me for the compliment but replied that she felt she could do more good in her current job. She went on to express she could be as much older friend and mentor as anything else and felt more comfortable and helpful in this role. She also made it clear she was not interested in greater social status, more money, or any other traditional trappings of success. "I just want to do my job and help others," she said. Interestingly, during my tenure as director of Counseling Services at this small, rural institution, her name was frequently mentioned by students or the staff as being the most helpful person on the campus. Furthermore, I can recall the odd professor whose arrogance caused a lot of hurt for the students we counseled. While constructive criticism certainly plays an important role in educating students, not all criticism falls into such a constructive category. Admittedly, I did not know the entire situation regarding the occasional student complaint about a faculty member, although a couple of names were regularly brought up as problematic by several students. This simple custodian was doing a far greater service to the students she encountered than these unnamed faculty members. In fact, when one considers it, the very term *custodian* lends itself very ably to human development. Jane walked the walk of a good custodian—one who cared for and effectively mentored the students in her care. There were indeed some faculty members who would have done well to have emulated her example. I can only hope some of the students I counseled found me as helpful, though I wonder.

For counselors, living by the ACA Code of Ethics (2014), or another related professional code, is essential for long-term practice. No doubt, it is imperative for counselors to understand and be able to refer to the code of ethics as a guiding document. Ethical practice is important in reducing liability and also in practice that is in the client's best interest. We must further understand that people are watching us as examples for the profession we serve. As we honor ourselves we honor the counseling profession, as we disgrace ourselves, we do likewise. This is not to say that counselors must take on the profession's banner in such a hefty, all-encompassing

178   *Healing the Divided Self*

manner. In fact, such a belief is unhealthy and impossible (Ellis, 1999). The more reasonable issues are living our professional lives consistent with our code of ethics and perhaps even more important understanding our own inner code of ethics. The next paragraph illustrates this case in point.

I was a very impressionable young counselor, freshly graduated from a program on the west coast. I had taken a job at a residential psychiatric facility serving children and adolescents. Proud of this challenging job, I worked very diligently to improve my skill and of necessity to impress my superiors. This administrator was someone I liked and respected from the onset. He was very intelligent and having served in a variety of clinical roles at the center for over ten years was well-seasoned. He particularly impressed me as someone who could related well to the children and adolescents in the center. Occasionally, we would be in the break room at the same time and I appreciated his willingness to inquire about my wellbeing, especially as pertaining to the job. I found myself observing his interactions with colleagues and the children. More and more I was impressed as this fellow was clearly the high watermark of what a therapist should ideally become. I longer to be like this role model and have the thoughtful answers to challenging adolescents (I worked with older boys) that I as a neophyte counselor clearly lacked at this point in my nascent career. I idolized this person and placed him upon a high pedestal in my mind. I recall thinking that perhaps one day I too could be so therapeutically gifted.

Then came that fateful day when my therapeutic world unraveled. This center's executive director was accused and later convicted of sexually abusing numerous children over a 20-year period. The initial news and later conviction, was like that of an earthquake rumbling through a community of unstable buildings and structures. Practically all of the top management were fired from their jobs, and numerous others quit in disgust. My role model, the man whom I held in such high regard, was also fired. He had not been accused of abusing any children, and child protection services made that clear. However, he had failed to intervene regarding the former executive director's questionable behavior. As the stories filtered through the media, my mentor's judgment seemed far less than what I had made it out to be. I wondered what had happened to this intelligent, skilled, seemingly compassionate clinician. A couple of years later, I happened to be taking a graduate psychology class with a former colleague and one of the longtime staff from the center. My former role model's name came up and my former colleague shook his head. While acknowledging the man's intelligence and the good things he had accomplished, he made the statement, "He failed to walk the talk." That is, this smart, skilled, likable, and successful person, was not the persona he projected to the outside world.

I relate this painful chapter from my past not as any way of scapegoating someone. I harbor no desire to gather stones, as managing my own behavior has been a full-time job. Nevertheless, this example from more than 30 years ago has served as a warning siren in my ears. I consider my former colleague's comment regarding a superior's failure to walk the talk. As one who served on the task force that revised the American Counseling Association's Code of Ethics (2014), the siren blares even louder in my ears. Weekly, I teach impressionable students, regularly make conference presentations, volunteer in overseas locations annually, and write and publish much prose regarding the counseling profession. I try to ask myself regularly, "Am I walking my talk?" The most honest answer I can come up with is the unimpressive, yet accurate statement that "I am doing my best." Likewise, if you are a professional counselor, counselor educator, counselor-in-training, or someone considering the profession, are you walking your talk?

The Heart of a Counselor

Although he is not a counselor, I continue to reflect on the writings of Parker Palmer. His book *Let Your Life Speak: Listening for the Voice of Vocation* (2000) is a brief, though rich and thought-provoking book for the philosophically minded counselor. Within just over 100 pages, Palmer describes ways in which teachers and other professionals can start to uncover their authentic self. He writes that vocation is not a goal one pursues, but rather a "calling" one hears (2000, p. 4). Most interestingly for counselors, Palmer writes of the problems and distortions of the ego ("ego" in the common sense, not the Freudian term). A section that particularly speaks to me comes in the first few pages in the book:

> Behind this understanding of vocation [inner truths] is a truth that the ego does not want us to hear because it threatens the ego's turf: everyone has a life that is different from the "I" of daily consciousness, a life that is trying to live through the "I" who is its vessel. This is what the poet knows and what every wisdom tradition teaches: there is a great gulf between the way my ego wants to identify me, with its protective masks and self-serving fictions, and my true self.
> (Palmer, 2000, p. 5)

Palmer's words could very well be written about counselors, teachers, lawyers, or any other profession. My own experience is that professionals in service occupations, and I include counselors within this list, must do their own due diligence to make sure they heed that inner voice of truth to which Palmer alludes, while discarding the masks of egoism and inflated self-importance. One can conceptualize this inner vocation in numerous ways. I choose to refer to it as the heart of a counselor and, although I am scarcely as eloquent as Parker Palmer, it is essentially a very similar process of discernment as is that of vocation to Palmer. To illustrate this point, I must return to my counseling practicum class of 1986. A very seasoned, thoughtful doctoral student was teaching my practicum class. There were four or five other students in the class, mostly female, with significant variation in age and experiences. Our instructor and supervisor, whom I will call Sue, had worked for over 20 years as a child and family counselor in California. She had a gift for initiating trust and my confidence in her grew as the term progression. Near the end of the practicum, one of the students asked what they should do when confused regarding treatment. Sue naturally referenced our code of ethics, and speaking with one's supervisor. She then went on to say that each of us has an inner counselor in a state of development. That internal sage's wisdom is honed through education and most especially through experience. This inner counselor is also influenced by our own values and

180   *Healing the Divided Self*

ethics, as well as our attitude. Consequently, this inner counselor develops an intuitive sense of how to guide us in therapeutic encounters. She continued that when faced with dilemmas in counseling, we should seek the counsel of this inner guide and learn to heed her calling.

I recall the small group of students, different as we were, finding that an interesting way to consider resolution. I recall a classmate from Asia querying, "How do you know whether to trust this inner counselor?" Sue's response was strikingly similar to Palmer. "I usually know when the answer comes from within my gut and not through my ego." To continue along this philosophical line, our ego represents our own insecurities and defenses—walls we construct to protect ourselves from the simple truths we feel too vulnerable to face. I understood Sue's comments were not about simply truisms and clichés, but that likely the "best" answers come from a place of being grounded in our own being, and not from an egocentric position as an all-knowing expert. As an individual, counselor, counselor educator, and professional consultant who has spent his lifetime climbing out of the abyss of doubt, Sue's words frequently return to me in times of self-doubt. This doubt is a natural human response to challenges we all face in our lives, whether when counseling clients, supervising staff or students, teaching in teaching in counseling programs, or providing consultation services. My six decades on terra firma have taught me that doubt is a reality and will make its presence known at times. As a counselor or counselor educator or related professional, doubt is my signal to step back and look within. Any forthcoming answers may not be easy or simple ones but they likely will be from a more grounded and less ego-driven place.

At this point, the topic of mindfulness usually emerges. One might well inquire, "So, is the heart of a counselor all about mindfulness?" The best answer possible is that "It depends on what is meant by mindfulness." For my part, I prefer John Kabit-Zinn's definition of mindfulness. He speaks of mindfulness as paying attention, on purpose, resent moment, intentionally, nonjudgmentally (2013). He goes on to write that he sometime adds the terms "self-understanding" and "wisdom." I have to think that discussions of wisdom are about as common as that of discussions regarding the heart of a counselor. That meaning, rare, though less so in the present day. Therefore, mindful counselors are grounded in present time, and paying attention with a nonjudgmental focus. Kabit-Zinn has less to say regarding what he means by the term "wisdom," but perhaps we could speculate that it involves a sense of compassion while understanding one's personal and professional limitations. Likely, a mindful counselor will also be aware of the importance of keeping healthy boundaries with clients, as well as with colleagues. Mindful counseling practice likely would imply letting go of perfection-seeking, removing the protective mask of egoism, and relating authentically to clients as a resource person walking alongside their journey and not some sage pretending to have all the answers.

Many years ago while attending a national counseling conference, I had an interesting experience during an educational session. Now, it is noteworthy to confess the actual topic of the presentation has eluded me as this was nearly two decades ago. Yet, what I retain was an exchange between the presenter and the audience. Early in the session, the presenter made a statement that went something like "We

Healing the Divided Self   181

can make no definitive statements," at which point someone in the audience percep- tively called back, "Except for the one just made." Then the verbal fireworks began! Yet, despite this somewhat antagonistic exchange, I was struck by the presenter's philosophical approach espousing no central truths. The presenter, upon regaining his composure, went on to more evenly and eloquently discuss the therapeutic need to train clients to question what they have been taught, particularly when what they have been taught no longer works for them. Regarding this latter point, I found myself in general agreement with the presenter. While the presenter likely was making the point from a post-modern perspective, I commenced thinking along broader lines. That is, is there any universal constant, either in therapy or beyond? My initial path towards the monastery and monastic life maintained a belief in a universal truth, although I had had my doubts. My experience is that sometimes essential truth often lies at the precipice between two competing points of view. To consider this matter further, let us examine it in the following paragraph.

Fritz Perls (1969) was known for comparing psychotherapy to that of peeling away the layers of an onion. You continue finding layer after layer, some tougher, some more fragile, and some that will leave you weeping. Naturally, my own spir- itual upbringing taught me about universal constants, as all spiritual approaches certainly do. But as counselors, as humans, and certainly as faculty, we tend to question everything. Perhaps the only universal constant is that of questioning, doubting, searching, debating, and thinking long on the vagaries and challenges of the human condition that is the constant. As counselors, whatever our spiritual beliefs are or are not, our job is to facilitate the client's growth through a process of attending, therapeutic presence, open-ended questioning, and promoting healing and emotional growth through the crucible of the counseling encounter. Perhaps, then, mindfulness may be the most important trait to maintain during counseling, teaching, or presenting to one's colleagues. That is, while providing therapy, teaching, or training, we should maintain a present-oriented, nonjudgmental, *wise person* approach that makes room for alternate beliefs as, we simply may not have precise, easy answers. In fact, as a counselor for well over two decades, I often find people's lives messy, unduly complicated due to deceptions, residual anger due to trauma or addiction or both, and many former clients, especially those mandated, often want nothing from me. "I don't want your fucking help!" as seemingly a legion of mandated clients, addicts and former inmates have screamed at me. What little wisdom I have developed, during the past 30-plus years since entering the coun- seling profession, lies in my ability to seek out the inner guide that Sue taught my classmates and me decades ago. For me, returning to my inner guide (or counselor) always involves briefly stepping back from the brink of conflict, ego defenses, anger and other baser emotions, and offering up a meditation for assistance. I recognize that while writing about mindfulness and related topics my prose may give the impression of sounding banal. While admittedly life has taught me I know very little, counseling experience has taught me therapeutic success is as much about human understanding and connection as about *DSM* diagnoses, treatment plans, or particular therapeutic approaches. Theoretical approaches, *DSM* categories, and developing sound treatment plans certainly are important in counseling—make

182 *Healing the Divided Self*

no mistake about it. My own belief, however, is they are not the sine qua non of successful therapy.

The heart of a counselor is a journey into deeper self-understanding, while simultaneously jettisoning the personal baggage of ego, hubris, and the need to be admired by clients, colleagues, or students. While I have never forgotten Sue's sage advice, I am sadly inarticulate in my ability regarding the *how* of developing one's inner counselor. You will simply have to walk that valley alone, with occasional guidance from faculty, knowledgeable elders, academic study, and perhaps more than anything else, an attitude that in all interactions—be they with clients, students, or colleagues—you have something to learn as well as impart.

Lessons Learned

I had been working in the counseling field for a few years, mostly doing contract and summer work as I went spelunking through my doctoral years. In addition to providing individual and group counseling for public organizations, such as child protection services, a homeless shelter, a pastoral counseling center, and a university counseling center, I taught as a graduate assistant in the separate departments of counselor education and psychology. My fledging career was challenging as everything was built around doctoral study and the Sisyphean task of writing the dissertation. One of my more interesting jobs was at a local agency that served a variety of human service functions. Although I was originally hired as a vocational-employment counselor, my duties quickly expanded to tutoring in their alternative school, teaching at the youth job club, interviewing displaced timber workers, marketing ex-convicts and other adults with a poor job history to potential employers, providing site visits for teen work experience, among various and sundry duties. I spent one year working at this agency prior to doctoral work and for five summers during my doctoral years it was my standing temporary job.

Despite the itinerate nature of my position and the widely varying range of my responsibilities, I had a generally good experience. Likely, my most memorable experiences lay in providing career counseling and teaching at the youth job club. Every one of my students (officially, "participants") had academic difficulties and many were high school drop-outs trying to earn a General Equivalency Degree, more commonly known by its acronym GED, and get a job. The occasional participant had spent time in juvenile detention and, sadly, a few likely matriculated to prison. I had initially been gifted the responsibility of teaching at the summer job club for teens when the full-time staff member had gone on stress leave during my first summer at the agency. No doubt, the job was stressful, as eight to ten teens, several of them rowdy, filed in ready to give the instructor a challenging time. Due to my seeming success in fulfilling this function, meaning no violence between participants, the agency assigned me to teaching Teen Job Club every summer (along with many additional responsibilities!).I had grown up in impoverished circumstances in rural Arkansas where rowdiness was simply a way of life. As a socially awkward adolescent who struggled to find his place in a family of six boys with grandparents who were overwhelmed, I understood adolescent angst and blues. My MO was to establish a relationship in the first day of class and keep working at it throughout the duration. As classes ran for three weeks, 1:00 to 4:00 p.m. every Monday through Friday, there was ample time to work on relationships. Frequently, I discovered the tough guy/ girl act merely papered over an intense vulnerability. My students were almost universally from impoverished, single-parent families, with some placed in foster care, and many have been emotionally, physically or sexually abused, if not all three. Substance abuse was the primary means of coping and several were under mandatory drug screenings at the local mental health authority. Such were my students! Coming from a family of teachers, I well understood that some students stand out in a teacher's—or counselor's—mind for a variety of reasons. More than anyone during those summers, Adam (pseudonym) was that student.

The first day of job club, he stomped into class wearing his animosity like a poorly fitting garment. Adam was a tall, muscular, bi-racial adolescent male who sported a shaved head, combat fatigues, and ebony storm trooper boots so shiny you could comb your hair in their reflection. Most notably, he wore a chain that hung from his earring to his lip piercing. His animus seemed to shout, "Let's see you fuck with me!" I merely nodded at his entry and began class with my usual spiel, and then asked the class to introduce themselves. Naturally, Adam, who sat fuming in silence, was the last to speak. "Just here because they made me," he replied with a snarl. "Well, glad you're here," I replied. He looked skeptical as ever at this. After all, to him I was a young, naive-looking, educated, white fellow who knew nothing of his world. Frankly, he was right about much of that.

The first day was simply going over expectations: come on time, no smoking—a common issue though none were old enough to smoke legally—nor other drug use, no profanity, fighting, and all were to respect the instructor. This list of "don'ts" always drew snorts and guffaws from the class. I explained to them that successful completion meant they would be placed in a paid work experience and such would also provide one credit towards a high school diploma. The money was a far bigger carrot, needless to say. Upon dismissing class, I noticed that Adam continued to stare at me with a mix of hostility and what I interpreted as indecision. After work, a colleague and I stopped by at the coffee shop across the street. This coffee shop was well known as an alternative, counter-culture shop, where many of the grunge high school and college crowd hung out. As I sat down with my colleague, I noticed Adam sitting across the room. He seemed surprised to see me. I nodded and after a brief hesitation, he nodded stiffly in return.

As the week progressed, I noticed a slight thaw in his demeanor towards both his classmates and myself. As I wished them all a good weekend, he almost started to wish me one in return. Nothing of note had occurred during the week, which in itself was noteworthy! No fights, screaming or otherwise, no one *caught* smoking, and almost everyone had been on time. Adam, oddly enough, was always the first to arrive, though he would sit in mute silence, black sunglasses on his eyes until class began. He had offered only minimal tests of my authority and seemed disappointed I had said nothing about the chain he wore across his face. Once I praised him when he volunteered an answer. "Whatever," he replied with that universal adolescent attitude. Later, as I was packing up and getting ready to go to the workout

184 *Healing the Divided Self*

center he knocked on my classroom door. "Forgot my shades," he snapped. "No worries," I replied. "Okay, well, see you Monday," he said. "Was there something you wanted to talk about?" I inquired sensing an opening. "No, just getting my shades," he answered before leaving. I recall wondering if I had just missed an opportunity.

The following Monday he was first to class as usual, but surprisingly his face chain was gone. His scowl, however, seemed to indicate his challenge for me to inquire about it. Somehow, my gut, or perhaps that inner counselor, told me I should not mention it. I went ahead with class, working on focusing the always active members of the class. Two of the adolescent girls were pregnant, one of the males had a pregnant girlfriend, and the rest were dealing with various and sundry personal issues such as unstable foster care placements. There were the usual jokes about what I did over the weekend: "Did you go to the old folks dance at the nursing home?" and such. There were the usual complaints from my co-workers regarding under-age smoking on the coffee shop's grounds across the street and the students being loud and disruptive when leaving class for breaks. By week two, however, most of those issues had abated. Adam had even made a friend. This friend was a slightly built Caucasian adolescent who seemed almost withdrawn. I noticed Adam even helping his classmate in putting together skills for his résumé. I offered to assist, but Adam was territorial of his new friendship, and so I simply praised the two for teamwork.

Week two ended with résumés and cover letters being printed. I explained week three would be mock taped interviews. They were excited, but also nervous about the prospect of being seen on tape, and fearful of how they might come across. "Don't worry," I counseled, everyone is going through it and it's a lot of fun." Indeed, the taped interviews were always the most popular part of job club. For the first time, Adam actually looked pleased. "So, I can show my friends, right?" I explained that would be up to him. Now remember, this was prior to iPhones and iPads and recording was not as simple nor ubiquitous as in the present era. There was the usual chatter regarding their girlfriends and boyfriends seeing them on tape. Adam even took a lead role in boasting how popular he would be after his performance, and even accepted a good natured ribbing.

The fateful third and final week arrived and we spent all week practicing and finally making recording each student in a mock interview of some 5 minutes. Everyone took the exercise seriously and dressed her or his best. A couple of the girls had their hair done and Adam's shy friend even wore a blazer ("I helped him pick it out at Goodwill," Adam bragged to all). While all were visibly nervous about being recorded, all were able to complete the exercise and everyone seemed to enjoy it. I had prepped them for viewing and critiquing the interviews by reminding them that, as it was their first recorded interview, they would need one another's support. As all were a little anxious, everyone was quite supportive. In fact, there was so much good-natured laughter emanating from the classroom, my boss even entered the room to check whether any real work was being done. My boss appeared to be pleased the students were behaviorally appropriate, but requested a little less volume.

When I inquired about what they had learned during the past three weeks, everyone, including Adam, had a handful of things they could recount. They were all happy and excited to be going into a paid work experience, though most would not get their first choice—something I had vainly tried to prepare them for. Regardless, the final day was a celebration with soft drinks and a graduation cake. Several were working on GED studies and others trying to complete high school diplomas. Everyone was upbeat though understandably anxious about their future. I praised them for their perseverance as 100% of the class had successfully completed job club, something that was rare. I invited all who wished to make any final statement about their experience and everyone spoke of feeling a sense of accomplishment, had praise for a class mate and several thanked me—something that always felt good. As they filed out, quieter than usual, Adam hung around.

"Just wanted to let you know I appreciated you being our teacher." I thanked him and reiterated how much I had enjoyed him and his classmates. A shadow of a smile creased his face before disappearing like a ripple on a stream. He fidgeted in an awkward manner with his hands. "You know, I never knew my dad," he began. "My mom is a real mess. The teachers at my high school just seem to dislike me. You're like the first adult I've had a good relationship with." I praised him for having the courage to continue with the class. "So, you must have come to class wondering if we'd get along." He chuckled at that. "So, how was it for you, growing up I mean," he inquired. Without going into detail, I offered that I had had a difficult childhood and adolescence, perhaps like most. He then asked what had been most difficult for me during that time. I considered his thoughtful question and replied that it had been the fear that I would never matter. He sat back, looking thoughtful. "Yeah man, that's what bothers me so much too. Like I won't matter, you know." He stood and extended his hand. We shook hands, and then he marched out, storm boots and all, minus his face chain and his animus.

Some period of time later my colleague from work and I attended a folk concert at the alternative coffee shop across from the agency. While I was ensconced in conversation during a break, someone approached the table and put a large mug of coffee before me. I looked up to see Adam, wide smile across his face. "That's on me. I'm making some money at my work experience. Thank you," he said. He smiled at my co-worker, who also recognized Adam. She was astonished he was so friendly and inquired what I had done to elicit such kindness in the otherwise angry young man. "I believe we understand each other," was my reply.

I understood Adam pretty well. There are many Adams out there—lost, wounded people anxiously wandering about, misunderstood by many, and pondering if they ever will matter.

13 Gazing into the Future

This chapter is devoted to completing the practicum/internship sequence and preparing for your job search. The first part of the chapter addresses termination of the field supervisor–intern relationship. The latter section will be devoted to preparing for the job search, including preparing a résumé or curriculum vitae (CV), letters of reference, cover letters, interviewing, and issues of licensure and credentialing.

Staying Vibrant in Your Career

Because the practicum/internship is all about preparing to become a professional counselor, this book would not be complete without some basic orientation to managing your professional counseling career. Although this section of the text is a brief overview (there are many more comprehensive job search books and websites available), it will provide some basic information and point the way for further information that may be helpful in assisting you in your career.

Designing and maintaining a successful career is more complex than when I entered the profession in the late 1980s. When I was launched into the field, the belief was that one should get a counseling job in a school or agency and maintain that job through licensure or other credentialing, and then think about moving up. If promotion seemed unlikely, then take another job with a different school or agency. Promoting oneself was through local and state associations, with the résumé or CV as the counselor's calling card (three to five references, naturally). Today, the career field has expanded in light years during the 32 years since I entered. For example, with social media outlets such as LinkedIn, a counselor's ability to connect with essentially the entire counseling world has become a reality. Online promotion, job search, recommendations, and applying for jobs have been streamlined considerably. Recently, I attended an international counseling conference in Australia. Students and faculty were able to network prior to as well as during the conference using an interactive application providing access to all conference attendees. There was even a site for those seeking jobs. No doubt, the ability to meet potential employers face-to-face will always be an advantage. That said, the exchange of information beforehand, as in résumés and CVs, introductions, references, and so forth, can speed up the process. There is little question that the counseling profession's future runs through technology, both in delivering counseling services and in hiring staff. The more facile the counselor is with technology, the more successful she will be in the profession. Further, the profession is making more use of technology with apps to assist clients in managing anxiety, depression, and the like. Distance counseling is on the increase and the days in which clients appeared at the counselor's door are becoming obsolete. In other words, for baby boomers like myself, this brave, high-tech counseling world is something we never could have envisioned. For those under 25, however, living through technology is akin to ducks thriving in water.

Next, we must explore avenues that can assist you in managing your future or existing career. First of all, do you have a clear direction? The next section addresses career planning, which I will refer to as "career visioning."

Visioning: A Key Ingredient in Career Success

As in a previous chapter, I wrote regarding the importance of visioning in one's career. Career professionals will tell you that the first step to success is the ability to visualize a desired goal. Surprisingly, many clients I have counseled and students I have taught do not have a clear vision for their career. Such a lack may set up a graduating counseling student or even a veteran for some degree of struggle and disappointment. Richard Nelson Bolles, author of the *New York Times* bestseller and iconic *What Color Is Your Parachute?*, restates a popular saying: If you don't know where you're going, you'll likely end up somewhere else. Thus, there is the need for visioning work regarding a career (and personal life as well). The second, and more important task, is to strategize on how to achieve the goal. One of the most popular methods for strategizing is creative visualization, or *visioning* for short (Capacchione, 2000). Successful people in every occupation tend to use some type of visioning process. Some notable visionaries are Nelson Mandela, Mohandas Gandhi, Martin Luther King, Jr., and Mother Teresa. Vision includes optimistic thinking, which is strongly correlated with success (Seligman, 1998). Now, your next responsibility is to consider the specifics of your career/life vision. In the sections, create a vision using the outline below.

Personal history: Briefly, how has your life's journey led you to your current location? Location being geography, career, family and anything else relevant.

Values: Now, consider your values and how they have influenced and helped direct your life. What are your five most guiding values? How do they inform your career and life choices?

Professional identity: What is your professional identity? Or, like some, your professional identities? How well does this identity line up with your values? What changes might you make if any?

Goals: What are your key goals for the net 5–10 years? Why did you select these as your goals?

188   *Gazing into the Future*

Action plan: What is your plan to achieve the goals you have set? How will you evaluate progress? How will you deal with failure and disappointment? Remember, resilience may be the most important ingredient in goal achievement. Furthermore, do not be afraid to revise and change goals as more important priorities may emerge.

Sample Action Plan

Okay, what is your primary goal regarding your career (or your life)? Now, devise a plan to achieve this goal. Set out specific steps towards this goal. The number of steps likely is correlated with the goals you have set.

Primary goal:
Steps to achieve this goal:
1.
2.
3.

Now, few if any endeavors go according to plan. You may need more time and some *successful* failures before meeting your goals. Some goals will not be met, while others will. What is more important is that you should set goals and aim to achieve them.

Remember, setting clear, measurable goals for your career or life helps you to plan and craft needed steps towards achieving your goals. You will need to be resilient as setbacks and disappointments are simply a part of life experience. My go-to mantra has long been, "This failure is one disappointment that brings me one step closer to my success." Frankly, my failures, while painful, have taught me far more than my successes. I would not be writing this book without the valuable lessons healthy failure has taught. Embrace and learn from your failures.

Thus, when creating a visioning plan:

1. **Be conscious of the present:** Start with the present but consider long term goals. Long term goals however are related to here and now decisions.
2. **Set a time frame:** Remember, long term plans are just that. Keep your goals in mind as life happens: marriage, divorce, children, moves, etc. When you are not having success, examine why. Do not be afraid of seeking advice from those you respect. If needed, consult a counselor or career coach.
3. **Be flexible:** Some goals will naturally change over time. Your goal of running a community clinic may lose out to a burgeoning interest in a private practice with trusted colleagues. Serving as ACA president may become less important than serving as president of your state counseling association. Remember, life is dynamic and change is occurring all the time.

Gazing into the Future   189

4. **Review your action plan periodically:** Keep score regarding goal achievement. What goals have you met? What has not been met? Why? What changes might be necessary?
5. **Be mindful:** Be grounded in your values. Make sure your set goals actually are congruent with your core values. Take time for daily gratitudes as this practice represents a practical "count your blessings" strategy. Daily gratitudes will help your mood and mindset. They have made a significant difference in mine.

Okay, as in a previous chapter, here are some basic techniques for career and life visioning:

Open-ended questions: "What do I want in my career?" and "Now that I know what I want career-wise, how can I create it?"

Meditation and mindfulness: Many people have a meditation practice that calms and centers them. Some people use meditation as part of the creative process. Remember also, part of mindfulness is practicing non-judgment towards oneself (Kabit-Zinn, 2013).

Visualization: When you picture yourself 5, 7, or 10 years down the line, what does that picture look like? What does your career involve? Where are you living? Who else is in the picture?

Focusing: This assists in clarifying how to plan and prioritize the preceding visualization process. For example, what needs to happen before you can open your own private practice?

Career journaling: For many people, journaling allows them the opportunity to document how their career is proceeding, what challenges, satisfactions, struggles, changes, failures, successes, and so on, they face. Not everyone finds journaling helpful, but for those who enjoy it, journaling can be a type of self-discovery regarding personal and occupational insights.

Collage making: As a counselor working with children and adolescents, then later adults, I used collage in treatment. Collage making can be fun and helpful in your career by helping you create a picture of your career dreams. Use a collage to explore your future dreams and goals. When you have completed it, share your collage with someone you trust and ask for feedback.

Informational interviewing: Choose two or three people whom you respect and who know you well. Ask them to address the following questions about you:

1. What qualities do you possess that will help make you successful in your career?
2. What steps do you need to take to realize your career goal(s)?
3. What is your strongest quality?
4. What is your chief weakness?
5. What are you most passionate about?

(Adapted from Hodges & Connelly, 2010)

Trends in the Counseling Profession

As I referenced earlier, the counseling profession has changed considerably since I completed my master's degree in the late 1980s. From my perspective, most of the change has been beneficial, with state licensure, expanding professional privileges, and a robust job market that suggests ongoing growth (Bureau of Labor Statistics, 2016–2026). Nevertheless, as counseling is a dynamic profession, there will always be marketplace changes. To manage your career, you will need to be aware of changes occurring in the broader field.

First, you need to keep a lifetime membership in the American Counseling Association (ACA) and also in your specialty organization (e.g., American School Counselors Association or ASCA, American Mental Health Counselors Association or AMHCA, etc.). I also encourage a membership in your state organization. No doubt, this requires some cost, but the return on your investment will be worth the price. Professional organizations advocate and lobby elected officials who pass laws that impact our profession, provide research journals (e.g., *Journal of Counseling & Development* and others), other publications (such as *Counseling Today*), national newsletters and regular emails updating members on important issues in the profession. So, keep those memberships updated as they do have a strong bearing on your career.

Another important resource for all counselors, regardless of specialty area, is the U.S. Bureau of Labor Statistics (BLS). The BLS runs ongoing occupational growth projections for thousands of occupations, including that of the counseling profession. It is important to note that projections are updated at periodic intervals so continuing to check the BLS website is essential (www.bls.gov/). The BLS has grouped the counseling profession into the following: school and career counselors, rehabilitation counselors, substance abuse, behavioral disorder, and mental health counselors, and the newest, genetic counselors. The BLS provides a number of counselors in the field for each counseling job type, as well as the job outlook for the next decade. The following are the current BLS figures for counselor specialty areas as at the time of this writing.

School and Career Counselors

Number of jobs, 2018: 324,500
Job outlook, 2016–2026: 8% growth (faster than average)
Employment change, 2018–2028: 27,200
Median salary: $56,310

Substance Abuse, Behavioral Disorder, & Mental Health Counselors

Number of jobs, 2018: 304,500
Job outlook, 2018–2028: 22% growth (much faster than average)
Employment change, 2018–2028: 68,500
Median salary: $44,630

Rehabilitation Counselors

Number of jobs, 2018: 119,700
Job outlook, 2018–2028: 10% growth (faster than average)
Employment change, 2018–2028: 11,800
Median salary: $35,630

Genetic Counselors

Number of jobs, 2018: 3,000
Job outlook, 2018–2028: 27% growth (much faster than average)
Employment change, 2018–2028: 800.
Median salary: $80,370

Now, you can see that the BLS has a tendency to group various counseling specialty areas with those that are distinctly different from one another. For example, mental health counselors and substance abuse counselors are quite different in treatment focus and philosophy. Furthermore, to be a licensed counselor (LPC, LMHC, LPCC, etc.) will require a master's degree. Substance abuse counseling has traditionally been less than a master's degree though the profession is moving towards a master's level profession (I see this clearly in New York State). Furthermore, a license provides a substance abuse counselor and the mobility to move into mental health counseling or into upper-level administration.

Here is another trend that I see at present in my role as professor, counselor educator, and international consultant and trainer. Trauma treatment has become very prominent in the field. Validated treatment approaches, such as EMDR, DBT, ACT, and others, have become popular in the mental health field. In our own program, we have infused trauma treatment education and training into our three-year program and likely our program is moving towards specializing in trauma counseling. At a recent international counseling conference I attended in Australia, educational sessions on trauma treatment were among the most common, and incidentally my own presentation was on addressing trauma. In western New York, many of the local mental health and addictions agencies have developed ACT and DBT treatment groups. Many of our graduate students have become trained while completing their 1,000 hours of field experience. Some graduates have received training in EMDR, another popular and efficacious treatment. You can expect this trend to continue and become more commonplace in the future as trauma is so ubiquitous.

So, current and emerging counselors will need to keep current with the latest trends in the profession. This means staying informed on issues highlighted in the literature of academic journals, national media, and in regular publications such as *Counseling Today*, and *Psychology Today* among others. It is also a wise idea to regularly check with the Bureau of Labor Statistics to review changes in marketplace demand for one's chosen counseling profession.

The Medical Profession's Example: Sub-specialties in Counseling

Naturally, the medical profession has been in existence far longer than that of counseling, which is a relatively new mental health specialty. The medical profession has become replete with numerous specialties such as general practice, neurology, urology, gynecology, psychiatry, and many others. In medicine, students graduate with an MD and are licensed as a physician. However, they also become board certified in their specialty area, such as pediatrics, psychiatry, neurology, and so forth.

Originally, there was primarily one recognized type of counselor and that was the school guidance counselor. The guidance movement was initiated by the federal government to help identify future scientists and engineers in the wake of the launch of the Soviet satellite Sputnik in the late 1950s (Remley & Herlihy, 2016). Guidance professionals in K-12 schools have evolved into the present-day school counseling profession, a large and instrumental profession. Since the 1970s, however, the counseling profession has especially broadened, with Clinical Mental Health Counseling, Clinical Rehabilitation, Addictions Counseling, Career Counseling and most recently, Genetic Counseling. Genetic Counseling is a separate profession, though certainly involves counseling patients on sensitive medical concerns, so I have opted to include this rapidly evolving profession.

What has also helped forge separate counseling specialty areas has been counselor credentialing, the most significant being licensure. Counselors are now licensed in all 50 states and three territories, and counselor licensure, like that in medicine is considered the required credential by the profession and most states. Originally, counseling was a self-governing profession with no licensure in any state or territory. Thus, a national credential was created to standardize education and training for counselors. This resulted in the creation of the National Board for Certified Counselors, Inc. (NBCC), developing the National Certified Counselor (NCC) credential in 1982 (Remley & Herlihy, 2016). Later, as states began licensing counselors, the discussion revolved around whether national certification would continue. In recent years, licensure has become the foundation credential, while certification has evolved into sub-specialty areas, much as in the case of medicine. As the counseling profession matures, it will be interesting to see changes in national certifications. For example, as trauma treatment has become so prominent in the field, it is likely that NBCC, or another organization such as the Center for Credentialing and Education (CCE), an affiliate of NBCC, will create a national trauma counseling certificate. One can examine the Certified Alcoholism and Substance Abuse Counselor (CASAC) credential has become very popular and is even required in most states and is sought even by licensed counselors. Expect to see similar credentials for trauma counseling, and likely other sub-specialties. There already is the Distance Certified Counselor created by the CCE, as online counseling has exploded in practice.

A cautionary note should be mentioned at this point. Be wary of any credentials advertised that are separate from established bodies such as NBCC, CCE, and those that do not require an examination, supervised hours in the field, or ongoing continuing education, if not all of these. So, be a good professional and consumer and check the standards involved. Certification will likely become more prominent and common for specialty areas in the future. You just want to ensure you are working towards a valid credential that will be recognized and not one where you have invested considerable time and money for naught.

The Counseling World Is Flattening

One of the most influential and insightful books I have read in the past 20 years is Thomas Friedman's *The World Is Flat* (2005). In the book, *New York Times* columnist Friedman illustrates the interconnectedness of the financial, social, educational, political, and other natures of a high-technological, postmodern era. While one might argue the toss regarding just how prescient Friedman has become given the current isolationist mood of many, without question he is not too far off regarding how technology has changed our world. For example, consider how financial markets are international and intertwined. As I have lived overseas, I have witnessed how trade between countries can impact economies far from home. I recall how a coffee fungus in Central and South American coffee-producing countries drove up the price at a local coffee shop I frequented because supply dwindled. This also had the effect of people losing their jobs due to suppliers and shops being less profitable. Consider also the field of education. Online college degree programs have become commonplace. Arizona State University has one of the world's largest enrollments, including thousands who may never set foot on the Tempe campus. Weekly, I notice online master's degrees such as counseling, social work, MBA programs, and numerous others being advertised on the internet, radio, and billboards. One of my colleagues runs a master's degree program in Educational Leadership. When the program was offered in traditional seat-time delivery, the enrollment dwindled to under 20. When the program went online however, the enrollment shot up to above 60. Currently it approached 100, with students as far away as California, British Columbia, and south Florida. Needless to say, these are regions a medium-sized, northeastern university could not have reached 15 years ago.

The impact of a virtual world means that traditional residential counseling graduate programs are essentially obsolete. This is not to say that all classes will be online only, and in fact I certainly hope not. What is clear to me is that hybrid programs, with some online classes, some with an online-residential ratio, and some entirely seat time will become the norm. Niagara University's Clinical Mental Health Counseling program, where I teach, was until recently an entirely traditional residential program. Now, we have three completely online courses, and a couple of others that are online–seat-time hybrids. When I taught in Australia on my last sabbatical, the counseling program had online courses for students in Hong Kong. I would expect we will offer more hybrid courses with a ratio of online to seat time. I also have colleagues at institutions whose counseling program is entirely online. When I entered my counseling program at Oregon State University in 1985, we could not have imagined that this would happen. The very notion would have been both heretical and science fiction in nature. Nevertheless, the revolution arrived

194 *Gazing into the Future*

some time ago and counseling programs have been transformed, though not always in the manner we expected.

I am writing this chapter having just returned from the 6th Annual Asian and Pacific Rim Confederation of Counsellors Conference (APRCCC) in Brisbane, Australia. During the conference I met faculty members and students from all over the Pacific Rim, including countries such as Australia, New Zealand, Fiji, Malaysia, China, Singapore, Taiwan, and others. I am informed the profession is beginning to grow in parts of Asia—a region many likely would not have considered in the past. One Australian professor informed me a good number of his students were from Asia and other were Asian-Australians. It will be curious to observe how the region develops with regard to increases in graduate counseling programs and more counseling professionals in the workplace across Asia. During a panel discussion at APRCCC, the CEO of the Australian Counselling Association mentioned that the counseling profession has experienced over 50% growth in the past few years and that job placement was robust. Such growth and expansion are certainly good news for the profession and illustrate the popularization of what was once a western-oriented profession.

Such growth and expansion do pose certain questions, of course. For example, given the significantly different cultural norms in regions such as Asia, how does that change the nature of counseling? Further, as many diverse cultures view the role of gender very differently than westerners do, what does this mean for the ethical practice of counseling (i.e., women viewed as subservient to men)? Sexual orientation and transgender issues are a non-starter in many countries to say the least. Many traditional Asian cultures accept the role of deferring personal decisions such as careers, marriage partners to elders, while westerners, and western counseling norms and ethics posit an individual-oriented decision-making process. Questions about these and many other cultural differences have largely remained unanswered. No doubt, counseling across borders, especially across the eastern-western cultural divide, will mean changes and adaptations in the counselor's role.

Finally, as a counselor educator, the most exciting prospect of a global counseling profession is the opportunity to partner with international programs on graduate student exchanges. Imagine what an internship in say, Malaysia, Hong Kong, or Ecuador could mean for a counseling student's development? Consider a counselor educator spending a semester or year on faculty in Botswana or the Philippines. Having taught in two Australian counseling programs, and conducted extensive volunteering in South Africa and remote, aboriginal Australia, I believe that the impact can be profound. My own vision of a global counseling profession would be a very interactive profession, whereby students and faculty regularly go on an exchange to institutions in diverse regions. Naturally, there are many logistical challenges to this, but that also was the case when international exchange programs began for undergraduate students. While many US faculty members have cautioned me regarding cultural challenges related to providing counseling services, most people I meet on international service trips have welcomed me into their communities. Certainly, there are challenges in language, culture, religion, and so forth, but for the most part these have not been insurmountable and the growth in the profession suggests as much.

So, here is a challenge for anyone reading this chapter. Ask yourself the following questions: What is my vision for my counseling career? Where do I wish to be in five years? In ten years? Would my vision involve international work? If so, how could I begin to lay a foundation for international counseling work? Where are my interest areas? What skills do I possess, or will possess, that might help make me viable in a different culture? Several years ago at the national American Counseling Association conference, former ACA president and president of the International Association for Counselling (IAC) Cortland Lee posed this question: "What is the value added of counseling on an international basis?" Based upon the growth evidenced at the APRCCC conference and what the counseling faculty in Asia and Australia and saying, the value added seems to be proving its worth. The cautionary note is that the profession remains overall small still and likely will need a good decade or more for growth and maturity. If I am writing a follow-up to this book in a decade, likely my report on the international counseling profession will record continued growth.

Technological Advances

Like all professions, counseling has been impacted greatly by twenty-first-century technology. Previously, I referenced the advent of online programs. While non-traditional virtual institutions such as the University of Phoenix, Walden University, and others were the primary domain initially, traditional residential institutions such as Arizona State University, the University of Maryland, and many others have followed suit and created large online degree programs for subjects including counseling. So, in the case of a single-parent living in rural Maine, she may be able to complete her master's and become a counselor without having to relocate and give up her job. Thus, the great advantage in online education is the ability to reach a wider audience that otherwise might not be able to attend a graduate counseling program. No doubt one of the largest beneficiaries in the postmodern, high-technology explosion is the higher education sector and students wishing to access it. Online education also has a flattening effect in that graduate education becomes a buyers' market. We can certainly debate the pros and cons of online education as the ubiquity in online graduate counseling programs could mean a watering down of programmatic and student quality, although I recall the same concerns being expressed when I was a graduate student when counseling programs were becoming more numerous. There are additional concerns, of course. Capella University declared bankruptcy in spring 2019, leaving thousands of students without a program. Many of these students were just shy of graduation as well. Fortunately, many established counseling programs stepped up and accepted Capella's former students taking most if not all academic credits earned. Anyway, buyer beware!

Well beyond counselor education training programs, counseling services have been significantly impacted through the advent of increased technology. When I was beginning my counseling program, distance counseling was over the telephone.

196 *Gazing into the Future*

Working the crisis line and also taking calls from college students while interning at a campus health center, I frequently counseled via the phone. Fast-forwarding to the present, counseling over the phone seems a quaint anachronism. Practically all agencies in my area make use of encrypted internet video packages to provide mental health services to needy populations. One of my interns counseled a shut-in through such a video program, eventually luring the client to the agency for face-to-face counseling. An Australian ex-patriot friend living in New York City uses such a program to speak with his psychiatrist in Sydney, Australia each month. These examples are not outliers but represent a burgeoning movement that will only become more common, and perhaps even the dominant service delivery method. For example, consider millennials and how hard-wired they are to technology. Now we should all have concerns regarding the level of smart phone addiction evidenced in young people. All my colleagues and friends have a story of observing young people texting each other while sharing a table or couch! This living through technology, though de rigueur, carries with it interpersonal isolation while ironically providing connections all over the globe! I recall on a recent four-week trip through Southeast Asia one young woman whose face was always riveted to her phone screen to the exclusion of World Heritage Area scenery!

The responsible approach to technology, then, is to create applications that both assist people in developing and maintaining emotional wellbeing, while encouraging them to "un-plug" from the Internet. On a weekly basis, I listen to a meditation app to help me stay grounded. Furthermore, this application encourages me to break away from technology at regular intervals. Many treatment providers also use such applications to assist their clients in maintaining sobriety, managing trauma, depression, eating disorders, and many other issues. Technology, then, is a medium that can be either helpful in maintaining mental and emotional health or in detracting from it. Just this week, I agreed to participate in the development of an application that assists people in building and maintaining resilience through encouraging physical activity, social interaction, and meditation. Once again, the critical issue is how well the counseling profession uses technology to support counseling services and overall client wellbeing. The risk, of course, is that we feed an addiction that can overwhelm clients during the very time we try to assist their recovery from addiction. By the very nature of using technology in counseling, there is an inherent paradox in such use.

Regarding ongoing training for students in graduate programs and professionals seeking ongoing training for continuing education, advancing technology offers many options. For example, through artificial intelligence, avatars could be used to train counseling students in intakes, assessments, group and individual counseling, relationship counseling, crisis intervention, and additional areas. We are a little early in the AI movement for this, but not far from such possibilities. Consider as well the implications for after-hours crisis intervention. A distressed person makes a crisis call and the initial screening is conducted by an operating system. The system, with a human-like voice, conducts the initial assessment regarding lethality. Then, using programmed decision trees, either refers the call to a live counselor or schedules the caller for a session the following day. To take the futuristic scenario further, the operating system, or simulated counselor, could actually conduct a session with the caller by monitoring voice tone, content of the call, optimistic versus pessimistic outlook, and lack of social connections to cite a few critical considerations. Readers may find counseling with a software-generated counselor to be unnatural. Consider, however, the realistic manner whereby millennials live and interact with their peers and the world through technology. Given this reality, is therapy with a simulated counselor really so far-fetched? Having been exposed to millennials in my classroom the past several years, my opinion is not at all! My comfort level with the notion of an operating system providing the initial assessment, intake, and preliminary counseling is one of discomfort, although this may reflect my age more than anything. Change is happening, so be prepared.

Ethical Concerns

When my colleagues on the Ethics Revision Task Force and I were revising the American Counseling Association's code of ethics, we struggled to address the technological aspect of ethical practice. During one discussion, a member of the ERTF stated the challenge of adequately crafting ethics for advanced technology that does not yet exist. Without question, I felt sadly inadequate to articulate a cogent way of covering ethical parameters the task force members could not begin to anticipate. The task force did, however, find the technological aspect to be one of the more fruitful discussions due to the fact that it was so interesting to speculate about. The discussions were part Jules Verne in nature, albeit with a counselor ethics flavor.

So then, what are potential ethical concerns related to advanced technology? What quickly comes to mind is counseling across international borders—something that is already occurring. Which country's laws take precedent? What about the variations in client privacy and confidentiality, as these likely will vary greatly. Some countries mandate gender inequality and might even prohibit a male counselor counseling a female. What if a client discloses she is a lesbian and wishes to address such, yet resides in a country where being an LGBTQ person is a capital offense? These are the more predictable questions, and, in fact, ones the profession is just now begging to grapple with. There are other ethical and legal quagmires.

Returning to the simulated counselor scenario, just as human counselors make mistakes, so will virtual ones. So, what is the legal responsibility for virtual counselors? One would assume the culpability falls onto whoever owns or supervises the virtual counselor, if not it fact both. The more pressing question in my mind is whether the virtual counselor can lower or increase liability. Then again, would the creation of virtual counselors even be ethical in itself? Thus far, there seems nothing in the current ACA code of ethics, not in any related ethical code (e.g., AMHCA, APA, NASW, etc.) that addresses the issue. Having trained and counseled in non-western countries and regions, one wonders whether virtual counseling would be an asset or a liability given sometimes significantly varying cultural norms. Naturally, the lack of available technology would be a concern, but assuming that deficit is addressed, would a person from rural Botswana feel more comfortable with the

198 *Gazing into the Future*

virtual counselor, or a live western one? Then we have the issues of counselor education training and supervision. So, gazing 20 years into the future, an underfunded counselor education program in a rural area lacks financial resources to hire another counselor educator, but a virtual counselor educator is cheap by comparison (no health care or retirement costs). The virtual counselor educator will then be programmed with doctoral-level information, experience, decision-making, and ethics. The virtual professor, who we will call Jane, joins a team of two human counselor educators. If technological advances were such Jane could instruct, provide feedback, grade assignments, and so forth, all the responsibilities of a human, could CACREP find she was a legitimate faculty member for accreditation? Given Jane might hold less bias than her human colleagues, would she be less of a liability and more an asset? Would students accept her legitimacy? Again, given the way younger people live through technology, one wonders if students in 2040 would not actually *prefer* Dr. Jane over their human faculty counterparts. While this may sounds far-fetched, didn't the internet and artificial intelligence once sound as much so? Travel by jet airplanes, much less automobiles, was once considered something out of Jules Verne. I recall that the first time someone mentioned a fax machine to me I thought they were poking fun at me.

The future has never been easy to discern nor reliably predict—Nostradamus claims notwithstanding. Given the quantum leap in technology in my lifetime, I can only expect to see even greater advances during the remainder of my life. The clichés regarding a rising tide and all boats comes to my mind. Meaning, the impact of technology is ubiquitous and will both shape and transform the counseling profession in ways we cannot imagine. The impact likely will flatten the profession with regard to international borders, culture, gender, sexual orientation, ethics, all areas of professional practice, and certainly counselor education program, to mention just some. Without doubt, technology will transform the profession in ways we cannot fathom at present. The larger concern way well be how well the counseling profession adapts to address what promises to be a rapidly shifting landscape. In 20 years, I hope to be writing about how the counseling profession has used technology to provide for a healthier populace and a vibrant profession.

Lessons Learned

The cliché that life happens is a cultural expression with roots firmly planted in the soil of my formative childhood and adolescent experience. Due to familial circumstances, my grandparents took custody of my four siblings and me, moving us from various relatives into their rural Ozark home in northern Arkansas. They did what they could to provide us a stable childhood, filling their house with love, despite living under significant economic hardship. That hardship was further exacerbated by having to feed and care for five young grandsons on a meager income. Fortunately, as our grandparents were resourceful people, and with help from extended family, they always found a way to survive and even thrive. Each birthday, were made to feel special with a cake my grandmother baked and a nice

Gazing into the Future 199

gift. At Christmas, they found a way to buy each of us something, albeit usually small and economically priced.

For me, however, there was no better material gift than that given by my aunt and uncle from Texas. Each Christmas, they bought us a one-year subscription to the *National Geographic*. During grade school, I began to read of far-away lands, cultures, and peoples. Growing up in an impoverished family that lacked even an automobile, my lone vehicle for travel lay between the pages of that iconic magazine, its exotic pictures my roadmap to the seven continents. During the chill of winter's icy grip and summer's oppressive heat and humidity, I would take the magazine down to the dirt-floor basement for comfort and privacy. Tempted by the shiny apple represented by glossy four-color photos, I would curl up on the bed, reading up on far-flung locations I longed to visit. I even complied a top ten list of exotic locations I planned to visit during my lifetime. But prior to such concrete plans, my pleasure was simply to leaf through the pages, inspired and at times mystified by what I saw and read. One day, while in primary school, my interest was piqued. The cover story was on Australia, with a focus on the remote Outback.

I had little awareness of Australia at this point. My grandfather, a former one-room school teacher and a geography buff, showed me Australia on the map he kept. He explained the indigenous culture, British colonization (to a limited extent), and spoke of its remote location, and how its deserts were sparsely populated. He knew little of the land's flora and fauna, however, other than the iconic kangaroos. I was intrigued and read and re-read the article. I discovered the aborigines likely were the world's oldest continuous culture, that Australia was the oldest, smallest, hottest, and driest inhabited continent. That their night sky constellations were different than those in the northern hemisphere, and like the British, the Australians drove on the left side of the road. This was all very interesting, but then I read about the School of the Air. I discovered that children living in remote regions attended school by watching a TV channel or listening to the radio. The children would be tutored most commonly by their mother, and answer roll call and the teacher's questions via two-way radio. In some cases, the teacher might be 500 miles distant from the remote cattle station the children lived on. I wondered if these kids ever got lonely, or who helped them if the parents were not good at math? What about birthdays and Christmas? Friends likely would be unable to travel great distances for a party, and Christmas in the desert, especially as it was summer not winter, seemed downright strange.

Essentially, my grandparents' tiny world was being expanded through the medium of a popular monthly periodical. I continued reading and found sick and injured were served by the Royal Flying Doctors service. This service was established by Sir John Flynn, a Presbyterian theologian who wanted to bring health care to the indigenous and whites living and working in the Outback. Reading the *Geographic* spurred me to check-out what few books my rural school and tiny county library possessed on the topic of Australia. Moreover, it was remote Australia, aka the Outback or "Bush country" to Australians, that most interested me. Eager for a more personal view, I queried my grandparents, teachers, and family friends to see if there was anyone in

200 *Gazing into the Future*

our area who have traveled to the far southern continent. To my disappointment, there seemed to be none.

Feeling dissatisfied, I did what I had learned to do whenever angry, sad, confused, or in need of wiser counsel and sought out my grandmother. She listened well as always and with few interruptions. As a woman who believed strongly in education, she encouraged my interest in all things academic and suggested I consult the *World Atlas* at the county library. I did so and found maps that explained the desert regions, wildlife unique to Australia, information on the indigenous cultures, its cities, and common crops. Feeling even more inspired, I returned home and found my grandmother puttering in the kitchen. I exclaimed my intent to visit Australia and many other countries profiled in my now favorite magazine. She had grown up impoverished herself, in a hard-scrabble existence, with a school offering eight grades, working hard from the time she was scarcely old enough to walk. Only later did I realize such experiences could easily have beaten down a less resilient person. It might have been tempting for someone like herself to express, "You can never see those places. They're too far and expensive." But she merely smiled, and said, "Yes, it's possible to go there. But you will need to be wise with your money and plan carefully." Later, I appreciated she did not discourage me, nor did she hand out the platitudinous and unrealistic "You can do anything you want" type of answer. Her counsel was both encouraging and at the same time, realistic. To a child growing up in severe poverty, raised by fiscally challenged grandparents, I needed healthy measures both of encouragement and realism. My grandmother had ample supplies of both.

"What might you do when you go there?" she inquired, looking up from peeling apples for a pie. "Besides just tourism," she added. I considered this and replied that I would teach something. She nodded. "Lots of teachers in our family. Maybe you will be another." Now, I had no idea what I might teach, as after all I was a second or third grader at this point in my burgeoning life. Nevertheless, the seeds of becoming an educator and realizing world travel were firmly sowed in the fields of my consciousness. The monthly *National Geographic* then became the greenhouse for irrepressible hopes. While I struggled academically, I began to exert more effort at my studies, realizing that college degrees are a requirement in order to teach.

Most people in my circle were not like my encouraging grandparents, and more than once I made the error of confiding to someone of my future plans only to be ridiculed with a sarcastic, "Sure kid, you going to fly down there by selling coke bottles!" or, "You're too dumb to go to college." Feeling a need for additional affirmation I spoke with my third-grade teacher, the unfailingly kind Miss Caldwell. She listened patiently and replied after a brief silence, that my grandmother had given me thoughtful counsel. "Don't let others discourage you too much," she added, "they may not feel so good about their lives." Then, she surprised me by talking about a college friend who had traveled to Australia! I left the encounter with my teacher buoyed by the possibility of actualizing my dreams.

I wrote down my future travel and educational goals, took them out and re-read them when I was discouraged and doubtful about achieving them. Somehow I had just enough faith, perhaps less than a mustard seed, but enough to keep me going forward. I went forward through years of working at two or three jobs a year while

Gazing into the Future   201

going through undergraduate and graduate school. Keeping hope alive was very difficult, especially during times when academic and occupational success appeared to flee from me. But I kept my dreams in the forefront of my mind and written on a piece of paper I kept for decades. Whenever discouraged or feeling I could not go on, I would unfold that crinkled piece of paper and remind myself of my goal. Eventually, I completed my doctorate, began to have moderate success, and in time began traveling internationally. One by one, I checked off countries and regions on my childhood list. Finally, in a watermark experience I landed a spot teaching at an Australian university during my first sabbatical. During a school break, I flew to Alice Springs in the dead center of the continent. I rented a sturdy mountain bike and with an acquaintance from Britain, cycled into the ancient West MacDonnell Mountain Range. We stood at daybreak watching the ancient rocks on the world's oldest continent change colors in magical fashion. I thought back some 40 years to when in grade school I had read the *National Geographic* cover story on the Outback. I considered my grandmother's and Miss Caldwell's thoughtful words, as well as those discouraging ones from others. As the sun made its ascent over the remote, antipodean continent, all words were stripped bare and, for a change, I could think of nothing save gratitude. I had finally achieved a childhood dream.

My takeaway lesson is that hope can be a somewhat fragile creature, much in need of care and nurturance through tumultuous, seemingly unpromising years of academic and economic struggle. My experience in achieving dreams represents more an exercise in resilience than in visualization, though the latter is of critical importance as well. Finally, the role of a counselor can be of critical important in visualizing, assessing, and realizing dreams. Although we had a school counselor who was very effective in some functions, he could also be gruff and speak with a barbed tongue. I would like to have spoken with him about my aspirations but did not trust he would value them based on our encounters. When I consider some 25 years of providing counseling services in the USA and abroad, valuing people's dreams has been a significant part of my job. Valuing does not mean unconditionally accepting all someone says, but rather helping them to explore their dreams and the ways they might pursue them. My grandmother and my third-grade teacher were worthy role models in this regard. Their message was validating and encouraging, while at the same time realistic. As counselors we must be both validating and realistic in our counsel: an Adlerian "Follow your heart but take your head with you in the process" type of approach. The "You can be anything you want" type of approach is unrealistic and likely ultimately discouraging when the economic, educational, familial and other realities emerge in life. So, plan carefully, be wise with finances, and find ways to keep your dreams alive, even when the reminder is a cheap, crinkled sheaf of paper torn from the corner of a pulp notebook.

I am completing this final chapter in the book having just returned from an international counseling conference in Brisbane, Australia. This coming summer I will return to the remote Northern Territory for service work in remote schools and communities. My work involves training teachers, counsellors, administrators, community elders, and others on addressing trauma, suicide prevention, preventing compassion fatigue, self-care plans, and other related topics. Perhaps more than anything else in my life, I am grateful at having realized the most valued part of my childhood dreaming. When I reflect back on my child self, sitting in my grandparents' dirt-floor basement, with *National Geographic* in my hands, I so want to whisper, "It was all worth it." I can almost feel the grit of the dirt floor, the oppressive July humidity, and the pounding of my child heart, excited at the prospect of a world previously unimaginable.

References

Alcoholics Anonymous (1993). *Alcoholics Anonymous* (4th ed.). New York: AA.

American Counseling Association. (n.d.). *American Counseling Association*. www.counseling.org/

American Counseling Association. (2016). *Licensure requirements for professional counselors*. Alexandria, VA: Author. www.counseling.org/knowledge-center/licensure-requirements/state-professional-counselor-licensure-boards

American Counseling Association. (2014). *Code of ethics*. Alexandria, VA: Author.

American Psychiatric Association. (2013). *Diagnostic and statistical manual of mental disorders* (5th ed.). Washington, DC: American Psychiatric Association.

Baer, R.A. (2003). Mindfulness training as a clinical intervention: A conceptual and empirical review. *Clinical Psychology: Science and Practice, 10*, 125–143.

Beck, A.T. (1967). *Depression: Clinical, experimental, and theoretical aspects*. New York: Harper & Row.

Beck, A.T. (1963). Thinking and depression: Idiosyncratic content and cognitive distortions. *Archives and General Psychiatry, 9*, 324–333.

Beck, A.T., & Steer, R.A. (1987). *The Beck Depression Inventory manual* (2nd ed.). San Antonio, TX: The Psychological Corporation.

Bergman, D.M. (2013). The role of government and lobbying in the creation of a health profession: The legal foundations of counseling. *Journal of Counseling & Development, 91*, 61–67. doi:10.1002/j.1556-6676.2013.00072x

Bernard, J.M., & Goodyear, R.K. (2004). *Fundamentals of clinical supervision* (5th ed.). Upper Saddle River, NJ: Pearson.

Bernard, J.M., & Goodyear, R.K. (2009). *Fundamentals of clinical supervision* (4th ed.). Needham Heights, MA: Allyn & Bacon.

Bolles, R.N. (2015). *What color is your parachute? A practical manual for job-hunters and career-changers*. Berkeley, CA: Ten Speed Press.

Boykiv, Y. (n.d.). The 5 steps you must take before firing an employee. www.inc.com/yuriy-boykiv/the-5-steps-you-must-follow-before-firing-an-employee.html. Retrieved July 31, 2019.

Boynton *v.* Burglass. 590 So. 2d 446 (Fla Dist. Ct. App. 1991).

Brach, T. (2003). *Radical acceptance: Embracing your life with the heart of a Buddha*. New York: Bantam.

Brott, P.E., & Myers, J.E. (1999). Development of professional school counselor identity: A grounded theory. *Professional School Counseling, 2*, 339–348.

Brown, L.S., & Brodsky, A.M. (1992). The future of feminist therapy. *Psychotherapy, 29*, 51–57.

204 References

Brown, K.W., & Ryan, R.M. (2003). The benefits of being present: Mindfulness and its role in psychological well-being. *Journal of Personality and Social Psychology, 84,* 822–848.

Butzin, C.A., O'Connell, D.J., Martin, S.S., & Inciardi, J.A. (2006). *Journal of Criminal Justice, 34*(5), 557–565.

Capacchione, L. (2000). *Visioning: Ten steps to designing the life of your dreams.* New York: Tarcher/Putnam.

Center for Credentialing & Education. (2014). www.cce-global.org.

Cillizza, C. (2019, July 15). George Will's startling assessment of Donald Trump. *The Point with Chris Cillizza.* www.cnn.com/2019/07/15/politics/donald-trump-george-will-presidency/index.html

Corey, G. (2017). *Theory and practice of counseling and psychotherapy* (10th ed.). New York: Cengage.

Council for the Accreditation of Counseling and Related Educational Programs. (2016). *CACREP accreditation standards.* Alexandria, VA: Author. www.cacrep.org/for-programs/2016-cacrep-standards/

Creative Spirits (n.d.). Aboriginal suicide rates. www.creativespirits.info/aboriginalculture/people/aboriginal-suicide-rates

Curran, L.A. (2013). *101 trauma-informed interventions: Activities, exercises, and assignments to move the client and therapy forward.* Eau Claire, WI: PESI Publishing and Media.

de Shazer, S. (1994). *Words were originally magic.* New York: Norton.

DiClemente, C.C. (2003). *How addictions develop and addicted people recover.* New York: Guilford.

Doherty, W.J., & Simmons, D.S. (1996). Clinical practice patterns of marriage and family therapists: A national survey of therapists and their clients. *Journal of Marital and Family Therapy, 22,* 9–25.

Duckworth, A.L. (2016). *GRIT: The power of passion and perseverance.* New York: Scribner's.

Duckworth, A.L., Eichstaedt, J.C., & Ungar, L.H. (2015). The mechanics of human achievement. *Social and Personality Psychology Compass, 9,* 359–269.

Duckworth, A.L., Peterson, C., Matthews, M.D., & Kelly, D.R. (2007). Grit: Perseverance and passion for long-term goals. *Journal of Personality and Social Psychology, 9* (1087–1101).

Dwyer, C., & Limbong, A. (2019, July 15). "Go back where you came from": The long rhetorical roots of Trump's racist tweets. National Public Radio. www.npr.org/2019/07/15/741827580/go-back-where-you-came-from-the-long-rhetorical-roots-of-trump-s-racist-tweets

Ellis, A.E. (2004). *Rational emotive behavior therapy: It works for me, it can work for you.* Amherst, NY: Prometheus Books.

Ellis, A. (2000). *How to control your anxiety before it controls you.* New York: Citadel Press.

Ellis, A.E. (1999). *How to make yourself happy and remarkably less disturbed.* Manassas, VA: Impact Books.

Epstein, M. (1992). *Thoughts without a thinker: Psychotherapy from a Buddhist perspective.* New York: Perseus Books.

Evans, F.B. (2012). Assessment in psychological trauma: Methods and interventions. In L. Levers (Ed.), *Trauma counseling: Theories and interventions* (pp. 471–492). Alexandria, VA: American Counseling Association.

Falander, C.A. (2014). Clinical supervision in a competence-based era. *South African Journal of Psychology, 44*(1), 6–17. doi: 10.1177/0081246313516260

Falander, C.A., & Shafranske, E.P. (2004). *Clinical supervision: A competency-based approach.* Washington, DC: American Psychological Association.

Feldman, G., Hayes, A., Kumar, S., Greeson, J., & Laurenceau, J.-P. (2006). Mindfulness and emotional regulation: The development and initial validation of the cognitive and

References 205

affective mindfulness scale-revised (CAMS-R). *Journal of Psychopathological Behavior, 29*, 177–190. doi: 10.1007/s10862-006-9035-8

Forgan, J.W., & Jones, C.D. (2002). How experiential-based activities can improve students' social skills. *Teaching Exceptional Children, 34*(3), 52–58.

Frankl, V.E. (1969). *The will to meaning: Foundations and applications of logotherapy.* New York: Penguin Books.

Frankl, V.E. (1965). *The doctor and the soul: From psychotherapy to logotherapy.* New York: Washington Square Press/Pocket Books.

Frawley-O'Dea, M.G., & Sarnat, J.E. (2001). *The supervisory relationship: A contemporary psychodynamic approach.* New York: Guilford.

Friedman, T.L. (2004). *The world is flat.* New York: Macmillan.

Garst, B., Schneider, I., & Baker, D. (2001). Outdoor adventure program participants impacts on adolescent self-perception. *Journal of Experiential Education, 24*(1), 41–49.

Gladding, S.T. (2019). *Family therapy: History, theory, and practice* (7th ed.). New York: Pearson.

Gladding, S.T. (2018). *Counseling: A comprehensive profession* (8th ed.). Boston: Pearson.

Goleman, D. (2005). *Emotional intelligence: Why it can matter more than I.Q.* New York: Bantam Books.

Gonzalez, J.M.R., & Connell, N.M. (2014). Mental health of prisoners: Identifying barriers to mental health treatment and medication continuity. *American Journal of Public Health 104*(12), 2838-2333. doi: 10.2105LAJPH.2014.302043.

Grande, D. (2017, December 6). Couples therapy: Does it really work? *Psychology Today.* www.psychologytoday.com/us/blog/in-it-together/201712/couples-therapy-does-it-really-work

Granello, D.H., & Granello, P.F. (2007). *Suicide: An essential guide for helping professionals and educators.* New York: Pearson-Allyn & Bacon.

Gray, K. (2019, October 17). Michigan mental health-counselors get final OK of bill that allows them to keep practicing. *Detroit Free Press.* www.freep.com/story/news/politics/2019/10/17/mental-health-counselors/4011114002/

Groves, E.R. (1933). *Marriage.* New York: Henry Holt.

Hahn, T.N. (2016). *The Miracle of mindfulness: An introduction to the practice of meditation.* Manchester, UK: Beacon Books.

Hayes, D.G. (2017). *Assessment in counseling: Procedures and practices* (6th ed.). Alexandria, VA: American Counseling Association.

Hayes, S.C. (2012). *Acceptance and commitment therapy: An experiential approach to behavior change.* Washington, DC: American Psychological Association.

Hayes, S.C., Stroshal, K.D., & Wilson, K.G. (2012). *Acceptance and Commitment Therapy: The process and practice of mindful change* (2nd ed.). New York: Guilford.

Haynes, R., Corey, G., & Moulton, P. (2003). *Clinical supervision in the helping professions: A practical guide.* Pacific Grove, CA: Brooks/Cole.

Healy, A.C., & Hayes, D.G. (2012). A discriminant analysis of gender and counselor professional identity development. *Journal of Counseling & Development, 90*, 55–62. doi: 10.1111/j.1556-66.2012.00008.x

Heller, S. (2014, March 28). Borderline personality disorder: The sufferer's experience. *Psychology Today.* www.psychologytoday.com/us/blog/resolution-not-conflict/201403/borderline-personality-disorder-the-sufferers-experience

Higgins, I. (2019, February 16). Suicide at crisis levels among aboriginal children as leaders fear it will become normal. *Australian Broadcasting Corporation.* www.abc.net.au/news/2019-02-17/indigenous-suicide-rates-at-crisis-levels-communities-say/10814874

Hodges, S. (2019). *101 careers in counseling* (2nd ed.). New York: Springer.

206   References

Hodges, S. (2002, November–December). Authentic values and ersatz standards: Making sense of college rankings. *Academe: Bulletin of the American Association of University Professors, 88*, 33–38.

Hodges, S., & Connelly, A.R. (2010). *A job search manual for counselors and counselor educators: How to navigate and promote your counseling career.* Alexandria, VA: American Counseling Association.

Hodges, S., Denig, S., & Crowe, A. (2014). Attitudes of college students towards purpose in life and self-esteem. *International Journal of Existential Psychology & Psychotherapy, 5*, 124–131.

Holloway, E. (1995). *Clinical supervision: A systems approach.* Thousand Oaks, CA: Sage.

Indeed (2017). www.indeed.com/career/licensed-professional-counselor/salaries.

International Association of Marriage and Family Counselors (2017). Code of ethics. Alexandria, VA: International Association of Marriage and Family Counselors. Author. www.iamfconline.org/public/IAMFC-Ethical-Code-Final.pdf

Ivey, A.E., & Ivey, M.B. (1998). Reframing DSM IV: Positive strategies from developmental counseling and therapy. *Journal of Counseling & Development, 76*(3). doi: 10.10002/j.1556-6676.1998.tb02550.x

Juhnke, G.A., & Hagedorn, W.B. (2013). *Counseling addicted families: An integrated assessment and treatment model.* New York: Routledge.

Kabit-Zinn, J. (2013). *Full catastrophe living: Using the wisdom of your body and mind to face stress, pain, and illness* (2nd ed.). New York: Bantam.

Kaplan, D.M. Tarvydas, V.M., & Gladding, S.T. (2014). 20/20: A vision for the future of counseling: The new consensus definition of counseling. *Journal of Counseling & Development, 92*, 366–372. doi: 10.1002/j.1556–6676.201400164.x

Kim-berg, I., & Szabo, P. (2005). *Brief coaching for lasting solutions.* New York: Norton.

Lambers, E. (2000). Supervision in person-centered therapy: Facilitating congruence. In E. Myers & B. Thorn (Eds.), *Person-centered therapy today: New fronters in theory and practice* (pp. 114–133). New York: John Wiley & Sons.

LaRose, J. (2018, February 12). U.S. personal coaching tops 1 billion, and growing. In *Marketresearch.com.blog.* https://blog.marketresearch.com/us-personal-coaching-industry-tops-1-billion-and-growing

Lau, M.A., Bishop, S.R., Segal, Z.V., Buis, T., Anderson, N.D., Carlson, L., Shapiro, S., & Carmody, J. (2006). The Toronto mindfulness scale: Development and validation. *Journal of Clinical Psychology, 62*(12), 1445–1467. doi: 10.1002/jclp.20326

Lee, C.C. (2019). *Multicultural issues in counseling: New approaches to diversity* (5th ed.). Alexandria, VA: American Counseling Association.

Levers, L.L. (2012). An introduction to counseling survivors of trauma: Beginning to understand the context of trauma. In L. Levers (Ed.), *Trauma counseling: Theories and interventions* (pp. 1–22). Alexandria, VA: American Counseling Association.

Linehan, M.M. (2014). *DBT skills training manual* (2nd ed.). New York: Guilford.

Linehan, M.M. (1993). *Cognitive-behavioral treatment of borderline personality disorder.* New York: Guilford Press.

Linehan, M.M. (1987). Dialectical behavior therapy: A cognitive behavioral approach to parasuicide. *Journal of Personality Disorders, 1*, 328–333.

Marmarosh, C., Holtz, A., & Schottenbauer, M. (2005). Group cohesiveness, group-derived collective self-esteem, group derived hope, and the well-being of group therapy members. *Group Dynamics: Theory, Research, & Practice, 9*(1), 32–44.

Maslow, A. (1968). *Towards a psychology of being* (rev. ed.). New York: Van Nostrand Reinhold.

Meany-Walen, K.K., Carnes-Holt, K., Minton, C.A.B., Purswell, K. & Pronchenko-Jain, Y. (2013). An exploration of counselors' professional leadership development. *Journal of Counseling & Development, 91*, 206–215. doi: 10.10022/j1556-6676.2013.00087.x

Myers, J.E., & Sweeney, T.J. (2005). *Counseling for wellness: Theory, research, and Practice*. Alexandria, VA: American Counseling Association.

Myers, J.E., Sweeny, T.J., & Witmer, J.M. (2000). The wheel of wellness counseling for wellness: A holistic model for treatment planning. *Journal of Counseling & Development, 78*, 251–256.

National Society of Genetic Counselors (n.d.). About genetic counselors. www.nsgc.org

Obergefell *v.* Hodges, No. 576 U.S. (Supreme Court, June 26, 2015).

Palmer, P.J. (2007). *The courage to teach: Exploring the inner landscape teacher's life*. San Francisco: Jossey-Bass.

Palmer, P.J. (2000). *Let your life speak: Listening for the voice of vocation*. San Francisco: Jossey-Bass.

Perls, F. (1969). *In and out of the garbage pail*. Moab, UT: Real People Press.

Peters, T.J., & Waterman, R.H. (1982). *In search of excellence: Lessons from America's best run companies*. New York: Harper-Collins.

Pinsof, W., & Wynne, L. (Eds.). (1995). Special issue: The effectiveness of marital and family therapy. *Journal of Marital and Family Therapy, 21*(4), 339–613.

Prochaska, J.O., Norcross, J.C., & DiClemente, C.C. (2013). Applying the stages of change. *Psychotherapy in Australia, 19*(2), 10–15.

Reardon, S.F. (2011). The widening academic achievement gap between the rich and the poor: New evidence and possible explanations. In R. Murnane & G. Duncan (Eds.), *Whiter opportunity? Rising inequality and the life chances of low-income children*. New York: Russell Sage Foundation Press.

Reeves, A. (2011, September/October). Therapy and Skype. *Family Therapy Magazine*, 48–49.

Remley, T.P., Jr. (1995). A proposed alternative to the licensing of specialists in counseling. *Journal of Counseling & Development, 74*, 126–129.

Remley, T.P., & Herlihy, B. (2016). *Ethical, legal, and professional issues in counseling* (5th ed.). Boston: Pearson.

Rogers, C.R. (1977). *Carl Rogers on personal power: Inner strength and its revolutionary impact*. New York: Delacorte Press.

Rogers, C.R. (1961). *On becoming a person: A therapist's view of psychotherapy*. Boston: Houghton Mifflin.

Rogers, C.R. (1951). *Client-centered therapy*. Boston: Houghton Mifflin.

Rokeach, M. (1979). *Understanding human values: Individual and societal*. New York: Simon & Schuster.

Ronnestad, M.H., & Skovholt, T.M. (2003). The journey of the counselor and therapist: Research Findings and perspectives on professional development. *Journal of Career Development 30*, 5–44.

Ronnestad, M.H., & Skovholt, T.M. (1993). Supervision of beginning and advanced graduate Students in counseling and psychotherapy. *Journal of Counseling & Development, 71*, 396–405.

Seligman, M.E.P. (2011). *Flourish: A visionary new understanding of happiness and well-being*. New York: Free Press.

Seligman, M.E.P. (1998). *Learned optimism: How to change your mind and your life* (7th ed.). New York: Knopf-Doubleday.

Smith, K.L. (2009). *A brief summary of supervision models*. Milwaukie, WI: Department of Counselor Education, Marquette University.

208 References

Stoltenberg, C.D., McNeill, B., & Delworth, U. (1998). *IDM supervision: An integrated developmental model for supervising counselors and therapists.* San Francisco: Jossey-Bass.

Stone, L.A. (1985). National Board for Certified Counselors: History, relationships, and Projections. *Journal of Counseling & Development, 63,* 606-606.

StopBullying.gov. (n.d.). *Prevention: Teach kids how to identify bullying and how to stand up to it safely.* www.stopbullying.gov

Tagnoshi, H., Kontos, A.P., & Remley, T.P., Jr. (2008). The effectiveness of individual wellness counseling on the wellness of law enforcement officers. *Journal of Counseling & Development, 86,* 64–75.

Thapar *v.* Zezulka. 994 S.W.2d 635 (Tex. 1999).

U.S. Bureau of Labor Statistics (BLS) (2018–2028). *Occupational outlook handbook.* Washington, DC: U.S. Bureau of Labor Statistics. www.bls.gov

U.S. Department of Defense (2005). *ASVAB counselor manual.* North Chicago, IL: U.S. Military Entrance Processing Command. Ward *v.* Wilbanks. Case No. 09-CV-11237 9E.D. (Mich. July 26, 2010).

Wheeler, A.M., & Bertram, B. (2019). *The counselor and the law: A guide to legal and ethical practice* (7th ed.). Alexandria, VA: American Counseling Association.

Williams, J.M.G., Teasdale, J.D., & Segal, Z.U. (2007). *The mindful way through depression: Freeing yourself from chronic unhappiness.* New York: Guilford.

Wrenn, G.C. (1962). *The counselor in a changing world.* Washington, DC: American Personnel and Guidance Association.

Yalom, I.D. (2008). *Staring at the sun: Overcoming the terror of death.* San Francisco: Jossey-Bass.

Yalom, I.D. (1998). *The Yalom reader: Selections from the work of a master therapist and storyteller.* New York: Basic Books.

Young, S.N. (2011). Biologic effects of mindfulness meditation: Growing insights into neurobiologic aspects of the prevention of depression. *Journal of Psychiatry & Neuroscience, 36*(2), 75–77. doi: 10.15031/jpm.110010

Ziv, S. (2014, November 12). Technology's latest quest: Tracking mental health. Newsweek. In R. Remley & B. Herlihy, *Ethical, legal, and professional issues in counseling* (5th ed.). Boston: Pearson.

Index

Accreditation Council for Genetic Counseling 52
ACT scores 84
action plan, career visioning 120, 121, 188–188, 189
action words 127–128
activist, counselor as 152–154
addictions counseling 43, 45–46, 71, 191; licensure 32, 33
adventure based counseling (ABC) 50–52
advocacy 154, 190
Affordable Care Act ("Obama Care") 152, 153
Alcoholics Anonymous (AA) 45
Amazon 111
American Art Therapy Association (AATA) 40, 50
American Association of Marriage Counseling (AAMC) 74
American Association for Marriage and Family Therapy (AAMFT) 74
American Association of State Counseling Boards (AASCB) 34
American Coaching Association (ACA) 53
American College Counseling Association (ACCA) 36
American College Personnel Association (ACPA) 35–36
American Counseling Association (ACA) 11, 35–36; affiliates 36, 44, 74; Code of Ethics 17, 18, 19, 76, 79, 87, 106, 107, 153, 154, 164, 165, 177, 178, 197; continuing education 78; definition of counseling 12; Governmental Affairs 154; history 14, 35–36; license portability 34; *Licensure Requirements for Professional Counselors* 32; lobbying 36, 154; Medicare reimbursement 16; membership 16, 36, 126, 136, 190; networking 123;

professional coaching 53; professional goals remaining 16; scope of practice 35; state branches 36; technology 109, 112
American Dance Therapy Association (AADA) 40, 50
American Mental Health Counselors Association (AMHCA) 11, 36, 37; license portability 34; lobbying 154; networking 123; professional goals remaining 16; scope of practice 35
American Music Therapy Association (AMTA) 40, 50
American Pastoral Counseling Association (AAPC) 48
American Personnel and Guidance Association (APGA) 11, 14, 36
American Psychiatry Association (APA) 35, 150
American Rehabilitation Counseling Association (ARCA) 16, 35, 36, 37, 78
American School Counselors Association (ASCA) 39, 44; continuing education 78; history 14; license portability 34; lobbying 154; membership 16; networking 123; professional goals remaining 16; scope of practice 35
American Society of Group Psychotherapy and Psychodrama (ASGPP) 40
Americans with Disabilities Act 153
animal-assisted therapy 50
appreciation, in collegial relationships 101
Approved Clinical Supervisor (ACS) 33
apps 196
aptitude 22–23
armed forces, counseling in the 49–50
Armed Services Vocational Aptitude Battery (ASVAB) 22, 23
art therapy 50
Assange, Julian 105

210 *Index*

assessment and testing 34, 35
Association for Adult Development and Aging (AADA) 37
Association for Assessment and Research in Counseling (AARC) 37
Association for Child and Adolescent Counseling (ACAC) 37
Association for Counselor Education and Supervision (ACES) 36, 37
Association for Counselors and Educators in Government (ACEG) 37
Association for Creativity in Counseling (ACC) 37
Association for Humanistic Counseling (AHC) 37
Association for Lesbian, Gay, Bisexual, and Transgender Issues in Counseling (ALGBTIC) 38
Association for Multicultural Counseling and Development (AMCD) 38
Association for Play Therapy 50
Association for Professional Executive Coaching and Supervision (APECS) 53
Association for Specialists in Group Work (ASGW) 38
Association for Spiritual, Ethical, and Religious Values in Counseling (ASERVIC) 38
attitude assessment 26
authenticity 6–7, 96–98, 175–176, 179
avatars 112, 196

Bateson, Gregory 74
Beck, Aaron 5, 89, 91
Beck, Judy 89
becoming a counselor 30–31; ACA 35–36; BLS 40; considerations 31; lessons learned 40–42; license portability issues 33–34; licensure 31–33; organizations 36–40; scope of practice 34–35; *see also* should I become a counselor?
behavioral disorder counseling 191
Bernard, J.M. 157, 164
Berra, Yogi 119
Bertram, B. 108
Board Certified Coach (BCC) 33
Bolles, Richard Nelson 133, 139, 147–148, 187
Borderline Personality Disorder (BPD) 7, 79–80
Bowen, Murray 28, 74
Boynton *v.* Burglass (1991) 109

Buddhism 10, 25
bullying 101
Bureau of Labour Statistics (BLS) 15, 40, 190–191, 192; addictions counseling 46; creative arts counseling 50; *Occupational Outlook Handbook* 22, 40; pastoral counseling 48; school counseling 44

career center 122–123
career counseling 190
career management 117, 146; beginning your career 145–146; trends in counseling profession 190–192; vibrancy 186–187; visioning 118–122, 187–190; *see also* job search
Center for Credentialing and Education (CCE) 33, 40, 192, 193; Distance Certified Counselor 106; online training 112; professional coaching 53
Center for Journal Therapy (CJT) 40
certification 192–193; becoming a counselor 30–31, 32–33; continuing education 78; distance counseling 106; genetic counseling 52; school counseling 30–31, 32, 33, 44; trauma counseling 47
Certified Alcoholism and Substance Abuse Counselor (CASAC) 32, 33, 192
challenge courses 51
chemical dependency counseling *see* addictions counseling
clinical mental health counseling (CMHC) 33, 35, 43, 45, 191
clinical rehabilitation counseling 35, 36, 46–47, 191
codes of ethics 17, 18, 19, 20; AAPC 48; ACA 17, 18, 19, 76, 79, 87, 106, 107, 153, 154, 164, 165, 177, 178, 197; lessons learned 82–83; professional coaching 53; virtual technology 112
Cognitive and Affective Mindfulness Scale (CAMS) 60, 62
cognitive-behavioral supervision 160
collage making 122, 189
collegial relationships 98–103, 155–156
Commission on Accreditation for Marriage and Family Therapy Education (COAMFT) 31
Commission on Rehabilitation Education (CORE) 47
confidentiality 76, 107, 109, 112
conflict 100, 101, 135
consent, informed 75–76

Index 211

continuing education (CE): groups, couples, and family counseling 78–79; *see also* training

correctional settings, counseling in 43, 49

Council for the Accreditation of Counseling and Related Educational Programs (CACREP) 13, 39; accredited programs 31, 32, 33; addictions counseling 45; affiliates 74; clinical mental health counseling 45; clinical rehabilitation counseling 47; diagnosis 35; ethics 153; liability insurance 36; license portability 34; merger with CORE 47; virtual counseling 198

counseling: defined 12, 34; meaning and purpose in 5–6; presence in 6–8; wellness model 13–14

Counseling 20/20 initiative 34

counseling organizations: lists of 36–40, 50; membership 126, 136, 190

counseling profession 11, 43; choosing a profession 54–55; ethics 17–18, 19, 20; exercising professional judgment 18–20; history 14–15; international perspective 193–195; lessons learned 20–21, 55–57; professional goals remaining 16; professional identity 11–12; recommended reading 55; specialty areas 43–53; state of the 15–16; trends 186–187, 190–192, 193–195; wellness model of counseling 13–14

counseling programs: addictions counseling 45; clinical mental health counseling 45; considerations 31; genetic counseling 52; licensure 31–34; online 111, 112, 193–194, 195–196; pastoral counseling 48, 49; school counseling 44; self-reflective questions 54–55; technology 111, 112, 193–194, 195–196, 198; trauma counseling 47

counselor: authentic v. divided self 174–176; ethics 17–18, 19, 20; exercising professional judgment 18–20; heart 179–182; inner life 173–174; as leader and activist *see* leader and activist, counselor as; lessons learned 182–185; numbers 15, 42; self-care 102, 166, 174; walking the talk 176–179; *see also* becoming a counselor; career management; should I become a counselor?

Counselors for Social Justice (CSJ) 38

couples counseling 69–71, 72, 73; case studies 75–77; challenges 73–75, 78; continuing education, need for 78–79

cover letter 123, 131–132

creative arts counseling 40, 50

Credentialed Alcoholism and Substance Abuse Counselor (CASAC) 45

credentialing 52, 53, 192–193; *see also* certification; licensure

cultural issues 17–18, 194

curriculum vitae (CV) *see* résumé

dance and movement therapy 50

de Shazer, Steve 95, 160

death 7–8

deep listening 6

Delworth, U. 158

Department of Veterans Affairs 49

detention facilities, counseling in 43, 49

diagnosis 7; and licensure 15, 16; lobbying 154; medical model 13; scope of practice 34–35

Diagnostic and Statistical Manual of Mental Disorders (DSM) 7, 13, 181; feminism 158; pastoral counseling 49; scope of practice 34, 35

Dialectical Behavioral Therapy (DBT) 79, 80

Dimensions of a Healthy Lifestyle (DHL) 62–67

disadvantaged students 55–57

disappointment, dealing with 138–140

discrimination model of supervision 157

Distance Certified Counselor (DCC) 33, 106, 193

distance counseling 105, 106, 186–187, 196; case study 106–107; ethical and legal considerations 107–111, 197–198; future 112; lessons learned 113–116; *see also* virtual technology

divided self 174–175

domestic abuse 18

Edison, Thomas 121, 188

education *see* continuing education; counseling programs; training

Educational and Vocational Guidance Practitioner (EVGP) 33

Eisenhower, Dwight D. 14

elderly populations 15

Ellis, Albert 25, 88, 89, 90, 91

emotional intelligence (EQ) 84–86; authentic feedback 96–98; case study

212 *Index*

87–88; collegial relationships 98–103; defined 86–87; lessons learned 103–104; making use of 87; management 156; Miraculous Question 95–96; self-talk 89–95; strategies 102–103
Epstein, Mark 60
Equal Opportunity Employment Commission (EEOC) 137
Erickson, Milton 74
ethics 17–18, 19, 20, 177–178; authentic feedback 98; codes *see* codes of ethics; collegial relationships 99, 100; couples counselling 75–76, 77; distance counseling 107; emotional intelligence 87–88; family counseling 76, 77; future 197–198; genetic counseling 52–53; informed consent 75; interview questions 135, 137; licensure 32; politics 153, 154; poor self-care 102; résumé 126, 127; scope of competence 69, 71; selection of potential counseling candidates 24–25; supervision 164–166; unethical practice 101
euthanasia 19–20, 109
existential therapy 7
expressive arts therapy 40, 50

failure 121, 188
family counseling 69, 71, 73; case study 76–77; challenges 73–75, 78; continuing education, need for 78–79; lessons learned 80–83
feedback: authentic 96–98; job search 140, 167
feminist model of supervision 158
firing staff 166, 167–169
Frankl, Victor 5, 67, 91, 96, 174
Frawley-O'Dea, M.G. 157
Freud, Sigmund 157
Friedman, Thomas 111, 193

Gandhi, Mohandas 119, 187
genetic counseling 52–53, 191, 192
Gestalt Therapy 7
Global Career Development Facilitator (GCDF) 33
goals, career 119–121, 187, 188–188; beginning your career 146; interview question 134–135
Goleman, Daniel 84, 86, 88, 96, 156
Goodyear, R.K. 157, 164
gossip 101
grade point averages (GPAs) 24

Graduate Record Examination (GRE) 23–24
gratitudes 59, 102, 104
group counseling 70, 71–73, 78–79
Groves, Luther 74

Haley, Jay 70, 74
Hayes, Stewart Chen 79
health *see* wellbeing
health insurance 34–35
heart of a counselor 179–182
Heller, S. 79
Hierarchy of Needs 13
hiring staff 166–167
history, personal 119, 187
Holloway, E. 162
hospitals, counseling in 43
Human Services-Board Certified Practitioner (HS-BCP) 33

identity, professional 11–12, 119, 187–188
informational interviewing 122, 189–190
informed consent 75–76
inner life of a counselor 173–174, 182–185
Institute for Life Coaching 53
insurance: health 34–35; liability 36
integrated developmental model (IDM) of supervision 158–159
interest 22–23
International Art Therapy (IAT) 40
International Association for Counselling (IAC) 39
International Association of Addictions and Offender Counselors (IAAOC) 38
International Association for Marriage and Family Counseling (IAMFC) 74, 76
International Association of Marriage and Family Counselors (IAMF) 38
International Coach Federation (ICF) 53
International Expressive Arts Therapy Association (IEATA) 40
International Society for Animal Assisted Therapy 50
internet *see* distance counseling; virtual technology
internship: completion 117–118, 145–146; international 194–195; supervision 156, 157, 163, 164
IQ scores 84, 86

jails, counseling in 43, 49
job hopping 127

job interview 133–138
job market: addictions counseling 46; clinical rehabilitation counseling 47; genetic counseling 52; military, counseling in the 50; school counseling 44
job offer 142–145
job search 117, 146; career center 122–123; career visioning 118–122; cover letter 131–132; interview 133–138; job offer 142–145; lessons learned 147–149; networking 123–124; preparations 118; recommended reading 146–147; references 125, 167; rejection, dealing with 138–140; résumé 126–130; self-reflection 117–118, 141
journaling, career 122, 189

Kabit-Zinn, John 58, 59, 180
Kim-Berg, Insoo 95
King, Martin Luther, Jr. 119, 187

labor market *see* job market
leader and activist, counselor as 150–152; hiring and firing staff 166–169; legal and ethical liability 164–166; lessons learned 169–172; management 150–152, 155–156; politics 152–154; supervision 156–166
Lee, Cortland 195
legal issues: collegial relationships 99; distance counseling 107, 197; exercising professional judgment 18–19; firing staff 168, 169; informed consent 75, 76; interview questions 135, 137; lessons learned 82–83; politics 153; supervision 164–166
Lennon, John 188
lessons learned 1; becoming a counselor 40–42; counseling profession 20–21; disadvantaged students 55–57; distance counseling 113–116; emotional intelligence 103–104; hope 198–202; inner life 182–185; job search 147–149; management and supervision 169–172; second chances 26–29; self-discovery 8–10; wellbeing 67–68
letters of reference *see* references
liability insurance 36
Licensed Mental Health Counselor (LMHC) 45, 47
Licensed Professional Counselor (LPC) 33, 45, 47, 154

licensure: addictions counseling 45; becoming a counselor 30–34; beginning your career 145; clinical mental health counseling 45; clinical rehabilitation counseling 47; continuing education 78; correctional settings, counseling in 49; and diagnosis 15, 16; distance counseling 108; history 14–15; lessons learned 40–41, 42; lobbying 154; military, counseling in the 50; portability issues 33–34; specialty areas 192; state of the counseling profession 15; substance abuse counseling 191
Linehan, Marsha M. 7, 48, 79, 80
LinkedIn 111, 123, 146, 186
listening 6, 101, 103
lobbying 15, 16, 35, 36, 47, 152, 154, 190
logotherapy 5, 67

malpractice 18–19
management 150–152, 155–156, 169–172
Mandela, Nelson 119, 187
marriage counseling *see* couples counseling
Maslow, Abraham 13, 91
matters of conscience legislation 109
McNeill, B. 158
meaning in counseling 5–6
Medicaid 15, 16, 152, 153
medical model 13, 14
medical profession 192–193
Medicare 15, 16, 152, 153, 154
meditation 102; apps 196; career visioning 122, 189; guided 60; heart of a counselor 181; lessons learned 68, 103–104; mindfulness 58, 59–60, 68
Meichenbaum, Donald 89
mental health counseling 36, 46
Merton, Thomas 103
military, counseling in the 49–50
Military and Government Counseling Association (MCGA) 38
Mindful Attention Awareness Scale (MAAS) 60–62
mindfulness 14, 58; career visioning 121, 189; in daily life 59–60; defined 180; DHL 62–67; heart of a counselor 180, 181; lessons learned 67–68; MAAS 61–62; nature of 58–59; trauma counseling 80
Minnesota Multi-Phasic Inventory, second edition (MMPI-2) 9
Miraculous Question: emotional intelligence 95–96; supervision 160, 161

214 *Index*

mortality 7–8
multicultural counseling 30
Munchin, Salvador 74
music therapy 50
Myers, J.E. 13

National Association for Drama Therapy (NADT) 40
National Association of Guidance and Counselor Trainers (NAGCT) 35
National Association for Poetry Therapy (NAPT) 40
National Board for Certified Counselors, Inc. (NBCC) 32, 39, 192, 193; affiliates 53; Distance Certified Counselor 106; networking 123; online training 112
National Career Development Association (NCDA) 39
National Clinical Mental Health Counseling Examination (NCMHCE) 35
National Counselor Examination 32
National Defense Education Act (NDEA) 14, 43–44
National Employment Counseling Association (NECA) 39
National Society of Genetic Counselors 52
National Vocational Guidance Association (NVGA) 35
Nationally Certified Counselor (NCC) 32, 33, 192
negligence 19
networking 123–124, 146, 186
North American Drama Therapy Association 50
nurse practitioners 13

"Obama Care" (Affordable Care Act) 152, 153
Obergfell *v.* Hodges (2015) 153
Occupational Outlook Handbook 22, 40
online counseling 43, 196
organizations *see* counseling organizations

Palmer, Parker 6, 27, 174–175, 176, 179, 180
pastoral counseling 48–49
patient-centered supervision 157, 160
pay *see* salary
Perls, Fritz 7, 181
Perls, Laura 7
personal history 119, 187
Peters, T.J. 150

physical abuse 18
physician-assisted suicide 19–20, 109
play therapy 50
politics 152–154
post-traumatic stress disorder (PTSD) 48
practicum *see* internship
presence 6–8, 101
prisons, counseling in 43, 49
profession *see* counseling profession
professional coaching 53
professional identity 11–12, 119, 187–188
professional networking sites 123, 146
professional organizations *see* counseling organizations
psychiatry 13, 35, 47
psychodynamic supervision 157–158
psychology: history of counseling profession 14; licensure 32; medical model 13; military 49; politics 153; professional coaching 53; professional identity 11, 12; scope of practice 34, 35; trauma counseling 47
punctuality 101
purpose in counseling 5–6

Quakers 1

recreational therapy 50
recruitment 15, 166–167
references 167; career center 122–123; requesting 125
registration *see* licensure
rehabilitation counseling 35, 36, 46–47, 191
rejection, dealing with 138–140, 148
relationship counseling *see* couples counseling
Remley, T.P., Jr. 32, 33
resilience: emotional intelligence 84, 85, 86, 92–93; groups, couples, and family counseling 73; job search 140, 148; selection of potential counseling candidates 24; self-reflective questions 92–93
respect 101
résumé 126–128, 131; career center 123; referral sources 125; sample 128–130; updating 145
Rogers, Carl 6, 13, 17, 91, 97, 98, 101, 160, 175, 176
Rokeach, Milton 119, 187
Ronnestad, M.H. 159–160
Rose-Baumann, Miriam 6

Sacks, Oliver 9
salary: addictions counseling 46, 191; behavioral disorder counseling 191; clinical mental health counseling 45, 191; clinical rehabilitation counseling 46, 191; correctional settings, counseling in 49; genetic counseling 52, 191; interview question 136; job offer, evaluation 142, 144; school and career counseling 44, 190
Sarnat, J.E. 157
SAT scores 84
Satir, Virginia 74
school counseling 43–45, 190, 192; distance counseling 110–111; history 14; licensure/certification 30–31, 32, 33, 44; professional goals remaining 16; trends 43
scope of practice 34–35, 154
second chances 26–29
selection of potential counseling candidates 23–25
self-actualization 7, 13, 84, 91, 176
self-care 102, 166, 174
self-determination 21
self-discovery 3–4, 8; lessons learned 8–10; meaning and purpose in counseling 5–6; presence, importance in counseling 6–8; vulnerability risks and rewards 4
self-reflection 1, 117, 160, 173–174, 175; attitude 26; authentic self 176; internship conclusion 117–118; job search 140, 141; leadership role 171–172; meaning and purpose 5–6; Miraculous Question 95–96; networking 123–124; resilience 92–93; selecting a counseling program 54–55; self-discovery 4, 8; should I become a counselor? 25; supervision 163
self-talk 88–91, 96, 102; authenticity exercise 98; conflict resolution 100; exercises 93–95; goal setting and progress measurement 91–93; job search 140, 148–149
Shakespeare, William, *The Tempest* 8
should I become a counselor? 22; attitude assessment 26; interest v. aptitude 22–23; lessons learned 26–29; selection of potential candidates 23–25; self-reflective questions 25
Skovholt, T.M. 159–160
Skype 107
social media 105, 140, 186
social work: history of counseling profession 14; medical model 13;

military 49; number of social workers 42; politics 153; professional coaching 53; professional identity 11, 12; scope of practice 34, 35; trauma counseling 47; Veterans Administration 47
solution-focused supervision 160–162
specialty areas 192–193; choosing between 54; common 43–53; trends by 190–191
state certification *see* certification
state counseling organizations 16
Stoltenberg, C.D. 158
Strong Interest Inventory (SII) 22, 23
Student Personnel Association for Teacher Education (SPATE) 35
substance abuse counseling *see* addictions counseling
supervisee-centered supervision 157–158
supervision 156–163, 166; legal and ethical liability 164–166; lessons learned 169–172
supervisory-matrix-centered supervision 158
Sweeney, T.J. 13
systems approach to supervision 162

technology 105–106, 193–194, 195–197; career management 186–187; ethical concerns 197–198; *see also* distance counseling; virtual technology
Teresa, Mother 119, 187
testing and assessment 34, 35
Thapar *v.* Zezulka (1999) 109
Thich Nat Hahn 103
Thinking for a Change Certified Facilitator (T4C-CF) 33
Three Cs 89–90, 91, 102
Toronto Mindfulness Scale 60, 62
training: beginning your career 145; *see also* continuing education; counseling programs
trauma counseling 47–48, 79–80, 191; credentialing 192, 193
Tricare 16, 49, 50
Trump, Donald 153

university counseling faculty 36
unsupportive colleagues 101–102

values, and career management 119, 187
values-based referrals 109
Van der Kolk, Bessel 79
Veterans Administration (VA) Medical Centers 15, 16, 47, 49, 50

216   *Index*

virtual technology 105, 106; future 111–112; *see also* distance counseling
visioning, career 118–122, 187–190
vulnerability 4

walking the talk 176–179
Ward *v.* Wilbanks (2010) 153
Waterman, R.H. 150
wellbeing: DHL 62–67; emotional intelligence 88–91; lessons learned 67–68; self-care 102, 166, 174; *see also* mindfulness
wellness model of counseling 13–14
Wheeler, A.M. 108
Whitaker, Carl 74
Will, George 153
Witmer, J.M. 13

Yalom, I.D. 8
YouTube 111